saur

Woodcut from a verse version by Giuliano Dati of the letter from Columbus to Ferdinand and Isabella announcing his discovery of the West Indies. Printed in Florence, 1493. British Library IA27798.

Great Collections and Collectors 1

A Guide to Americana

the American collections in the British Library

by
Gregory Palmer

K · G · Saur

London · Edinburgh · Munich
New York · Singapore · Sydney · Toronto · Wellington

© Gregory Palmer

All rights reserved. No part of this publication may be reproduced, stored in a retrieval system or transmitted in any form or by any means, electronic, mechanical, photocopying, recording, or otherwise, without permission in writing from the publisher.

K. G. Saur
is an imprint of Butterworths.

British Library Cataloguing in Publication Data
Palmer, Gregory, 1938–
A guide to Americana: the American collections
of the British Library.
1. Great Britain. National Libraries.
British Library. Department of Printed Books.
Stock. Americana. Acquisition.
I. Title.
025.2'9'73
ISBN 0–86291–475–2

Printed and bound at the University Printing House, Oxford
Printed on Acid free paper.

Contents

Foreword   vii
Acknowledgements   ix

Introduction   1
Part One: The Formation of the Collections
  1. Early Americana and the Foundation of the British Museum Library   11
  2. The American Collection of the National Library, 1846 to 1886   37
  3. Copyright Deposit and American Books after 1886   64
Part Two: Locating Americana
  4. The Catalogues   91
  5. Microfilm Collections   101
  6. Picture Research   106
  7. American Maps   112
  8. American Music   118
  9. Americana in Languages other than English   120
  10. Official Publications   124
  11. Newspapers and Periodicals   130
  12. American Manuscripts in the British Library   151
  13. The Manuscript Collections   157
Appendices
  I – Sample Catalogue Entries for Americana   187
  II – Books in the British Library Relating to America Published between 1493 and 1525   195
  III – A List of American Books Acquired by the British Library in 1837   205
  IV – American Publishers Depositing Books in the British Library 1850–1950   207
  V – Original Files of American Newspapers Published Before 1820, in the British Library   209
Bibliography of Sources   222
Index   239

Foreword

Acceptance of the significant rôle played by American literature and scholarship in British academic life to-day is axiomatic: American studies, for so long an object of academic suspicion, no longer need to be vindicated. This is still a relatively recent development. Until the Second World War, recognition of American cultural developments was hardly widespread in Britain despite the growing presence of universities which by any European standard were undoubtedly great. American studies were regarded simply as part of English literature and history, and a somewhat minor part at that. The founding of the American Trust for the British Library with the specific objective of filling some of the numerous gaps in the collections of the National Library is witness to the attitudes and neglect of the past.

It is easy to attribute the change in academic awareness to the rise to superpower status of the United States and the decline of Britain as a world power. It is less easy to trace in any detail the cultural implications of the inferior status which Britain continued to confer on its wayward offspring long after Independence. This Mr Palmer has done in his pioneering investigation of the growth of the holdings of Americana in the National Library. His review of accessions and acquisitions policies since its foundation as the British Museum Library in 1753 confirms in an all too uncomfortable way the indifferent, even negative, attitudes of the British towards this former colony. Important as the holdings undoubtedly are for the history of the United States, this is more likely to be an accident of history or the consequence of some great collection coming to the Library than to any positive policy towards the acquisition of American material. Ironically, the one period of positive interest by the Library in acquiring American imprints, during 1840–1880, is the work of two 'foreigners'. It reflects the far-sightedness of Panizzi and the diligence of the American Henry Stevens who between them laid the foundations of the American collections of today.

Mr Palmer's study does more than trace the growth of the Library's American collections. He brings fresh historical insights into the workings of the Library and lays open aspects of its policies and development which go far beyond the expectations of his original brief. He demonstrates that there is much more to be read from library catalogues than author, title and imprint. They tell also of great events, of social change and economic development, of American achievements as well as of British attitudes and Library policies. The book trade calendars a nation's conscience as well as its cultural and historical achievements. The collections of a great national library not only stand as the archives of its printed word, but also as a commentary on world affairs. Mr Palmer puts a new slant on the commentary and gives it to us in a highly readable form.

F.W. Ratcliffe
Cambridge University Library

Acknowledgements

This book had its origin in my term as a consultant to the British Library between 1980 and 1983. My brief was to advise the Library in drawing up lists of American materials which it would acquire with funds provided by the American Trust for the British Library, and to prepare for publication a handbook to the American collection. I was employed by the Trustees of the British Library Endowment Fund and my post was funded by the Leverhulme Trust; I was thus given the privileged access to the collections enjoyed by members of the Library's staff, and was allowed to continue this privilege after my contract expired.

Advising on improvements to the existing collection implied criticism, although that might have been of decisions made a century ago; but in an institution with such a strong sense of its traditions as the British Library, such criticism coming from an outsider could easily have been misunderstood, and I am grateful for the generosity and courtesy of those senior members of the Library's staff with whom I dealt most closely – Alexander Wilson, who was then Director General, Robert Fulford, Keeper of Printed Books, Ian Willison and Philip Harris, Deputy Keepers.

Anyone who writes on the history of the British Library will be in the debt of Philip Harris, and I would like to acknowledge, in addition, his helpfulness in my day-to-day work at the Library. Ian Willison has taken an interest over a number of years in the American collection of the British Library and it was largely due to his original analysis of its strengths and weaknesses that the project on which I was employed was initiated.

Robert Parker, my assistant, was later taken on to the permanent staff of the Library. His bibliographic skill and conscientiousness, and in particular his knowledge of the cataloguing and shelving of books in the British Library, were such that his contribution to our joint effort was in no respect subordinate to my own; the Library would indeed have been at a loss without his services as the work of the American Trust has progressed.

Other members of the staff of the Library provided information or assistance on particular matters: Robin Alston, Eighteenth Century Short Title Catalogue; Stephen Green, newspapers; Philip Brown, nineteenth century bookselling; Harold Whitehead, books in Spanish, Portuguese and Latin American books; Michael Maclaren-Turner, Russian, Ukrainian and Hungarian; Robert McFarlane, Dutch; David Paisey, German; Tom Geddes, Scandinavian; Howard Nelson, Chinese; Laurence Dethan, French; V. Nersessian, Armenian; Hanna Swiderske, Polish; Denis Reidy, Italian. Chris Wootton wrote the programme for the analysis of the results of a survey of American books acquired between 1850 and 1950; most of the work on the survey was done by Robert Parker, who also provided information on American music.

Ilse Sternberg, at present in charge of American books, read the manuscript on behalf of the Library and made several useful comments. The chapter on the catalogues was read by Frank Fletcher who corrected several mistakes. Dominic Griffiths has given me much help with the use of the catalogue.

I must also acknowledge that the British Library has allowed me to reproduce items in which the Library owns copyright. Hugh Cobbe, then Head of Publishing, Robert Fulford and Ian Willison assisted me in arranging publication. It was my choice that publication was not by the Library; parts have been read by various members of the staff and their comments generally incorporated; while acknowledgement is made for the assistance I have received from the Library, this is an independent book. I worked with the staff of the Library for two and a half years, but I have held a reader's ticket for twenty, and I write as a user of the collections.

I have debts to people outside the British Library. My association with the Institute of United States Studies of the

Acknowledgements

University of London has been fruitful; the Director, Professor Peter Parish, made comments on the manuscript. I have talked often with Alison Cowden, Librarian of the Institute, and with Dr Howell Daniels, about American books. The British Association for American Studies supported a Colloquium on American Studies that I organised at the British Library in 1982, and Professor Charlotte Ericson and Dr F. Ratcliffe of Cambridge University read a draft of the manuscript and made useful suggestions. Douglas Bryant, Executive Director of the American Trust for the British Library, told me about the American Trust at Harvard in 1980, which led to my association with the British Library, and although it was not strictly part of the Trust's project, has encouraged the publication of the Guide.

My wife Ann and son Ned took great interest in my work at the British Library; they share my interest in American books, and have helped with several tasks.

Introduction

Why should the national library of Britain have an American collection? An answer might be attempted by explaining the historical reason for why it does. The expansion of England's power and influence throughout the world that took place between the beginning of the seventeenth and the end of the nineteenth centuries has made English the most widely used of world languages; the contraction of British power that took place with American independence made it in effect an international language, an effect that was even greater after the loss of the second British empire. When power diminished, influence remained; but there is no Académie Anglaise and trustees of the language have been customary and self-appointed: among them Samuel Johnson, the Oxford dictionaries and lately the BBC in England, Noah Webster and H.L. Mencken in America.

The need for a national archive of the English language that would include all works in English was recognised by Antonio Panizzi when, in the 1840s, he was establishing the doctrine of a national library. Such a library, in Panizzi's view, could not be parochial; it must include the major works of the languages and cultures which were close to the traditions of Britain, and also represent to some extent those that were not; but its first duty was to English books, 'that is books in English including those of America, and works relating to England . . . the Museum is the library of the English nation, and there ought to be in that library every book that was printed, either by Englishmen or in English, or relating to England'.

Panizzi made these remarks to a select committee of Parliament in 1860. Fourteen years earlier he had appointed an American, Henry Stevens, to be agent for American books, and to 'sweep America' for books for the British Museum

Library, and since then seven thousand books had been received.

There were thus two overlapping justifications for an American collection: both the foreignness *and* the Englishness of the United States; and policy since has hovered between these two. Early European works which relate to the discovery and settlement of America, and which came to the Library during its first century, are present in the collections because they trace the overseas expansion of European and particularly British power; this part of the collections is dealt with in Chapter One of the present guide. The collection of American imprints, English books by Panizzi's definition, that were received between the 1840s and 1880s as a result of his plan for a national library, reflects the widest extension of the policy of American acquisition; the character of this part of the collections is the subject of Chapter Two. Between the 1880s and 1950s, the collection of Americana was seldom a specific policy objective, and the works received were mainly those that had been published by British publishers, or distributed in Britain by the agents of American publishers. These books and the means by which they were acquired are discussed in Chapter Three.

The intention in the first part of this guide is to give an indication of the kind of books, and as far as possible the numbers, that the British Library acquired during the different phases of the publication of Americana: the era of discovery and settlement; the period which saw the establishment of printing in the British colonies and the growth and achievement of independence; and third, the development of the mature culture and the publishing industry that supported it.

Each chapter consists first of a consideration of the full extent of American material from which the Library's collection could have been formed, and which might have been represented in character if not in number; then the state of bibliographical knowledge of the time is described; and finally the response of the Library and the consequences of its policies.

Some internal documents relating to the administration of

Introduction

the British Museum and its former Department of Printed Books have been used: minutes and papers of the Trustees, papers of the Department of Printed Books, registers of acquisitions, and invoices from booksellers. These are referred to in the text and noted in the bibliography of sources. Several printed books and two unpublished theses have also proved fruitful sources and they are likewise referred to where material from them has been used. But the main source of information has been the books themselves. The date and means of acquisition of each volume are recorded in the Library's stamp and the books are classified and shelved according to the rules of several successive systems. Direct access to the shelves has made possible investigations that could not have been carried out using the catalogue alone.

The second part of the guide is concerned with the means of locating Americana in the British Library – printed books, pictures, maps, books in foreign languages, music, government publications, newspapers and manuscripts.

Where possible, the titles of books have been given, drawn from the catalogues, the shelves, the registers and booksellers' advertisements, in the belief that these titles, while they make up a very small part of the collections, give, as no exposition can, an impression of their character.

No discussion of the American collection of the British Library can proceed without introducing Antonio Panizzi and Henry Stevens. Antonio Panizzi came to England from Italy in 1823 as a political refugee. He had been sentenced to death as contumacious by a court in Moderno, a charge that in the non-legal sense of the word might have been made against him by some of his contemporaries later in his career. He had useful connections in Britain, with Lord Brougham for example, and was for a short time Professor of Italian in the University of London before joining the staff of the British Museum Library in 1831. He became Keeper of Printed Books in 1837 and occupied the office until 1856 when he was appointed Principal Librarian, which was the designation at that time of the chief of the entire Museum. He retired in 1866 because of ill health and died in 1878. Panizzi's time was one of great upheaval at the

British Museum. He is remembered today mostly for the round Reading Room, the building of which he supervised; but in library circles his successful advocacy of the cause of the national library is well recognised. Panizzi's career is fully described in Edward Miller's *Prince of Librarians* (1967).

Henry Stevens, an American by birth, was a bookseller in London and a supplier of books to the British Museum between 1845 and 1886, the year of his death. He was in partnership for much of that time with his brother, Benjamin Franklin Stevens; their father, Henry Stevens senior, of Barnet, Vermont, was a notable New England bibliophile. Henry Stevens junior arrived in England from the United States in 1845 carrying letters of introduction from Jared Sparks, among others, and despatches for the American Minister (the head at that time of the diplomatic mission), Edward Everett, who had himself been Professor of Greek at Harvard and thus a teacher of Emerson, and editor of the *North American Review*. The following year the historian George Bancroft came to London as American Minister; Stevens had already been collecting books for him in the United States and, when Bancroft arrived, was already engaged in locating and copying documents relating to American history at the State Paper Office, the predecessor of the British Public Record Office.

The forty years of Stevens' residence in Britain were years of great vigour in Anglo-American cultural relations, although they were years in which, no doubt, equally as much misunderstanding was created as was common comprehension. During these years books that were not merely American, but distinctively American, like *The Scarlet Letter, Moby Dick,* and *Uncle Tom's Cabin*, became best sellers in Britain, and many other long-forgotten fiction and non-fiction titles were imported or republished.

For seventy years after Stevens' death, the British Museum followed a 'passive' policy of American acquisition in which it relied on the receipt by copyright deposit of American books published or distributed in Britain, supplemented by exchange of official publications, and the purchase of a few academic monographs, mainly the works of the university presses.

The collection of original American works deposited in the British Library might thus be regarded as itself the documentation of an aspect of Anglo-American cultural history to which no retrospective amendment could or should be made. This would be, of course, to ignore the needs of a working research library: but if the collection is observed in a historical fashion, then even retrospective improvements can be seen to have reflected the Anglo-American interests of their time. The intention of the historical sketch of the American collections that follows in the next three chapters is to give a sense of coherence to the collections which they lack physically, being dispersed amongst the other English books, and which cannot be derived from any definition of the term Americana. This word is itself historically relative and its use will be explained as the history of the Library's collection is being described.

The catalogue entries to individual works often give an insight into the structure of the collection. Those of three works, William Hubbard, *Narrative of the Indian Wars*, Sebastian Brant, *Narrenschiff* (Ship of Fools), and Harriet Beecher Stowe, *Uncle Tom's Cabin*, are given in Appendix I.

Three bibliographies must be constantly referred to by students of Americana: they are so well known that they are frequently referred to by the name of the author only. Their titles are given here in acknowledgement as well as explanation. They are: Joseph Sabin, *Bibliotheca Americana: A Dictionary of Books Relating to America, from its Discovery to the Present Time* (29 vols, 1868–1936); Charles Evans, *American Bibliography: A Chronological Dictionary of All Books, Pamphlets and Periodical Publications Printed in the United States of America 1639 to 1800,* (14 vols, 1903–1959) supplement R.P. Bristol, (1952); and a work that is still in progress, John Alden, *European Americana: a Chronological Guide to Works Printed in Europe Relating to the Americas, 1493–1776,* (1980 –).

It is finally necessary to say something about the institution itself, although there are two adequate sources of information:

Edward Miller's *That Noble Cabinet* (1973), and more concisely, P.R. Harris's *The British Museum Reading Room* (1976).

The British Museum was founded by an Act of Parliament in 1753 to administer the collections of books, manuscripts, antiquities, scientific specimens and curiosities which had all come by different means into public ownership, having previously been in the possession of Sir Robert and Sir John Cotton, the two Harleys, Earls of Oxford, and Sir Hans Sloane. At the time of its foundation, the printed books and manuscripts commanded the most serious respect, and the objects the least. Since that time, although the scientific specimens have been removed to the National History Museum, material culture has become as serious a branch of history as that based on written sources. In 1973 the departments of Printed Books, Manuscripts, and Oriental Manuscripts and Printed Books were separated from the Museum to become the major part of the Reference Division of the British Library. Further reorganisation took place in 1985, and the American collections described here are now subsumed under British Library: Humanities and Social Sciences. No scheme of organisation (or name) is immutable, but the book collections themselves have persisted through the changes with little disturbance.

This guide refers only to those parts of the present British Library that were formerly parts of the British Museum. The terms 'Library' and 'Museum' are both used in the text, which ever seems most appropriate.

The American Trust for the British Library was established in 1979 to assist the Library financially in remedying weaknesses in the American collection. Its contribution will be of great service to scholars, but as most of the material donated by the Trust will be microfilm, it will not substantially affect the collection of original publications and manuscripts which are the main subject of this guide.

There is no reason why scholars or readers should confine their attention to a single library; London is particularly rich in specialist libraries, several of which contain significant

American collections. The American collections of these and other libraries in Britain are described in Peter Snow, *The United States: a Guide to Library Holdings in the United Kingdom* (1982), and those of the various libraries of the University of London are described in Alison Cowden, *American Studies Collections in the University of London* (1981). The libraries of Oxford University (the Bodleian and Rhodes House Library) and Cambridge University have had the privilege of copyright deposit and in the nineteenth century, like the British Library, received books from Henry Stevens. They also have large holdings of American periodicals and official publications. Their American collections must rival those of the British Library within the confines of their more specialised academic purpose. But they, and most of the other London libraries, are not 'public libraries' in the sense that the British Library, although it places some restriction on its use, nevertheless is. This guide is not intended in its tone nor in the information it contains to be a strictly academic publication.

Part One
THE FORMATION OF THE COLLECTIONS

1.
Early Americana and the Foundation of the British Museum Library

Printed books and the discovery of America – the origin of Americana

On 15 February 1493, Christopher Columbus, sheltering from a storm off the Azores with his ships the *Nina* and the *Pinta*, wrote two letters: one to Luiz de Santagel, Chancellor of the Royal Household of Aragon, and the other to Gabriel Sanchez, Crown Treasurer, announcing the discovery of the New World. Fearing shipwreck, he enclosed a copy of the text in a barrel and ordered it thrown into the sea. The barrel has never been found, but three weeks later, on 4 March 1493, Columbus landed at Lisbon and sent the letters with a messenger to the Court of Spain. The original copies have not survived, but the text has; the Santagel letter was printed in Spanish in Barcelona a few weeks later, possibly while Columbus was still in the city waiting on his royal sponsors, Ferdinand and Isabella. A Latin translation (it is not known if there were two separate Spanish originals) was printed in Rome soon afterwards, and Latin editions followed in Antwerp, Basel and Paris before the end of the year. A verse paraphrase in Italian by Giuliano Dati was issued in Rome and Florence in 1493, and during the following years these and other translations and versions continued to appear, often appended to other works. The 'Columbus letter' remained the major printed work on America until the publication of Vespucci's *Mundus Novus* in 1503/1504, his account of his third voyage. The next most significant item of early Americana after these two works also appeared in 1504 – an unauthorised Italian translation of Peter Martyr's 'first decade'. In 1507 the book in which the name America was proposed, Martin Waldseemüller's *Cosmographiae*, was published to accompany a globe and a world map on which the New World was delineated and named.

The New World was mentioned, sometimes just in passing, in a number of works published in the decades following its discovery; the most notable was *Narrenschiff*, the Ship of Fools, by Sebastian Brant. This reference was only a few words concerning the discoveries of the Spanish, although it was expanded slightly in the English version. It was not part of the main theme of the book, which is a humanist satire, but it is through printed remarks such as these that one can see how quickly the news had spread. Within a few years of its discovery, the New World became a matter for comment among educated people throughout Europe. On the periphery of Americana are works concerned with the *morbum gallicum* and tobacco, and fictitious works such as Thomas More's *Utopia*.

In total, printed works relating to America make up a very small proportion of all the books published before about 1520, but as the century proceeded the number of references and the number of books devoted entirely to America increased. One is therefore inclined to look for a link between printing and the New World starting with the three great inventions 'unknown to the ancients' that, in Francis Bacon's words, 'changed the appearance and state of the whole world'. They were printing, gunpowder and the compass; the connections, while undeniable, are complicated, but their nature explains the character of early printed Americana.

News of the New World was received by a Europe intellectually in transition; in the production of books this meant at first the conversion of manuscript books, published and widely distributed none the less, into printed texts. Thus the old form set the pattern of the new: biblical exegesis, religious service books, geographies and grammars, fabulous and real adventures, often mixed together in the same text, and compendiums of knowledge. Old knowledge was seldom dropped even when it had become untenable, and printers added new information in successive editions as scribes had been able to do in individual copies before the age of print. Ptolemaic *Geographies* illustrate this; they had existed for three hundred years as manuscript books, then from the late fifteenth century appeared in print. An edition printed in Rome in 1508 reproduced a version of the previous year, but with the addition of the Ruysch map which showed the New World. Further editions appeared in 1511, 1513, and 1514, all with new American material, reflecting the increase in knowledge as exploration continued.

Columbus was himself associated with this transformation of knowledge. He was, in partnership with his brother, a bookseller and a publisher of maps. Geographical and astronomical texts were of particular concern to the mapmaker; these frequently took the form of the scholastic *summa*. At the end of his *Suma de Geographia*, Martin Fernandez de Encisco wrote:

> This suma was extracted from many authorities. It comes from the wisdom of the Bactrion History, the two Ptolemies, Eratosthenes, Pliny, Strato, Josephus, Anselm, the Bible, the General History and many other writings, and from our own day to day experience which is the mother of all.

The compiler of a *summa* might attempt to reconcile the discrepancies between his diverse sources and in doing so to advance knowledge. New information came in the fifteenth century not only from observation but also from the recovery of classical texts such as the *Almagest*, the Ptolemaic treatise on astronomy. This had been translated from Arabic into Latin in the twelfth century, but was retranslated directly from Greek by the German astronomer Johannes Müller (Regiomontanus) in 1496. The compiler of a *summa*, whether manuscript or printed, could make a gloss on those discrepancies that defied reconciliation, and could shade off into the vague or fabulous at the end of a chapter which might have begun with sound knowledge. The maker of maps and navigational manuals for Renaissance mariners could not do this because mariners required workable maps and tables.

Much speculation has arisen from Columbus's certainty about the western route to the Indies, a certainty sustained through twenty years of awaiting the opportunity for the voyage, and the vicissitudes of the voyage itself. Speculation about his grounds for certainty has of course to be constrained by the nature of the sources: the commentaries of his friend La Casas, and his son Fernando. His contemporaries suggested that Columbus sailed westward not to test a theory, but to get to the Indies, faith indeed on his part in the authority of texts and in the reconciliation of Christian and classical knowledge.

Columbus was wrong. Plato had known that the earth was spherical and Eratosthenes had measured its circumference accurately to a distance of fifty miles. Medieval Christian cosmology and *mappamundi* had been misleading, and his acceptance of the authority of the Church fathers had led Columbus into a gross underestimate of the earth's circumference.

But, nevertheless, Columbus crossed the Atlantic westward in the latitude of favourable winds still used by sailing vessels, and returned by the northerly route to the Azores, where his unsuccessful westward-sailing predecessors had met headwinds. He navigated with apparent precision on the first and later voyages, around the islands and mainland shores of the Caribbean, and he took with him a printed book, the *Ephemerides* of Regiomontanus. On the third voyage an event occurred, reported by the chronicler of the voyage, Fernando Columbus, which has become a regular literary device and which represents the divergence between the print and oral cultures, at the cleft of which Columbus stood. On the night of 29 February 1504 an eclipse of the moon occurred, as predicted by Regiomontanus's tables. According to Fernando, Columbus used his knowledge to intimidate the Jamaican Caribs at whose mercy Columbus and his crew had been cast by shipwreck. Columbus observed the eclipse from an elevated position among the frightened natives; then at its darkest moment he retired leaving them apparently at the mercy of his power over the natural world. But *were* they impressed? It was not, of course, the first eclipse they had seen; there had been two in

1502, and they might have shared some of the astronomical knowledge of their mainland neighbours. The true significance of the story, and of its persistent use by writers, is that it was the European discoverers of America and their literary heirs and successors, rather than the non-literate Caribs, who were impressed by printed books – the power of the book. What Columbus was probably doing was trying to calculate his longitude, the most difficult problem facing the navigator of his time, using a printed book – Regiomontanus's tables; this would have been in theory possible, if the tables were accurate enough. (John Donne in 'The Valediction of the Book' wrote 'but to conclude/Of longitudes, what other way have we/But to mark when and where the dark eclipses be?')

If Columbus had been even moderately successful, he would have been able to discard his lifelong conviction that he had been at the edge of Asia.

The drama that was yet to unfold, of European domination of the New World, has caused historians to invest the moment of discovery with a significance of which contemporaries were unaware. A nineteenth-century bibliographer wrote of the geographical work of Pomponius Mela published in 1493 that it 'pasted up into one little book all the knowledge and all the ignorance respecting our globe that could be collected from the ancients as well as medieval writers, so as to start fair with the new light to be let in by Columbus.'

This could not be more wrong. News of the New World was added to the existing body of written knowledge without displacing it, and medieval works with a geographical reference like *The Mirrour of the World* by Gautier of Metz and *Polichronicon* by Ranulf Higden continued to be printed without modification well into the sixteenth century.

Print has from its beginnings been exploited for the authority it can give to a text as well as being a means of dissemination; thus laws and proclamations were printed, often in type that resembled the previous handwritten scripts. The 'Columbus letter' can thus be read as a quasi-legal document, establishing the priority of the Spanish discovery, and the rights of Columbus to his promised share of the benefits. The claim required the support of the Holy Roman Empire, hence the printing in Rome of the Latin translation possibly made by Bernardino Carvajal, the Spanish ambassador, who made a public oration on the subject on 19 June 1493.

The dual opportunities offered by print, of dissemination and authority, were irresistible to the fraudulent or rival claimant. The *Nuremberg Chronicle* published in 1493 was subsequently put forward as evidence that Diego Cam and Martin Behaim had reached the American mainland before Columbus. A forgery by Jan Van Doesborch, a printer of Antwerp, printed a genuine account of the voyage to India of a German called Balthazar Springer but placed at each end of it short passages of Amerigo Vespucci's previously published *Mundus Novus*, thus misleading a Keeper of Maps of the British Museum in the last decade of the nineteenth century into the belief that he had discovered a previously unknown voyage of Vespucci's.

Accounts of voyages followed a manuscript tradition, that of Sir John Mandeville and Marco Polo. Mandeville's *Travels* had become, as far as was possible before literacy was widespread, a popular book. But much in such accounts was hearsay, speculation or invention, and careful selection and editing were necessary if reliable records were to be had; fortunately comparison of texts and the production of a canon was also in the medieval tradition. The first and possibly the greatest of these editors was a churchman, Pietro Martire de'Anghiera, known in English as Peter Martyr. His eight *Decades* were followed by similar collections of narratives compiled by Giovanni Battista Ramusio, Theodor De Bry and Levinus Hulsius. Richard Eden, Richard Hakluyt and Samuel Purchas continued the tradition in English.

The medieval chronicles appear among early Americana when their later entries refer to the discoveries, although most of the text is likely to precede them. The bibliographer Henry Harrisse described them as 'beginning *a mundi incunabulis*, and ending with the year when the manuscript was intrusted to the printer. Every two or three years additions were made and new editions published under the name of the author who had given celebrity to the work, even after he was dead and buried within the walls of the monastery which had been his only sphere of action.'

Pictures are an important part of early Americana. At first woodcuts, and later, engravings, were used to ornament texts. But pictures did not always convey reliable information; those of Theodor De Bry with their portrayals of Amazons, and of Indians munching on severed limbs, were the cause of much misunderstanding.

Printed Americana was late to appear in England, as indeed was an interest in exploration and colonisation, but no doubt manuscript books, such as Roger Barlow's *A Brief Summa of Geographie*, and European publications circulated. A book in English, the first to describe America (which it rendered as Armenica) and titled *Of the Newe Landes*, was published by Jan Van Doesborch in Antwerp probably in 1520. Thomas More's *Utopia*, which contains a reference to Vespucci and is itself set in the New World, was first published in Latin in Louvain in 1516, and in English in London in 1551. A work of fiction, *A New Interlude and a Mery of the Nature of the Four Elements* by John Rastell, made a passing reference to the naming of America; the date of publication was again about 1520. Two English versions of the *Ship of Fools* were published in London in 1509, by Richard Pynson and Wynken de Worde. *A Lytel Treatise of Astronomy* by Anthony Ascham in 1552 referred briefly to America in order to illustrate the reversal of the seasons in the southern hemisphere. Two translations by Richard Eden provided the first two works of substance relating to America and printed in England. The first was *A Treatise of the Newe India*, 1553, which was a translation of a work of Sebastian Munster, published first in Basel in 1544, to which is owed the English use of the Latin form of the Admiral's name – Columbus. The second contained a translation of Peter Martyr's first three *Decades*, Oviedo's *Historie of the West Indies*, Pigafetta's account of Magellan's circumnavigation and extracts from several other sources.

Printing therefore has its place in the annals of early America and references that are slight, fraudulent, dubious or merely incorrect entitle the works in which they appear to a place in the canon of early Americana. (A list of works of early Americana in the British Library is given in Appendix 2.)

The establishment of printing in America

From the middle of the sixteenth century, European works were joined by books printed in the New World. The first American printing was done in Mexico City in 1539 or 1540 by Juan Pablo. In 1550, a type foundry was set up and by the end of the century 116 titles had been printed. A press followed in Lima in 1584, and presses were established in two towns in Ecuador during the seventeenth century. It was the authority of print that was sought by the early printers of Spanish America; the works were thus related to the law or the church, and printing was strictly controlled.

The same was in general true of the origins of printing in the territory that became the United States, in contrast to Europe where printing had its origins in private enterprise. The words of William Berkeley, Governor of Virginia, in 1671 are often quoted as an amusing aside, but they were intended seriously in an age in which religious and political authority were closely identified:

> I thank God we have not free schools nor printing, and I hope we shall not have these three hundred years. For learning has brought disobediance and heresy and sects into the world; and printing has divulged them and libels against the government. God keep us from both.

But printing had already begun in New England, at the press of Stephen Daye at Cambridge, Massachusetts. This press had been brought to America in 1638, eighteen years after the voyage of the Mayflower, under the auspices of Harvard College, and it was operated by Stephen Daye and his son Matthew until 1649, then by Samuel Green until 1692. It remained the only press in the British colonies until John

Foster began printing, also with official permission, in Boston in 1675. As late as 1690 an attempt to print a newspaper was suppressed by the authorities, and the only surviving copy of the paper, *Public Occurrences*, printed by Benjamin Harris, is that sent by the Governor to the British Government to justify his action. (It is now in the Public Record Office at Kew.)

The material printed by Daye's press was similar to what had been published in Spanish America, relating mainly to the church and to the law. Two ephemeral works, 'The Freeman's Oath' and an almanac for 1639, were followed in 1640 by the first substantial book published in British America, *The Whole Book of Psalms* (usually known as the Bay Psalm Book), the theology of which was orthodox puritanism – 'The altar of God needs no polishing.' But American printing was slow to expand during the rest of the century.

It would be wrong to assume that there was no intellectual life in America and that the colonials were of necessity preoccupied with labour for the first century of settlement; George Sandys translated ten books of Ovid's *Metamorphoses* in Virginia in the 1620s.

For very good reasons most American books were printed in England until the last decade of the seventeenth century. To risk an investment in a printing enterprise of any scale, the printer needed a secure supply of paper, and although it could be imported, it was the most expensive item in the production of a book and required a lot of capital to order or to stockpile sufficient against a speculative future need. Paper was made at that time from clean linen rags, and it was not until 1690, by which time Philadelphia had become a sufficiently large and prosperous city to provide a constant supply, that a paper mill could be established in America. The bibliography of American books printed in America before 1700 therefore must be supported with that of books of American origin or interest printed in England.

As the settlement of North America became a rival in interest to exploration during the mid-seventeenth century, so books about America began to report on the progress and affairs of the colonies, and material matters of interest to colonists and promoters. The emigration of the Puritans was an event relating to the religious history of Britain, and thus theological controversy, even if it had its origins in the affairs of New England, was of interest to Englishmen who had remained at home; theological books were, even if originally disseminated in manuscript or printed in America, often reprinted in England.

The dates of first printing in each of the colonies give the impression of a steady expansion in the late seventeenth and the first half of the eighteenth centuries (the date of first settlement or founding of colonies in parenthesis):

Massachusetts (1620)	1639
Virginia (1607)	1682
Maryland (1634)	1685
Pennsylvania (1681)	1685
New York (1625)	1693
Connecticut (1639)	1709
New Jersey (1664)	1723
Rhode Island (1636)	1727
South Carolina (1670)	1731
North Carolina (1653)	1749
New Hampshire (1629)	1756
Delaware (1682)	1761
Georgia (1732)	1762

The time that elapsed between the first settlement and the beginning of printing varied greatly from colony to colony, which suggests unique reasons for the establishment of printing in each place. But conflict between printers and the colonial authorities was a common cause of the spread of printing because printers were often forced to take their presses to more hospitable or safer places. In the eighteenth century printing was spread wider when the authorities countered dissent by sponsoring the establishment of presses in the provincial capitals.

No reliable information is available on the output of the colonial presses as a whole, although there is information for particular presses over limited periods. This has led to speculation that estimates made by counting surviving copies and other works known with certainty to have been printed could understate the total output by a factor of almost five times. The best one can do is to make cautious use of the statistics of titles included in Charles Evans' *American Bibliography*. Taking Evans' figures by decades through the seventeenth and eighteenth centuries (but ignoring those from the later Bristol supplement which are counted on a different basis), it can be seen that the increase from year to year of items known to have been printed was far from constant:

Numbers of titles listed in Charles Evans *American Bibliography* by decades.

1639–1649	29	1720–1729	1,158
1650–1659	27	1730–1739	1,220
1660–1669	90	1740–1749	1,983
1670–1679	131	1750–1759	2,076
1680–1689	224	1760–1769	3,017
1690–1699	401	1770–1779	5,146
1700–1709	539	1780–1789	5,609
1710–1719	647	1790–17991	14,453

It is tempting to try to link the variations with the political events, in particular those of the eighteenth century. The most significant figure here would appear to be that for the last decade of the century, which shows the greatest increase of any over the previous decade: two and a half times. One might conclude that this reflects the fruit of independence, a flourish in the publication of American books. But the figures might be misleading and really reflect another aspect of independence – the interest that Isaiah Thomas and his fellow book-collectors were beginning to take in the history of American printing. Thomas and others sought out American imprints, and their collections have subsequently become available to bibliographers. Thus a higher proportion of the titles of books printed this decade would have been known by Evans, and the higher figure for the decade might result from this better knowledge as much as from more printing. This is confirmed by adding in the parallel figures from the Bristol supplement which diminishes the rate of increase at several points between 1639 and 1799, and particularly that of the last decade.

No one can doubt that the scale of printing in the British colonies and the United States was small at the beginning of the eighteenth century and large at the end, but one has to be cautious about attributing too much directly to factors such as non-importation in the 1760s or independence in the 1780s and 1790s.

Nevertheless, G. Thomas Tanselle has shown (in Bernard Bailyn and John B. Hench, eds., *The Press and the American Revolution*, 1980) that, as they are represented in the Evans/Bristol bibliographies and indexes, the number of items printed, the number of presses working and the separate places where printing took place increased dramatically during some of the years of the Revolutionary period. But his tables also show a considerable return to normality by 1783; an increase of one half in the number of places of printing and a doubling of the number of printers in the two decades between 1764 and 1783 (34 and 112 respectively in 1783) is what we would expect if a constant rate of increase had taken place since 1700.

Much of the increase beyond the trend which apparently took place during the mid seventies can be accounted for by the printing of pamphlets of varying length – broadsheets, proclamations and so on. Tanselle noted indeed a slight drop in the printing of almanacs, a printer's staple, during the early years of the war. Tories as well as Whigs were printers; the second most prolific publisher of pamphlets between 1764 and 1783 was James Rivington, a New York Tory and King's Printer. The period of increased printing, 1774 to 1779, included the most mobile period of the war, and perusal of local records suggests that a great deal of printing, in terms of numbers of separate items, usually followed a change of government. These items were generally short and ephemeral: forms for oaths of allegiance, loyal addresses to the new authorities, lists of banished and proscribed people, proclamations by the army commanders.

This kind of printing, although it had diminished by 1783, must have made up much of the output of items printed between 1790 and 1799 and during the first two decades of the nineteenth century, while the institutions of national and state government were being established.

But English printing of books relating to America remained important through the Revolutionary period. In *The American Controversy: A bibliographical study of the British pamphlets about the disputes in America 1763–1783* (1981), Thomas Adams records 700 British pamphlets wholly or largely concerned with the subject.

English books in America

Colonial intellectual life was based on books imported from Britain. Jeremy Condy, a Boston bookseller of the 1760s, visited England to enlarge his stock, and maintained a close relationship with Joseph Richardson, a London bookseller; as did David Hall of Philadelphia with William Strahan of London, and Henry Knox of Boston with Thomas Longman. The first libraries in the American colonies had been parish libraries established by the Rev. Thomas Bray in the first few years of the eighteenth century, under the auspices of the Society for the Propagation of the Gospel. During the century, men of intellectual or social aspirations – lawyers, planters, merchants – acquired collections of books; inventories of the losses of Loyalist refugees in the Revolution include some quite large ones, perhaps the creation of two or three generations. These collections were generally of British books, consisting largely of classical authors, histories and contemporary fiction. Such libraries created and perpetuated an American taste which American printing, as it expanded in the eighteenth and nineteenth centuries, would try to satisfy.

Thus in 1744 Cicero's *Cato Major* was published in America, and three editions of Richardson's novel *Pamela*. Joseph Addison's play *Cato* was published in Boston in 1767 (English editions had been available since 1713), *School for Scandal* in 1782 and a complete Shakespeare in 1794. All of these were familiar in British editions before they were printed in America, and indeed the American editions were usually typeset from an imported printed copy. British authors did not enjoy full copyright protection in the United States until 1891, and the reprinting of British works, especially in collections, cheap editions and 'home libraries', continued until then.

The character of colonial printing

It is not true, therefore, to say that American colonial publishing produced works of a predominantly practical character because it served the needs of a pioneer society. What did predominate were works of *local* interest whose market was in the colonies and the West Indies, in particular those like newspapers and almanacs that had to reach the market quickly. These works included legislative printing (ie votes and proceedings of the assemblies), laws (editions of New York laws were issued by William Bradford in 1694, 1710, 1713, 1719 and 1726), epitomes of laws, ready reckoners, primers, and works relating to local political controversies (like George Keith's *Truth Advanced* (1694), the first book printed in the city of New York), and Peter Zenger's *Brief Narrative of the Case and Trial of John Peter Zenger Printer of the New York Weekly Journal* (1736), the account of his trial for seditious libel. Zenger's book was reprinted in London in 1738 (a year in which *Areopagitica* was also reprinted), not because of interest in colonial affairs but for its defence against censorship. It was reprinted again in London in 1752, and then again in 1765 while John Wilkes was in exile in France and his conviction for libel was a popular political issue. Reprinting of political tracts in London, often subsidised by the interested parties, was essential if they were to influence Parliament.

Children's books, poetry and, after 1765, plays were printed in the colonies, a mixture of reprints of books that had previously been imported and original works. Popular books of a sensational nature were, while they had an English counterpart, of purely local interest, for example narratives of the experiences of captives of the Indians, and works such as *An account of the discovery of a hermit, who lived about 200 years in a cave at the foot of a hill, 73 days journey westward of the Great Alleghany Mountains* (1786) by James Buckland. These are reminiscent of English works of the previous century or earlier.

Humour and satire often have a local reference and a local style, and, like poetry, they were published both in newspapers and magazines, and also on their own; short publications were often reissued as volumes binding up unsold pamphlets.

It must be noted that printers made much of their living from jobbing work and stationery, and like most other colonial professional and business men had other interests. This perhaps explains how the numbers of printers named in surviving imprints can fluctuate from year to year. There were no publishing fortunes in the eighteenth century, although there were 'lineages' of apprenticeship and family. Governments were often bad payers, and the printer could do little but petition the assembly for his money. Newspaper subscriptions were difficult to keep up, and religious publishing, outside New England and Pennsylvania where it was precarious for doctrinal reasons, had strong competition from the Society for the Propagation of the Gospel, which did its publishing in London. The first English Bible was not published in America until 1782.

The expansion in American printing that occurred in the last decades of the eighteenth century continued into the early decades of the nineteenth. Its general character did not change, but the places where printing took place proliferated as settlement moved westward and new territories and states joined the original thirteen. Educational publishing – schools and college textbooks and encyclopedias for home use – was particularly associated with westward movement, and Cincinnati, strategically placed when rivers were the highways, emerged as the centre of western publishing.

Charles Evans proposed 1820 as the closing date of his *American Bibliography*, although he didn't get beyond 1800, and 1820 has often been taken as the end of the 'early period' of American printing. But the selection of any date is arbitrary, and it is convenient, if one is to consider the American collections of the British Library, to extend the early period to the 1830s and 1840s, when important changes occurred at the library itself.

Early bibliographies of Americana

'Americana' is unusual among bibliographical categories in that it has been in use during the time of the creation of most of the works it refers to; it is self-conscious like belles-lettres, rather than an abstract category like 'useful arts' and it is neither useful nor possible to define it precisely. The first list of American books was published in 1545 by Karl Gesner in *Bibliotheca Universalis*: it was not followed until 1629 when Antonio de León Pinelo's *Epitome de la Biblioteca* was published.

The first list of English Americana was White Kennett's *Bibliothecae Americanae Primordia* published in 1713. It has a connection, though a somewhat vague one, with the origins of the British Museum Library. Kennett was, like Columbus, associated with a period of transition, but this time a transition from the mentality of the Renaissance to an intellectual style that is familiarly modern.

But to explain this it is necessary to return briefly to the sixteenth century. While Spanish explorers were challenging medieval knowledge with their discoveries in the Americas, in Britain the contents of the medieval libraries were being dispersed. Although this was accompanied by excesses of antipopery, it had, paradoxically, a less destructive aspect. Looted manuscripts sometimes passed into secular libraries, such as the King's Library, and some Oxford and Cambridge colleges, and others were scattered widely in private hands; Archbishop Matthew Parker later acquired one collection of manuscripts for the King's Library from a baker in Canterbury. It is in the challenge posed by this situation that modern book and manuscript collecting had its origin.

Antiquarian collecting of these dispersed documents and books during the following century had a political slant: the antiquarian historians hoped, particularly by the examination of charters and such documents, to reveal an unchanging and fundamental English constitution. Sir Robert Cotton (1571–1631) and Sir Robert Harley, 1st Earl of Oxford (1661–1724), whose collections later became foundation collections of the British Museum Library, were among these early antiquarians. At the end of the seventeeth century, this particular viewpoint, which had had its apotheosis in Sir Edward Coke, was challenged; the political legacy of the Civil War required a more subtle view of the English constitution. White Kennett was prominent in this new movement. In his *Parochial Antiquities...* (1695), which has earned him the title of the father of parish history, he was concerned not to show that English institutions had existed since time immemorial as the early collectors had believed, but to find their particular origins and to trace their development. Kennett's purpose thus made him dependent on the great antiquarian collections. He used the Harleian (Sir Robert Harley's collection) with the help of its librarian Humphrey Wanley; in his own words 'where I wanted [ie lacked] authorities, I resolved my conjectures should be short and modest'. In his contribution to *The Compleat History of England* (1706) Kennett also relied greatly on documents, in this case mainly printed; he was able to make use of the library of his friend Archbishop Tenison.

When Kennett was asked to write a history of the Society for the Propagation of the Gospel, which had been founded to promote missions in the British settlements in America, he imagined his task to be the same in principle as that of his earlier histories. The difference was that the libraries he had used before did not contain an adequate collection of American books; Kennett would have to create one himself.

28 Americana and Foundation of the British Museum Library

Kennett expected this library to document the origins and development of the American communities: in his own words

> the first discovery of the regions...the several expeditions and voyages made to every coast and port and river, the advances and settlements there made, the tyranny and cruelty of the Spaniards in Mexico and Peru...above all...the relations and journals of our own countrymen upon those seas and coasts, their discoveries and observations, their settlement of plantations and colonies, their improvements in trade and strength, their conversation with the natives, and their endeavours to bring them civility and religion.

The collection he assembled is believed to have contained 330 volumes when he presented it to the Society in 1713 which, with the addition of works that he encouraged his friends to present, represented 1216 books, broadsides and manuscripts. This collection of American books was the basis for the *Primordia*, which is an analytical catalogue – ie the general works it contains, such as Hakluyt's and Purchas's collections of voyages, generate several entries under various subjects. Sir Hans Sloane, a physician, was among the friends of Kennett who contributed books to the library of the Society for the Propagation of the Gospel: a copy of his *Catalogus plantarum quae in insula Jamaica sponte proveniunt* (1696), and later a *Voyage to the Indies...* (1707). Sloane had travelled to the West Indies where the Society founded a library and a college, and took an interest in the work of the Society, advising them on the health of their missionaries. (He said they should avoid rum punch and have 'frequent resort to the bark', ie quinine.)

The books listed in the *Primordia* correspond very closely with the canon of Americana described earlier in this chapter. Its very existence and Kennett's activities and his connections with other book collectors suggest some general interest in the collection of Americana in London at this early date; its title is the origin of the bibliographical use of the term 'Americana'.

Kennett had hoped to promote the foundation of a public American library when he published the *Primordia*; he mentioned the names of Tenison and Bodley in the dedication and expressed the hope that the library of the Society for the Propagation of the Gospel might become not only a place of reference of American matters, but also a 'common fund and treasury of all the remains of that country', a repository for books and manuscripts. There was no national repository that he could have honoured with his gift of American books, although the idea of one had inspired several keepers of the Royal Library, and several proposals had been made. Kennett died in 1728 and although his American collection did not remain intact, his name is commemorated in the present library of the Society for the Propagation of the Gospel.

The founding of the British Museum

Twenty five years after Kennett's death, an Act of Parliament was passed founding the British Museum. This was a response to the will of Kennett's friend, Sir Hans Sloane, which offered his museum collection and library of books and manuscripts to the Crown for the sum of £20,000. To these the Act added the Cotton Library (which included the collections of the antiquarian, Sir Robert Cotton and the book collector, Arthur Edwards) and the Harleian manuscripts. Before the British Museum opened in 1759 it had also received the Royal Library (later known as the Old Royal Library) which brought with it the right to a copy of each book published in Britain. Kennett's American collection remained with the Society for the Propagation of the Gospel (and his British collection in the library of Peterborough Cathedral) until 1916 when, by then seriously depleted, it was offered to the British Museum. Only eighty volumes were accepted and the rest, which would have duplicated books already in the collection, were sold. But these were a valuable addition to the collection, and both its foundation and its strength in American books were in part the result of Kennett's enthusiasm for bibliography and the establishment of libraries.

Rede's Bibliotheca Americana

In 1789, the year in which the first United States Congress met, another American bibliography was published in London, *Bibliotheca Americana*, which had the same chronological arrangement as the *Primordia*. The author, who was not named, claimed that it derived from research 'in the British Museum and the most celebrated public and private libraries, reviews, catalogues etc.' It derived mostly, examination proved, from the Ayscough Catalogue, an early catalogue of the British Museum Library, and it included books printed after 1713. The *Bibliotheca Americana* was widely thought to have been compiled by the Reverend Arthur Homer who issued a prospectus for such a work, but it has subsequently been established to have been compiled by Leman Thomas Rede, a hack writer who had in some manner which remains unknown acquainted himself with the general situation of American publishing:

> In North America every science has not only reared her head, but flourishes with a degree of vigour in the New World that threatens to surpass the old. Their orators, lawyers, physicians, historians, philosophers and mathematicians, may be fairly opposed to our most successful cultivators of science and the liberal arts; and poets have lately put in claims, backed by productions that evince a very slender inferiority...

But, nevertheless:

> All publications of consequence, in point of size and expence, are executed in Europe and generally in London, Dublin or Edinburgh. The few that have been printed in America are badly executed... Law books have the most rapid sale...the French have taken uncommon pains to introduce their language and literature, but without success.

Rede's *Bibliotheca* has been unjustly maligned; a review that appeared in the *Gentleman's Magazine* in 1789 drew attention to its dependence on the *Primordia* and hinted that it might not be accurate. But the fact of its publication in that year is important. It was a commercial publication, which suggests sufficient interest in collecting Americana in the area served by the London book trade to absorb several hundred copies; it is not a rare book now. Its form is also important: it is a chronological catalogue, and it includes European (particularly British) as well as American imprints. The bibliography was preceded by an essay on 'the present state of literature in those countries'– like the *Primordia* it included North and South America – which gives the whole book a sense of having as its purpose the study and understanding of America. The bibliographer Henry Harrisse said that it had been compiled in fact 'to supply data to an American gentleman who proposed to write a history of America.' Broadness of scope (and the consequent difficulty of precise definition) and practical purpose were thus established in the bibliography of Americana. The words of the subtitle serve for later bibliographies as well: 'the most curious and interesting books, pamphlets, state papers etc. upon the subject...'

Because most of the work for the *Bibliotheca* is likely to have been done in the British Museum Library, it gives some impression of what Americana the Library might have contained towards the end of the eighteenth century.

The early American works in the Library at this time probably came with the Old Royal Library which had contributed about 9,000 printed books to the British Museum on all subjects, and the Sloane collection which had contributed about 40,000; neither the purchase of English printed books nor receipt of copies required under the copyright law proceeded on any scale before 1814. Some hint of the strength of the collection of early Americana at this time is given by the fact that the books received from the library of Thomas Grenville in 1847 duplicated a large proportion of the existing collection, although it had been the policy of the Library during the years of large-scale purchasing before the collection was received not to buy books that were expected to come with the Grenville Library.

Gifts and bequests of collections to the British Museum Library, some of them quite large, continued after its foundation, and this remained the major mode of acquisition of early printed books until 1845 when for the first time Parliament provided funds sufficient to remedy gaps in the collection of earlier works. Parliament would provide money for a particularly notable purchase before 1845; otherwise the principal source of money for the purchase of books was a fund that had come with the Cotton Library (originally a part of the bequest of Arthur Edwards). It seems likely that some Americana would have come with these acquisitions, particularly Italian books and works on geography and topography. The King's Library, the private library of George III which was passed to the British Museum in 1823, and the Grenville Library, have printed catalogues which list a great many American works; the King's Library is particularly rich in maps and military plans.

Private collections can thus be said to have characterised the British Museum Library until the early decades of the nineteenth century, but the consequences of this should not be exaggerated. The foundation collections, the Royal and the King's Libraries and the Grenville Library, were the only collections that the Library was obliged to take in their entirety and it was possible therefore that a policy of selection existed for other acquisitions. Most of the collections from which acquisitions were made were themselves specialised, and they represented very diverse subjects – books in Hebrew, Civil War tracts, Garrick's collection of plays, the Burney newspaper collection – which suggests considerable individuality, if not eccentricity, on the part of the collectors. They were not all statesmen/antiquaries like the Harleys and Thomas Grenville. Of the policy of collection in the eighteenth century, if such a surmise is correct, there is little direct evidence, other than of course the books themselves, so far as they can be collectively identified. But a clue to the kind of thinking that was current at the time is given by the advice of Dr Samuel Johnson to King George III's librarian, Frederick Barnard, which is quoted in the printed catalogue of the King's Library published in 1820

(Johnson's letter was dated 1768). He was addressing himself to the question of 'ransacking other countries' for books:

> English literature you will not seek in any place but England. Classical learning is diffused everywhere ... But every country has a literature of its own which may be best gathered in its native soil. The studies of the learned are influenced by forms of government and modes of religion, and therefore, those books are necessary and common in some places which, where different opinions or different manners prevail, are of little use, and for that reason rarely to be found.

He goes on to talk specifically about Italy for which place Barnard was about to depart, to recommend philosophy, law, curiosities of local publishing, topography, local history, and maps, for which he made a strong plea ('you will form a more valuable body of geography than can otherwise be had'). He advocated also the acquisition of titles in specialist subjects from 'the collection of an eminent civilian, feudist [civil and feudal law] or mathematician' because the books will be less likely to duplicate those of other collections acquired. The catalogue of the King's Library shows how well the librarian was guided by this advice.

If one adapts Johnson's advice to American books, bearing in mind Rede's account of American publishing, then the Library might have cautiously selected American imprints in science and the liberal arts as well as the American history and topography and 'local' printing that made up the staple of the printers' output, ie serial publications: periodicals and newspapers, annual registers and almanacs. There is no practical way of finding out what specific titles were acquired in any particular year in the eighteenth or early nineteenth century, but if the method of acquisition remained substantially the same until the 1840s, which is likely, then a guess as to the general character of acquisition can be made by using some lists which fortunately survive for later years.

Between 1837 and 1849 the titles of all books acquired were entered with their provenance in yearly registers. The list in

Appendix III is of American imprints acquired in 1837. The register of acquistions in which these titles were entered included books bought, books received as gifts and those sent on from the Stationery Office where they had been collected from the publishers under the provisions of the Copyright Act.

The register reveals another piece of information: almost all the American imprints received in 1837 were purchased from a bookseller in Covent Garden named Richard Kennett who had issued several catalogues of American books. Little is known of Kennett other than that he was certainly not a direct descendant of White Kennett, and that, although he was an Englishman, he named a son born in 1836 Benjamin Franklin Kennett. (Kennett used a medallion of Franklin on his American catalogues.) The registers, which run only from 1837 to 1849, record purchases from Kennett until 1842 but after 1839 they were confined to continuations of periodicals, and almanacs.

In 1842 a large number of American imprints, 556 volumes, were purchased from another London bookseller, William Pickering. Pickering supplied a further 245 volumes in 1843. There were no large American acquisitions in 1844, and in 1845 modest purchases were made from Pickering and from the firm of Wiley and Putnam. After that great changes occurred in the British Museum Library which will be the subject of the next chapter.

These purchases of American imprints were made in blocks rather than as single copies. They were mainly of recently published works, and while Boston, New York, Philadelphia and Baltimore predominated among places of publication, such places as Cincinnati, Columbus, Albany and New Orleans were also represented.

In their composition they fitted well Dr Johnson's advice to the Royal Librarian in 1768: they included medical science, civil engineering, technology, geology (all subjects in which Americans excelled), books 'influenced by forms of government' (ie law and political economy), works, particularly periodicals, reflecting 'models of religion', and books that 'may best be gathered on the native soil' – collected writings of

Washington and Franklin, biographies, local antiquities and the lore of the Indians.

Textbooks and encyclopedias, staples of American printers, were present in considerable numbers, but literature was scarcely represented other than in periodicals, and occasional volumes of essays and poetry. But much of the fiction printed in the United States was still at this time British in origin, and therefore in Johnson's words best sought in England.

A small but significant group of American books came to the Library in 1841 and 1842 from the sale of the library of the American Loyalist, George Chalmers. Chalmers had collected books, official documents and newspapers when he was living in Maryland, for the writing of his book *The Revolt of the Colonies*. (He suppressed publication in 1782 when, after the resignation of Lord North, he was offered a position in the Board of Trade.) The British Museum had an agent at the sale of Chalmers' library (which included a number of important English books) and it is significant that several files of American newspapers – the *Boston Gazette* was one – were among the items purchased. (Some early American newspapers had also come to the Library with the Burney collection in 1818.)

A report on the 'Origin, progress and present state of the [British Museum] library of printed books', which Panizzi had compiled, no doubt with the assistance of his colleagues, and which was published in 1846, commented on American history and literature. On the first, it repeated James Grahame's remark in the preface to his history of the United States, published in 1827, that he had had to go to Gottingen for American books; and on the second, commented that in all types of literature printed in America including scientific (but excluding theology) the collections were 'very incomplete'. Most American imprints that were present, the report stated, had been 'recently acquired'. This referred to purchases made since 1837, that is, to the substantial purchases of American imprints from Kennett, Pickering, and Wiley and Putnam.

There is no particular reason to believe that Grahame's comment was fair, or that he had any great knowledge of the

British Museum's collections; many scholars since have said the same sort of thing to justify their travels. Furthermore, his opinion was out of date by 1846.

Both Grahame and the report of 1846 were speaking of American imprints. Their remarks probably underestimated these, and they certainly ignored the strength of the collections of British and European Americana in the Library at that date.

The period of private collection, during which the British Museum Library might be thought of as a very large country house library, ended with the report of 1846, although, as the increased scale of purchasing after 1837 shows, the changes had been anticipated for several years. It can be seen from the acquisitions registers and from the catalogue of the Chalmers sale (the Library has a copy marked with the names of purchasers) that the foundations of a collection of American imprints had already been laid, mostly acquired, it is true, after 1837: but if one is prepared to speculate on the basis of Rede's *Bibliotheca*, it included works selected from the private collections that became available to the Library before that date. When added to the American books of European origin that the Library possessed, this gave it in 1845 a far from insignificant American collection.

2.
The American Collection of the National Library, 1846 to 1886

Growth and character of American publishing in the nineteenth century

While the general character of American publishing during the first three decades of the nineteenth century was not remarkably different from that of the last decade of the eighteenth, changes were beginning which would by the end of the century have transformed it entirely. Part of the explanation of these changes must be simply the increase in volume of the industry, in both numbers of separate titles, and sizes of editions. Thus in 1820 total book production in the United States was worth two and a half million dollars; in 1850 it was worth twelve and a half. Such an increase in scale presupposes a change in the organisation of the industry, even if it was not the cause. The most extensive change was the evolution of a new kind of publishing firm. These new entrepreneurial firms did not replace the local printers and publishers who continued to be associated, as they had been in the past, with the production of newspapers, and who had spread by mid-century to the Pacific coast. The new firms were, like the printers and booksellers of the previous century, concentrated in Philadelphia, New York and Boston, and for the same reason – distribution. New York publishers tended to specialise in reprinting British works; Sir Walter Scott and, later, Dickens and Thackeray accounted for millions of volumes. The Boston publishers, whose distribution was inland by railway to the northern states (the region now called the midwest), had access to a great deal of intellectual capital in the Transcendentalists, and in the New England colleges and academies. Philadelphia continued to be a centre of medical publishing, but shared political publishing with

American Collection of the National Library, 1846 to 1886

Washington after the Federal capital was moved there in 1800. Cincinnati, the first western publishing centre to emerge, was located on the interior water routes; its publishers reprinted eastern-published books and specialised in the growing educational and school book market.

Several publishing firms established before 1850 survived into the twentieth century, among them the following:

Harper and Brothers	New York	1817
D Appleton and Co.	New York	1825
Truman and Smith (American Book Company)	Cincinnati	1830
Tichnor and Fields	Boston	1832
J B Lippincott	Philadelphia	1836
Little and Brown	Boston	1837
A S Barnes	Hartford and New York	1838
Dodd and Mead	New York	1839
Wiley and Putnam	New York	1840
Scribner	New York	1846
Van Nostrand	New York	1848

The separation of partners or merger of firms was common throughout the century and it generally reflected the evolution of enterprises of a distinctive nature; unlike British publishers, these American firms were general publishers with respect to the kind of books they produced, and also in many cases they did their own printing. As the pattern emerged, they ceased to print for other publishers, but, because of the large editions they were required to print (50,000 in the case of a popular novel), they were in the forefront of new technologies such as stereotyping and power presses.

The chief characteristic which distinguished them from the firms that preceded them was that their distribution went beyond the locality to a mass market. This obviously influenced the kinds of book they published: well-known authors, standard textbooks, subjects of universal interest such as the Indians, geology, medicine, religion and history. Pamphlet publishing, commemorative volumes and gift books remained, as they still do, in the hands of small firms, and certain types of book, such as religious tracts, which went to a specialised market or which did not need to defray the costs of publication, were published by societies, which nevertheless resembled commercial companies in their scale and organisation.

The contract between author and publisher changed as scale increased. In the eighteenth century each book was produced as a separate enterprise and often the author paid at least for the paper. Such an arrangement, with its opportunities for wilfulness on the part of authors, was obviously impossible as publishing became industrialised. Publishers – George Putnam and Alexander McClurg, for example – were advocates of authors' copyright, so that authors would legally assign their rights to publishers and so reduce the anarchy that had resulted from reliance on 'courtesy of the trade', where a heavy investment in typesetting could be wiped out by legal piracy. But some disorder continued during most of the century because of the scale of reprinting of British works; until the International Copyright Agreement of 1891, British authors did not have the copyright of their works in the United States and could not therefore assign exclusive rights to an American publisher.

The profession of authorship became possible in the United States when sufficient money was generated by publishing to support it; the turning point occurred at about mid-century, although Washington Irving, Nathaniel Hawthorne and James Fennimore Cooper made money from writing before that. Cooper has been said to have been the first American writer of imaginative literature to have lived on his earnings. A royalty payment to authors of about ten per cent became standard. The lack of an international copyright agreement until 1891, which meant that American publishers were not legally obliged to pay royalties to British authors, does not seem to have discriminated against Americans; Irving, Cooper, Longfellow, Hawthorne, Dana and Poe took their place alongside Scott, Dickens, and Thackeray as best selling authors. Professional authorship was not confined to fiction. 'Parson' Weems, a book agent for Mathew Carey the Philadelphia publisher, had given biography a bad start with his *Life of Washington* in 1800, but Jared Sparks restored scholarly standards in his *Library of American Biography* (1834–1874), in which sixty notable Americans were dealt with by some equally notable authors in twenty-five volumes. Alongside these were collections of historical documents; Jared Sparks was again a pioneer in his *Diplomatic Correspondence of the American Revolution* (1829–1830) and *Writings of George Washington* (1834–1837). The histories of towns and of states had continued from the eighteenth century, but they were joined in the nineteenth by a vogue which outdid them both in numbers: county histories. These were then, and remain, repositories of useful information; they were generally large, of a regular format, and produced by specialist publishers.

The academic profession had not previously been a source of authors of commercial books until writers such as Francis Lieber, the founder of the *Encyclopedia Americana*, and Oliver Wendell Holmes brought both professions together. Toward the end of the century university presses were founded, the first being Cornell in 1869. Children's books, 'juveniles' as they are known in the trade, sometimes rivalled fiction in the number of titles produced each year, and religious and medical books continued to make up a large proportion of non-fiction books published.

Industrialised publishing required heavy promotion. Emerson

might have lectured in the mid-west to promote his ideas, but sales of his books did not suffer by his sallies from Concord. Tours by authors, nationwide advertising and, above all, magazines published by book publishers themselves, in which novels and travel books in particular were serialised, helped to create a mass market.

The establishment of new firms continued in the second half of the century: Houghton Miflin in Boston and Rand McNally in Chicago in 1864; Ginn and Co. in Boston in 1867; and in New York: Henry Holt in 1868; E.P. Dutton and the Macmillan Company of America, an offshoot of the British firm, in 1869; Funk and Wagnall, and Thomas Crowell in 1876; and the Century Company in 1881.

The onset and progress of the Civil War checked the growth of commercial publishing, although it stimulated the production of pamphlets; but as with the upheavals of the previous century, the trend continued none the less.

The increase in the number of book titles published each year throughout the century is undeniable, although it is not easy to arrive at accurate figures. It is believed that until the 1840s about one hundred book titles came from American presses each year. If the figures seem low compared to the Evans' figures for American *imprints* each year, it is because Evans included all printed works; his is a record of printing, not of book publishing. A more comparable figure with those of Evans is that of 25,000 items printed between 1820 and 1849 recorded in Orville Roorbach's *Bibliotheca Americana*. But as book publishing and jobbing-printing became distinct activities after the 1840s, accurate figures for book publishing alone became available. Thus in 1853, 879 book titles are recorded; in 1855, 1,092; and in 1859–60, 1,350. In 1869 an estimated 2,602 book titles were published; for the rest of the century a continuous series is available from the annual totals published in the *Publishers Weekly*: 1880, 2,076; 1890, 4,559; 1900, 6,356. Pamphlets possibly account for fifteen to twenty per cent of these annual totals.

Reprinting of British books remained a feature of American book publishing throughout the century but the balance apparently changed at about mid-century. It was estimated by Samuel Goodrich, who under his pseudonym 'Peter Parley' did much to expand the market for American books, that in 1820 seventy per cent of books published in America were by British authors; but in 1856, when Goodrich published his *Recollections of a Lifetime* the proportion of British authors had fallen to twenty per cent. Within these broad trends, both fiction and educational books were increasing in proportion to the total, and, in both cases, American authors were becoming predominant.

The market for mass-produced books was extremely competitive; more so in fact for reprints than for American books. At the beginning of the century a novel might sell for a dollar or a dollar and a half, and a school book for fifty cents. For half a dollar, John Tebbel points out in his *History of American Publishing*, you could buy a pair of shoes, and a dollar, a day's wage for a labourer, would buy five loaves of bread. In 1886 a writer in *Harper's Magazine* observed that 'For the price of a box of strawberries or a banana you can buy the immortal works of the greatest genius of all time in fiction, poetry, philosophy, or science'. This was brought about by the advent of the 'cheap library', although the items chosen for the second comparison might also say something about the changed attitude to books in a more affluent society and one in which the puritan ethic had been much eroded. In 1885 D. Appleton and Co. sold novels for twenty-five cents each, and in 1886 twenty-six cheap libraries were advertised in the *American Bookseller*, offering books at five to twenty-five cents a copy.

Cheap book production (the subject of a study by R.H. Shove in 1937) began in the 1840s with the weekly *Brother Jonathan*, which serialised foreign novels. Its success was emulated by others, and the publishers of these periodicals began eventually to issue whole books, cheaply produced, as 'extra' editions of the journals. This brought them into direct competition with the book publishers, who responded by issuing their own magazines and lowering the prices of their books. The quality of these cheap books caused concern to the publishers of the better class of books, but quality improved during the century. The Aldine company was established in Boston in 1885 to issue cheap books of good quality – 'honestly made cheap editions'. The very name they chose, with its historical associations, indicates a degree of self-conscious pride in their products, which were advertised at thirty cents a volume.

The 'cheap libraries' consisted largely of fiction and contained a large number of reprinted foreign titles, but they did put the classics of European and American literature into a very large number of American homes. 'Dime novels', books with no pretension to quality as literature, were cheaply produced and cheaply sold alongside the books of greater intellectual merit. Outside of the cities where there were specialist bookshops, books were sold in dry goods stores or by travelling salesmen. They were sold wholesale to the trade at book auctions, held mainly in New York and Boston, which meant that they might be sold retail at much less than the publisher's advertised price. Because the competition was more intense in the cheapest and least-regulated part of the market, ie foreign reprints, American authors were slightly favoured, and thus, with the other factors at work, cheap book production probably helped the growth of the American literary profession.

Bibliography and book collecting

The bibliography of Americana was inaugurated in the United States by Isaiah Thomas who published his *History of Printing in America* in 1810 and founded the American Antiquarian Society at Worcester, Massachusetts in 1812. His own collection became the basis of the Society's library. Orville Roorbach, a bookseller in Charleston, South Carolina, spent twenty years collecting information for *Bibliotheca Americana* (1849), a catalogue of 25,000 American imprints after 1820. He issued several supplements before his death and his efforts were continued briefly by Charles B. Norton, who in 1851 founded *Norton's Literary Advertiser* which became in 1872 the

Publishers' Weekly. James Kelly followed the scope and format of Roorbach's *Bibliotheca from 1861 to 1871* in his *American Catalogue of Books Published in the United States* (2 vols, 1866–71). Since 1872 the *Publishers' Weekly* has published a weekly trade list; in 1876 the founder and editor of the *Publishers' Weekly*, Frederick Leypolt, established the *American Catalogue of Books* which continued until 1910.

Unlike the catalogues of Americana issued by the London bookseller Obadiah Rich in the 1830s and 1840s, or those of Henri Ternaux in Paris in 1837, these were trade bibliograpies, that is, after Roorbach's first retrospective volume, they recorded current titles announced by publishers. This form of bibliography was accompanied after 1867 by the *Publishers' Trade List Annual*, the index to which eventually became a separate publication, *Books In Print*. Two names closely associated with that of Leypolt were R.R. Bowker and Adolf Growall. Bowker was the most notable bibliographical publisher in the United States in the nineteenth century (his firm continues to the present) and Growall ran the *Publishers' Weekly* during the latter half of the nineteenth century.

Leypolt and Bowker introduced high standards into current bibliography in the book trade, but retrospective bibliography was also well served. In 1866 Henry Harrisse published *Bibliotheca Americana Vetustissima*, which not only listed the titles of more than 300 books or shorter printed items relating to America and published between 1493 and 1551, but reproduced the titles in the original form, extracted and translated the passages concerned with America, and accompanied the whole with an erudite and often witty commentary. Two years later the first part of Joseph Sabin's *Dictionary of Books Relating to America* appeared. Sabin died before the work was complete – 'killed by a dictionary', a friend commented. These two publications, notable as they were, were only part of an enormous amount of bibliographical activity. Harrisse was the author of ninety-one scholarly publications, while Sabin, a bookseller and book auctioneer in New York, was a noted cataloguer. Retrospective bibliography would be pointless without the book collectors; Isaiah Thomas,

Jared Sparks, Peter Force and Samuel Drake collected libraries of Americana early in the century in pursuit of their historical writing and publishing. But the later years of the century saw the rise of the mega-collectors, men with not only a bibliophiliac obsession, but the means to satisfy it even at the inflated prices that their own competitiveness had produced. The first of these was George Brinley, a descendant of Massachusetts Loyalists, whose collection of 9,500 books, which included a *Bay Psalm Book* and a *Gutenburg Bible*, was sold at a series of auctions between 1879 and 1893. The auctioneer at the first of these sales was Joseph Sabin, who crowned his career with the sale of the *Gutenburg Bible* to a New York lawyer for $8,000. (The purchaser later sold it to his rival bidder for $16,000.)

The collection of James Lenox of New York numbered 11,870 items when it reached the New York Public Library, to which Lenox bequeathed it. Like Brinley, Lenox did not confine his enthusiasm to Americana. The catalogue of the John Carter Brown collection, compiled by the Boston bookseller John Russell Bartlett and published 1875-1882, contained more than 2,200 titles relating to America. The collection was eventually established as a private library in Providence, Rhode Island.

Henry Stevens

These collectors operated from necessity through agents and dealers, both in acquiring books in America, and, if their ambition ran to the really rare and expensive, in obtaining books from Europe as well. The most sought-after and the most famous of these agents was Henry Stevens of Vermont, as he liked to style himself, who ran his business from London, but who dealt at one time or another with all the notable American collectors. He wrote a small commemorative book on his chief customer: *Recollections of Mr James Lenox of New York* was published after Lenox's death. Stevens' father had been a relatively modest book collector and antiquarian in

Barnet, Vermont, and he was able to establish both his sons, Henry and Benjamin Franklin, in the book trade.

Henry Stevens was not a particularly good scholar or bibliographer, but through lack of the right temperament rather than of the love or knowledge of books. None of his numerous publications on the bibliography of Americana are of any real use today. But his enthusiasm for books and his ebullience of personality, which can be noted even on the title pages of his own books, made him known to everyone in the world of books on both sides of the Atlantic: to Sparks and Bancroft among the scholars, Lenox and Carter Brown among book collectors, Leypolt and Bowker among bibliographers, and Melvin Dewey and Antonio Panizzi among librarians. As their agent he was responsible for placing many of the most valuable works in the collections of Lenox and Carter Brown; but it is as agent of the British Museum for the supply of American works between 1846 and 1886 that his activities are of most relevance to the present purpose.

Antonio Panizzi and the British Museum

The British Museum Library of the nineteenth and twentieth centuries is very much the creation of Antonio Panizzi; this is due in part to his position in the Library's own historical self-consciousness. The principles that he laid down, the rules for the catalogue, the enforcement of copyright deposit, the provision for an annual sum for purchasing, are all properly traced back to him, although in their detail they often owe much to his contemporaries such as Thomas Watts, or successors such as Richard Garnett. But the historical self-consciousness adds more; his origins, with a hint of the romantic revolutionary, his personality and his epic battles have appealed enormously to later librarians drawn increasingly into the embrace of bureaucracy.

The Library to which Panizzi was appointed as an 'extra assistant' in 1831 did not command great prestige, although its size – about 240,000 volumes (of manuscripts and books) – was not inconsiderable by the standards of the time. There was an air of amateurism about its administration, and the pecuniary and physical conditions for the staff were bad; the professional loyalty of the Keeper of Printed Books, the Reverend Henry Baber, was divided between the Library and the Church. In 1837, as the result of reforms that he had himself helped to initiate, Baber resigned from the Keepership, and Panizzi succeeded him. Panizzi continued in this office until 1856, then served as Principal Librarian – head of the entire Museum – until bad health forced his retirement in 1866.

Three innovations of the 1830s marked the beginning of the modern Library: authority to buy books was passed from the Trustees to the Keeper in 1830, 'unfettered' grants of funds were made by Parliament after 1833, and the alphabetical author catalogue was begun in 1834. Expenditure on printed books rose between 1833 and 1837 from £1,359 to £2,883 per annum, and between 1837 and 1842, £18,000 was spent on printed books, the number of works acquired being 20,000. During these years the Library moved into a new building designed by Sir Robert Smirke to replace its original premises, Montague House.

Although it had reached a considerable size by the 1840s, the collection, because of the haphazard nature of its acquisition, had both great strengths and great weaknesses. While the philosophy of private collection had been predominant, this had not mattered; but from the mid-1830s, this ideal had been replaced by the concept of a national library that would be not a treasure house but a public reference library. This more mundane ideal had been honoured by the parliamentary grants made available to continue the acquisition of periodicals that had come with the Banks' (Sir Joseph Banks) and King's Libraries, but if it was to be achieved for non-serial publications, not only had a greater number of current English and foreign publications to be acquired, but money would have to be provided for retrospective acquisitions, to fill the gaps that existed between the disjoined subjects that had aroused the enthusiasm of the private collectors.

This ideal of a national library was very much in the spirit of the time, which combined a scientific approach to scholarship with intense nationalism. Both Munich and Paris had larger libraries than England, but England was, in the early years of the Victorian era, on the threshold of a period of national self-confidence in which politics and culture increasingly became the domain of the urban middle classes. The intellectual and political hospitality of an older tradition, which had brought Panizzi to Britain as it would later bring Karl Marx, was not entirely compatible with nationalism; Panizzi was several times accused of favouring the purchase of foreign books, and Queen Victoria herself wondered if a foreigner should be at the head of a British institution.

The philosophy that underlay the creation of a modern national library transcended the carping criticisms of parochial colleagues and politicians. In his report of 1846, Panizzi, in drawing attention to the deficiencies of the Library in particular areas, gave by implication his view of what the collections should have contained. In all subjects – law, philosophy, history and the sciences – the collection of foreign works was assessed, and no special plea was made to complete the collection of English works; the most notable omission from his report was any reference to works on technology except in so far as they might have been included in serial publications. In those languages and literatures that were significant in the humanist tradition the collections were in general strong, and attention was drawn to the absence of particular works, such as those that might appear in a published bibliography or the catalogue of another library. But in some other cases, such as slavonic and oriental books, there had been no collection at all until 1837 when Panizzi had begun to allocate to them some of his scarce funds. In the case of Chinese works, there was an uncatalogued collection, but further purchases had been made and an assistant appointed because 'the new relations with China' (the Treaty of Nanking in 1842 had opened the Chinese ports to British trade) had made increasing the Chinese collection 'more desirable as well as more easy'. Thus to the traditional purposes of the humanist library in which the collection of, for example, Roman law was important was to be added the purpose of furthering British national objectives.

The purchasing of American books at mid-century

American books had two claims on the Library's attention: they were a branch of English literature and they served the practical purposes of a national reference library. Only a very cursory investigation of the American collection had been carried out in compiling the report of 1846 – comparison with a circular issued by the bookseller Wiley and Putnam – and the report is rather careless in its treatment of Americana, barely remarking for example on the quite substantial purchases that had been made since 1837. Although not published until 1846, it had in fact been written at the beginning of 1843, just at the time when American books were being received from William Pickering, the largest acquisition of Americana until 1846. Yet for three years after that little more was done; both funds and a practical means for acquiring American books were lacking.

Both became available after 1846. The report made a request for an annual parliamentary grant for book purchasing of £10,000 to be used for both current and retrospective acquistions, and Parliament agreed to the request. Panizzi liked to purchase books through agents who were knowledgeable in both the book trade and the subject and who could in return for the business be expected to acquaint themselves with the Library's particular needs. This opportunity in respect of Americana presented itself in the person of Henry Stevens, and Panizzi grasped it immediately; in the last four months of 1845, Stevens had prepared a list of 10,000 American works lacking from the collection, and in 1846 he was asked to supply them. So closely did Stevens suit the Library's need, in fact, that one wonders if his arrival in the British Museum Reading Room on 28 July 1845 with a letter of introduction from Jared Sparks was as much of an accident as he later liked to say.

Panizzi and Stevens were rather different in personality, and although Panizzi's early letters to Stevens seem warm enough, his careful checking of Stevens' prices and calculations of commission due suggest some lack of trust. It is likely that Stevens' initial attachment to the Library was through Thomas Watts (later to be Keeper of Printed Books) rather than Panizzi. When Stevens arrived in London, Panizzi was away, and Stevens and Watts began to look together at the American collection. Watts had also apparently been responsible for the earlier American acquisitions. Stevens and Watts were close in age. Panizzi was 48 years old and well-established when Stevens arrived in London at the age of 26; he moved in quite auspicious social circles and was for a number of years pressed to accept a knighthood, which he eventually did. Panizzi was a political emigré, a category to which some glamour was attached, and was a man whose talents of every kind exceeded those of Stevens, as they did, it must be admitted, those of many of the people around him. Stevens seems never to have gained social acceptance in Britain; although he was ubiquitous in the book and library world, he was regarded as a shopkeeper. His jokes – putting 'blackballed Athenaeum', or the letters 'GMB' (Green Mountain Boy) after his name on the title pages of his books perhaps hid considerable resentment of British stuffiness. Yet, if his business practices had sometimes seemed rather sharp, Stevens' knowledge of Americana was legendary in both the United States and Britain. When a stranger entered Joseph Sabin's bookshop in New York and asked a question that showed some specific knowledge of the book he was looking at, Sabin asked 'Aren't you Henry Stevens?' When asked how he had known, Sabin said 'There is not another man in the United States who would ask that question.'

The initial list of 10,000 desiderata that Stevens compiled in 1845 is a puzzle. It no longer survives, although it has been said to have been used by Roorbach possibly with later Stevens' lists for his *Bibliotheca Americana*. Sparks warned Stevens in 1846 that there were American books that 'you will find...in no Bibliotheca' and that 'it would...be no easy task to ascertain what books have been published [in the United States] within the last twenty years'. John A. Wiseman, in a study of Henry

Stevens (United Kingdom Library Association thesis, 1973), notes that in 1845 the bibliographical work of Roorbach, Kelly, Sabin and Evans was still in the future.

The printed catalogue of the Library Company of Philadelphia and an article 'On the literature of the United States' published in the *Encyclopedia Americana* were used by Thomas Watts to draw up an American desiderata list in 1839 – it would have been from this list that the 1842–1843 purchases were made – and the circular issued by Wiley and Putnam had been used to evaluate the American collections for the survey done in 1843. So it seems that Stevens must have brought lists with him from the United States where he had already been collecting American imprints. He interpreted his brief from Panizzi to allow him to include almost anything; he told Charles Coffin Jewett, who had gained great renown for cataloguing Brown University Library, that he was to get

> all the historical works about the western hemisphere, even down to the little sketch of a country church or parish, all the American poetry, novels and polite literature generally, all voyages and travels, all school books and works on education, all periodical literature, including one or two files of the leading newspapers of each state, all the theology, scientific and medical works, all books about the Indians and Indian language, all public documents of the general government and also of each of the states, all laws, reports, trials and judiciary proceedings, all pamphlets, 4th July, funeral, fast, thanksgiving political, civil, religious, historical and critical etc., all geographical, topographical works.

In fact the only class of publication excluded was, as he had to advise his agent later, reprinted English works.

The Stevens' purchases

The first group of books purchased from Stevens, 330 volumes, are entered in the register of acquisitions under the date

30 July 1846; the total cost, which included Stevens' commission of ten per cent was £58 11s. The first fifty titles give a good impression of the whole, and they are reproduced here exactly as they appear in the register:

Adams, John, *American Constitution*, Vols 1–3, Philadelphia 1797.
Novanglus and Massachusettensis Essays, Boston 1819.
Eulogies on Adams and Jefferson, Hartford 1826.
Fisheries and Mississippi, Washington 1822.
Adams' Correspondence, Boston 1823.
The Moral Reformer, Vols 1, 2, Boston 1835.
Austin, B.J., *Constitutional Republicanism*, Boston 1803.
Memoir of the Reverend G. Hall, Andover 1834.
Balfour, N., *Observations on the Scriptures*, Charlestown 1810.
Barlow, J., *The Columbiad*, Philadelphia 1807.
Barnard, D.D., *Discourse on the life of S. van Rensselaer*, Albany 1839.
Beek, John B., *Medical Researches*, Albany 1835.
Bellamy, J., *Letters*, London 1761.
Belsham, Rev. Thomas, *American Unitarianism*, Boston 1815.
Birkbeck, M., *Journey in America*, Philadelphia.
Hochetaga Depicta, Montreal 1839.
Brackenbridge, H.M., *Voyage to South America*, Vols 1, 2, Baltimore 1819.
Bradford, A., *History of Massachusetts*, Vols 1–3, Boston 1822.
Breck, S., *Pennsylvania*, Philadelphia 1818.
Bridgeman, T., *Gardiner's Assistant,* New York 1832.
Brown, S.R., *Western Gazetteer*, Auburn 1817, 1820.
Burns, *Conspiracy*, 1811.
Caldwell, Charles, *Memoirs of the Honourable N. Greene*, Philadelphia 1819.
Burroughs, S., *Memoirs,* Hanover 1798.
Catalogue of the Harvard University Library, Vols 1–3, Cambridge 1832.
Catalogue of Harvard University Library, Supplement, Cambridge 1834.
Callender, J.T., *History of America*, Philadelphia 1798.

American Collection of the National Library, 1846 to 1886

The Christian Baptist, Cincinnati 1835.
Carey's American Pocket Atlas, Philadelphia 1813.
Chauney, Charles, *Thoughts on Religion*, Boston 1743.
Clark, Thomas, *History of the United States*, Vols 1–2, Philadelphia 1814.
Cogswell, William, *Christian Philanthropist*, Boston 1839.
Cummings, S., *The Western Pilot*, Cincinnati 1833.
Currie, William, *Diseases of America*, Philadelphia 1792.
Dana, E., *Geographical Sketches*, Cincinnati 1819.
Darby, William, *Discovery of America*, Baltimore 1828.
——, *Florida*, Philadelphia 1821.
——, *Gazetteer of America*, Hartford 1833.
First Settlers in Virginia, New York 1806.
Dawes, R., *Valley of the Narhaway*, Boston 1830.
Depons, F., *Voyage*, Vols 1–3, New York 1806.
Douglas, William, *Historical Summary*, Vols 1–3, Boston 1749.
Dunlap, William, *History of the American Theatre*, New York 1832.
Dwight, Theodore, *Lessons in Greek*, Springfield 1833.
Dwight, S.E., *The Hebrew Wife*, New York 1836.
Edwards, B.B., *Memoir of the Rev. E. Cornelius*, Boston 1833.
Featherstonehaugh, G.W., *Geological Report*, Washington 1835.
——, *The Republic of Cicero*, New York 1829.
History of the County of Berkshire, U.S., Pittsfield 1829.
Findley, William, *History of the Insurrection of Pennsylvania*, Philadelphia 1796.

History and biography (54 titles) predominated among the subjects covered by the first batch of books from Stevens followed by: travel, geography and topography (43 titles); religious works (36 titles); politics and economics (20 titles); fiction, poetry and belles lettres (15 titles). There were also several volumes of library catalogues, several government reports on roads and internal improvements, some railway and canal company reports, reports of private institutions, sermons, orations, law books and a few school books. About 80 items out of the 330 could be described as pamphlets, and there were five titles of periodicals.

Hawthorne's *Twice Told Tales* was included (but not the first edition), an edition of Hubbard's *Indian Wars*, Thomas Hutchinson's *History of Massachusetts Bay* published in 1764, a seven volume edition of Shakespeare published in Boston in 1844, and Weems' *Life of Washington*, again not the first edition.

The following places of publication were recorded: Philadelphia (68 titles), New York (67), Boston (39), Washington (24), Baltimore (18), Albany (6), Cincinnati (5), New London (4), Toronto (3), Hartford (3), Charleston (2), Andover (2), Cambridge (2), and twenty-three other places with one title each.

The years of publication were:

before 1800:   24   1820–1829:   79

1800–1809:   35   1830–1839:   72

1810–1819:   50   1840–1846:   6

A further 1,578 volumes from Stevens were registered with the date 23 October 1846, and 916 on 10 December. The total number of volumes received from Stevens and recorded in the registers until they ceased in 1849 was 8,066 (there were of course fewer *titles*), and the total cost to the British Museum was £2,184, which averages to about five shillings and five pence a volume. This price made them roughly a dollar a volume.

In addition to the books sold by Stevens to the Library, he was able to procure several quite large gifts of official publications from the Federal and state governments which must be taken into account in estimating Stevens' contribution to the American collection. It is also likely that the Library subscribed eventually to about 200 periodicals on Stevens' advice, which were continued after he had stopped gathering books for the Library.

The 'Stevens' Catalogue'

After the acquisitions registers stop in 1849 it is not easy to identify the American books supplied to the Library; although the actual invoices were retained, it is not practical to search through them for American imprints. But in 1856 Stevens was allowed to print a catalogue of Americana in the British Library up to the end of that year, using the Library's catalogue slips to compile it. He did this just before a planned visit to the United States to buy books, and it is likely that its usefulness to him for this purpose was uppermost in his mind when he compiled it. Although printed in 1856, it was not published for another ten years. It is not now an accurate record, and might not have been at the time. It records the titles of books *printed* in the United States, which as the century progressed ceased to be an adequate definition of Americana, but it does give some idea of what happened in the years between 1849 and 1856. Stevens recorded 12,050 titles (which represented 16,826 volumes) in this *Catalogue of American Books in the Library of the British Museum at Christmas 1856*; 1,158 imprints had been placed in the Library between 1837 and 1845, Stevens had added 8,066 up to April 1849, and it is unlikely that there were more than a few hundred in the Library before 1837. (A guess of three to four hundred fits some later figures for the development of the collection rather well.) Therefore one might assume (although this has to be very speculative) that 7,000 more were added in the seven years until the end of 1856. This figure sounds plausible, especially if it is assumed that the rate diminished over the period. (American purchases were 2,824 in 1846, 2,641 in 1847, 1,652 in 1848, and 849 up to April 1849. The acquisition of foreign books in general diminished during these and subsequent years because of a reduction in the government grant, which had dropped from £10,000 per annum in 1846/7 to £2,000 in 1854/5, and shortage of space in the Library itself.)

Stevens' journey to the United States in 1857 was traumatic for his business. Using the services of his brother Frank

(Benjamin Franklin Stevens) he bought large numbers of books in 1857/8, despatching them to London in anticipation of an increase in acquisitions that would follow the opening in 1858 of the new Reading Room and the extra book space that accompanied it. But the increase did not materialise, at least not in American books. Stevens might have shipped to England as many as 20,000 items; he gave that figure to John Russell Bartlett, the historian and bibliographer, in November 1859, when it was still uncertain how many of them the Library was going to take. In 1858/9 the purchase grant was restored to £10,000 per annum; of the £5,000 that was reserved for current publications, £500 was spent on American works. A considerable part of this must have been required for periodicals, transactions of learned societies and what the Library calls 'works in progress', that is publications issued in series.

After failing to sell to the Library many of the books that he had shipped to England, Stevens attempted to sell them to other libraries in Britain, but his business didn't recover from the setback and he became insolvent just before the Civil War, when for several years the output of American books was disrupted in any case. In 1863 Henry sold his stock and his business to his brothers Frank and Simon, retaining for himself the British Museum agency, which he estimated brought him £500 a year. But even this was apparently conducted by the new firm which was actually run by Frank.

It is difficult to understand why in 1858 and 1859 the Library did not repeat its massive American acquisitions of 1846 and 1847; both the funds and the opportunity were once again available. There might be a clue in the change of keepership in 1856. P.R. Harris, writing about the acquisitions system in the nineteenth century (*British Library Journal*, 7, 1981, 120), said: 'Panizzi's years as Keeper (1837–56) were the revolutionary period in the history of the Department of Printed Books. After such a turbulent time consolidation was needed and this was provided first by John Winter Jones who was Keeper from 1856 to 1866.' Winter Jones was followed in 1866 by Henry Stevens' old ally, Thomas Watts; perhaps it is significant that Henry Stevens' *Catalogue of American Books* compiled before

1856 from the Library's own catalogue slips lay fallow for the ten years of Winter Jones' keepership. (Watts died after only three years as Keeper, before, Harris says, he had time to make his mark.)

Acquisition of the Grenville Library

In 1847 the American collections had received an addition which was quite independent of the work of Henry Stevens, but not of Panizzi – the gift of the library of Thomas Grenville. Grenville had been a Trustee of the British Museum and a friend of Panizzi, and had possibly played some part in Panizzi's original appointment to the Museum. Grenville's collection had been built up over fifty years in the usual manner of private collections, largely by purchases from the sales of other libraries, and it contained 20,000 volumes, among them, according to the catalogues in 1842 'the earliest and most curious specimens of typography . . . first and best editions of the classics . . . Homers, Ariostos, books printed on vellum' and so on. It also contained 'an assemblage of early voyages and travels from the original editions of Marco Polo and Contarini, Columbus and Vesputius, to the collections of De Bry, Hulsius, Hakluyt and Purchas, forming such a complete chain of uninterrupted information on the subject as no other Library can furnish.'

Thus its chief contribution to the American collection was in early European imprints, but there were a few American imprints as well, of Christopher Saur (Sower) the German printer of Pennsylvania and works of William Hubbard and Cotton Mather. Although it was incorporated into the main catalogue the collection was given a distinctive stamp, a pressmark preceded by the letter G, and was shelved together rather than being distributed to the general library. It brought a number of duplicates to the Library, most of which have been retained. But three rare items of Americana were exchanged, one through Henry Stevens and the others through Obadiah Rich, although both ended up in the collection of James Lenox (and hence the New York Public Library); a duplicate of Thomas Hariot's *Virginia* was exchanged for Giuliano Dati's verse version of the 'Columbus letter', and Hakluyt's *Diverse Voyages* together with Fernando de Soto's *Florida* for Joseph Ames's *Typographical Antiquities*.

No single acquisition of early Americana on the scale of the Grenville Library, either of European or American imprints, has since become available to the Library, and it is unlikely that it ever will again.

Redefinition of Americana

By the middle of the nineteenth century the Library's collection of early Americana had more or less reached its present state, although rare works have been acquired from time to time: Edward Winslow's *Good Newes from New England*, for example, from the Holkham Hall Library (originally the library of Sir Edward Coke) in 1952. Recent acquisitions have been predominantly of modern imprints. This leads to a difficulty of definition. To Panizzi and Stevens, surveying as they did the body of American publishing up to the 1840s, the terms Americana and American books could mean the same thing, that is: American imprints. But as the century progressed and the output of American presses increased it became less useful to regard all American imprints as collectable Americana. This was obviously partly a matter of scale – American imprints were no longer scarce – but it also reflected increased sophistication in book collection and library acquisition and the growing internationalisation of the predominantly scientific part of the English language culture. American universities, scientific institutions and publishers were themselves a major force in this last process.

The difficulty is in defining what should still be regarded as Americana after mid-century. Oliver Wendell Holmes' *On the Contagiousness of Puerperal Fever* is indisputably Americana although it is a medical book on a problem not confined to America. But it has a particular place in the history of

American medicine, just as the Japanese books of Lafcadio Hearn have a place in the history of American interest in the East. The term Americana must thus be confined, in the case of works published from the middle of the nineteenth century onwards, to those that convey something distinctively American or whose subject matter is some aspect of America. The Library has continued to use the term American books to mean American imprints, a fruitful source of confusion.

Acquisition of Americana, 1850–1890

For the years after the acquisitions registers ceased in 1849, there is no direct evidence of the growth or character of the American collection apart from the Stevens' Catalogue. But there is fortunately, in the shelving and pressmark system in use from the 1850s to the 1950s, the possibility of making estimates of both. This system, known as the 'elastic' system because of the facility for expansion that it contained, was devised by Thomas Watts to serve the Library after the move from Montague House. It was subject classified, like several others in vogue at the time, and, like the widely known system later devised by Melvin Dewey (the Dewey Decimal System), the books were shelved in subject classes subdivided in appropriate ways, usually from the general to the particular. The presses were numbered consecutively, the shelves given letters from the top down, and the books numbered along the shelf. As the number of books grew, the shelfmarks ceased to have any significance other than as an abstract designation of subject, like the Dewey Decimal System, and the system was extended as the collections grew but following the logic of subjects not of bookshelves. Thus an old shelfmark might read:

   8175   number of press, ie bookcase
   g   shelf g
   17   position along shelf

60 American Collection of the National Library, 1846 to 1886

But as the subject group outgrew the original presses a shelfmark might be 08175 ggg 55. The prefix O referred to swinging presses attached at one time to the ends of rows.

Place of imprint was not considered in classification of a book, but where it was appropriate subjects were subdivided by country. The table which follows refers to the American sections of such subdivisions and the number of books in each. It should be noted that there are a great many American imprints shelved in subject classes that are not divided by country – the sciences in particular. It will be assumed for the reasons given above, and as a practical matter as well, that these books, the overwhelming number of which were published after 1850, are not to be considered Americana.

Numbers of books in the American subdivisions of the pressmark system in use 1850 to 1950:

Theology	8,680	Biography	15,200
Law	6,200	Belles lettres	8,330
Philosophy and Science	7,220	Fiction	17,700
History	5,760	Academies	23,600
Topography	6,660	(transactions of learned societies)	

A more detailed examination of one section of the American collection, 5,033 books classified as American politics and pressmarked 8175-7, included in the philosophy and science section (see table above), allows some conclusions to be reached about additions to the American collection between 1850 and 1890. Of the 2,673 books in this category, published before 1890, 2,188 were published in the United States, 284 in Britain, 83 in France and 23 in Germany. (Discrepancies in the totals of these and the following figures are accounted for by incomplete title pages.) If one considers only United States imprints, they were acquired at an uneven rate over the period:

American Collection of the National Library, 1846 to 1886

	Number of books	Percentage purchased	Percentage donated
1851–1860	51	71	29
1861–1870	1,374	98	2
1871–1880	578	64	36
1881–1890	185	74	25

A closer look at the decade 1861–1870 shows that of the 1,349 American imprints in this section purchased by the Library, 657 were acquired in the two years 1863/4 and 586 in the years 1867/8. These two pairs of years correspond with visits to the United States by Benjamin Franklin Stevens. In the following decade almost one third, 114 out of 367 purchased, were acquired in the single year 1875, but the pattern is less extreme. Of these three groups of acquisitions a large proportion were pamphlets rather than books:

	Number of pamphlets	Total US imprints
1863–4	640	657
1867–8	547	586
1875	103	114

The 1875 acquisition is partly accounted for by donations of collections of pamphlets; 203 were received in this way during the decade, two fifths of the total number. It appears, then, that the firm of B.F. and H. Stevens supplied a fairly constant number of current books each year, about 200 in all subjects, and that twice in the 1860s, following Frank's trips to the United States, large collections of pamphlets were sold to the British Museum.

A comparison of the date of publication of the monographs published in the United States and the date of acquisition shows that in the decade 1851–60 almost all monographs acquired had been published more than two years previously. In the decade 1861–70 the proportion was about half; and in 1871–80, three quarters were published within two years of publication. This indicates that the trend was away from retrospective acquisition, gap filling, towards concentration on current publications. In the decade 1881–90 retrospective acquisition had virtually ceased.

It appears reasonable that the need for retrospective acquisition should diminish during the period that attention is given to it, and that it might have been therefore quite proper to place less emphasis on it in the later decades of the century. It can be estimated that in the 1850s the Library acquired about seven per cent of American books published; in the 1860s twenty-four per cent; in the 1870s twenty-eight per cent; and in the 1880s nine per cent. This estimate leaves out the three large purchases of 1863/4, 1867/8 and 1875. It might be assumed that these went some way to fill gaps in the current purchasing of previous years. But there has been no year of large retrospective acquisition since 1875, and as the level of current acquisition began to diminish after then, one might expect the adequacy of the Library's collection of American imprints to be less after that date.

There is no obvious reason for the decline. The book purchase grant of £10,000 per annum introduced in 1846, after being cut to £2,000 per annum in 1854/5, was restored to its earlier figure of £10,000 in 1858/9 and remained almost constant until 1886, although it was reduced from £10,000 per annum to £9,750 between 1883 and 1886, and for the last years of the decade was in 1887 (for year ending 31 March) £10,000, 1888 £6,200, 1889 £8,200, and 1890 £9,275. In 1872, an average year for American acquisition, of the purchase grant of £10,000 probably less than ten per cent was spent on American books (£547 was spent on new publications which represented three quarters of the American books acquired) so that one might not expect that the amount available for

American Collection of the National Library, 1846 to 1886   63

American books would be responsive to small reductions in the total grant. It was also a period when American publishing was expanding, American authors were commanding attention in Britain, and American books were cheap.

One wonders if the explanation of decline really lies in the mechanism for American acquisition, in that the Stevens firm had by this time become fully anglicised and was no longer an adequate agency for the supply of American books. A most ingenious solution to the problem, if indeed it was a problem, was devised during the 1880s, bringing in a large number of American books by copyright deposit. This became the dominant mode of acquisition of American imprints until the 1960s.

3.
Copyright Deposit and American Books after 1886

Growth and character of American publishing after the 1880s

The political conflicts of the last two decades of the nineteenth century in the United States might not have proved as divisive as those earlier in the century, but equally profound changes were taking place. The period has been regarded as one dominated by materialism, yet three or four hundred books in theology and religion were published each year, and in 1894, not an untypical year, 370 novels written by Americans were published. The period also saw the growth of trusts and of organised labour, yet many of the major publishing firms remained in the hands of their founders or their founder's sons, and, although several merged, new firms were being continually established. In 1898, for example, 250 new firms announced their existence. The American Book Company, a textbook publisher created from the merger of several existing firms in 1890, aroused talk of a trust, but it did not prove big enough to dominate the market.

Eastern domination began to decline. The pioneer years in the west had ended – in 1890 the Superintendent of the United States Census declared that the frontier had finally disappeared – but they were followed by years of consolidation. Chicago had recovered from the fire of 1871 to manufacture more than a million books in 1880. Ambrose Bierce in his *Devil's Dictionary* defined reading as: 'The general body of what one reads. In our country it consists, as a rule, of Indiana novels, short stories in dialect and humor in slang.'

As remarkable as the efflorescence of the Hoosier novelists in Indiana was the Bohemian Club in California which had numbered Mark Twain and Robert Louis Stephenson among its members: both of these places were centres of publishing and many of the writers had been associated with newspapers and magazines. Newspapers and magazines were indeed, over the whole country, a major vehicle of literary publishing; the number of literary periodicals published rose from 428 in 1883 to 1,051 in 1893.

The list of new books issued by Robert Clarke of Cincinnati in 1880 gives the flavour of western publishing:

Virginia G. Ellard, *Grandma's Christmas Day*, A Poem, $1.
Karl Robert, *Charcoal Drawing Without a Master*, $1.
A.L. Vago, *Modeling in Clay*, $1.
M. Louise McLaughlin, *Pottery Decoration*, $1.
——, *China Painting*, 75¢.
John James Piatt, *Pencilled Fly Leaves*, Essays in Town and Country, $1.
Dr John D. Jackson, *The Black Arts in Medicine*, $1.
R.H. Taneyhill, *The Leatherwood God*, 30¢.
G.W. Manypenny, *Our Indian Wards*, $3.
Rev. C.P. Maes, *Life of Rev. Charles Nerinckx*, $2.50.
Dr G.E. Walton, (Trans.), *Hygiene and Education of Infants*, 25¢.
Insect Lives, $1.
H.J. Mettenheimer, *Safety Book-keeping* $1.
Family Expense Book, 50¢.
Benner's Prophecies of the Future Ups and Downs in Prices, $1.
Levi Coffin's Reminiscences, $2.
F. Hassaurek, *Secret of the Andes*, A Romance, paper, 50¢, cloth $1.
Louise W. Tilden, *Mission Band Exercises*, 25¢.
——, *Karl and Gretchen*, A Poem, 75¢.
J.P. MacLean, *The Mound Builders*, $1.50.
——, *The Antiquity of Man*, $1.
——, *Mastodon, Mammoth and Man*, 60¢.
A.J. Conant, *Footprints of Vanished Races in the Mississippi Valley*, $1.50.
M.F. Force, *Some Early Notices of the Indians of Ohio*, 50¢.
——, *Prehistoric Man; Darwinism and Deity; The Mound Builders*, 75¢.

Robert Clarke's books, like those of other small publishers, were distributed in the east by the large firms – Putnams, Dodd and Mead, Lippincott and Co. – and by the bookshop chains that these publishers ran. Authors, if they showed talent, followed the books. Thus the lists of the New York publishers contained each year a larger number of American authors; in its summary of publishing in 1880 the *Publishers' Weekly* noted books by W.D. Howells, George Washington Cable, and Lew Wallace (*Ben Hur*). It also noted an increase in professionalism (most books announced had actually appeared in print), and recorded 'phenomenal sales' of the best titles. Fiction was the largest single category in 1880, but had fallen from the 25 per cent it had once been to 16 per cent. Many of the non-fiction titles that the *Publishers' Weekly* thought worthy of particular mention in 1880 were reprints of foreign works: Justin McCarthy's *History of Our Own Times*, and books by Herbert Spencer and Louis Blanqui; but an American book, Henry George's *Progress and Poverty*, was also on the list.

Social problems that had been overshadowed earlier in the century by the issue of slavery were aggravated subsequently by the rapid growth of commerce and industry, by the growth of population in general and of immigration in particular – five and a quarter millions between 1880 and 1890 – and by the expectations that prosperity had generated among all classes of people. In the 1880s and 1890s these provided the occasion for much writing in all subjects. Thus fiction retained its preeminence, but was itself increasingly concerned with social questions, purveying a radicalism that was not to everyone's taste. The *Publishers' Weekly* commented on the books of 1895: 'the new woman or anti-marriage novel reached its climax of repulsiveness'.

Religious writing too, which was in most years of the two decades prolific, was influenced by the spirit of social concern; temperance became a frequent theme; baptism by immersion had been the corresponding interest for earlier writers. Both fiction and non-fiction attempted to describe small towns and real people, and even frontier wit was pressed into the service of a more serious purpose.

After reaching a plateau in 1886, the number of titles reported by publishers each year remained fairly constant at about 5,000 until 1899, dropping only in those years that saw a general decline in business confidence, but this apparent stability masked a trend towards American authorship which the changing interest of readers made inevitable. In 1890, of the 835 new novels published, about half were written by Americans; in 1893, 370 novels were by Americans and 297 by foreigners, and of the 5,134 books published, 2,803 were by American authors.

In 1900 the total number of titles published in the United States rose to 6,356, the beginning of an increase that took it, with somewhat uncertain progress, to 10,901 in 1909. The total remained close to this figure until the 1950s but with several large fluctuations: up to 13,470 in 1910, and down to 6,548 in 1945. In 1909 fiction gave way temporarily to general literature, ie essays, collected works and so on, as the largest category of publication, and in 1914 and 1919 fiction was almost equalled in volume by books on religion and also on sociology and economics. Scientific and technical works doubled their proportion of 5 per cent in 1880 to 10 per cent in 1910, and remained at this level until the 1950s.

These figures are all taken from the *Publishers' Weekly*, and are of publications notified to them. They include books imported from Britain and thus not, under the manufacturing clause in the Copyright Act of 1891, eligible for United States copyright, and also pamphlets which in 1920 made up a quarter of all works published. The figures exclude periodicals and also schoolbooks which might be thought by the twentieth century to be of little bibliographical or academic interest. Some idea of the real output, as opposed to that of interest to the book trade, can be gained from the copyright deposit figures from the Library of Congress for 1920. The *Publishers' Weekly* reported 7,446 works eligible for copyright in 1920. The Library of Congress reported the following copyright deposits for 1920:

printed volumes	18,156
pamphlets and leaflets	30,638
newspapers and magazines	57,870
plays	3,063
music (pieces)	44,566
maps	3,026

The considerable difference between the number of works published and the number entering the book trade suggests an increasing gap between large-scale commercial publishing, which had become more intensely concentrated in New York, and local printing. After a period towards the end of the nineteenth century when mergers were more common, new firms began to be established again in New York in the first three decades of the twentieth century:

Doubleday	1897
Doran and Co.	1908
McGraw Hill	1909
Alfred A. Knopf	1915
Boni and Liveright (Modern Library)	1917
Harcourt Brace	1919
Simon and Schuster	1924
Viking Press	1925

John Day	1925
William Morrow	1926
W.W. Norton	1926
Random House	1927
Farrar and Rinehart	1929

The total number of books manufactured each year in the United States had, by the 1920s, reached 200,000,000, and a bestseller by then might be expected to sell a million copies. Not all were fiction; Will Durant's *Story of Philosophy* (1926) sold more than a million.

The bestseller lists compiled by Frank Luther Mott (*Golden Multitudes*, 1947) reveal the names of most of the major New York publishers; a bestseller could make a firm into a major publisher overnight of course, as Hervey Allen's *Anthony Adverse* did to Farrar and Rinehart. They also show that American publishers in the twentieth century were providing books of a cosmopolitan appeal that might be expected to have a British market, just as books by Rudyard Kipling, J.M. Barrie, Conan Doyle and Anthony Hope had been bestsellers in America in 1890s. As well as the increased stature of American authors, the quality of American books had increased; the 'cheap libraries' had petered out in the 1890s, yet American books were still cheap in comparison with those produced in Britain. American universities had established international reputations by the end of the nineteenth century, and several set up university presses: Chicago in 1891, Columbia and Pennsylvania in 1869 and 1874 respectively, Princeton in 1905, and Yale in 1908.

Development of the Anglo-American book trade

American authors had been attracted to Britain by the recognition that its literary tradition was theirs also; John Quincy Adams, appointed Minister to Britain after the end of the war of 1812, cut a piece of wood off Shakespeare's chair at Stratford on Avon as a souvenir. Emerson, Poe, Hawthorne and Melville had all spent some time in Britain, and later in the century Henry James made his home there. Before the American Copyright Act of 1891, which gave reciprocal copyright protection, it was possible for an American to copyright a book in both countries if he published first in Britain, was at the time on British soil (Canada would do), and as an American citizen he also fulfilled the requirements for copyright registration in the United States. Many of Mark Twain's and Bret Harte's books, among others, were first published in Britain for this reason. But if they did not do this, American authors had the same problem as their British counterparts in reverse, and popular works like *Uncle Tom's Cabin* and the *Peter Parley* books were widely pirated in Britain.

The *Publishers' Weekly* commented in February 1872:

> The number of reprints or reissues of American books by English publishers cannot but strike anyone who looks over the lists. Such houses as Macmillan and Co., Sampson Low, Routledge and others reproduce the works of well-known authors by an arrangement either with them or with their American publishers.

But if Longfellow, for example, could enjoy no copyright protection in Britain other than what might be conveyed by the phrase 'author's edition' printed in his books by his own chosen English publishers, Routledge, why should not American publishers export to the British market the books that they had themselves printed of American authors, books that they could print more cheaply in America anyway? There was no British prohibition or duty on imported books.

Copyright Deposit and American Books after 1886

This obvious trade was organised by British agents who were in some cases publishers themselves. They operated, as their successors still do, by purchasing a number of copies outright from the American publishers, in return for a sole agency for those titles that they had purchased. In some cases, but by no means all, the British agent stamped his own name on the title page or elsewhere in the books purchased, but this did not confer British copyright protection on such books.

The best known of the firms conducting an American agency was Sampson Low. They announced the following titles as new American books in 1889 (stocks were held of most of the titles):

Aldrich, T.B., *The Queen of Sheba*, Boston, 2s 6d.
Babcock, W.H., *An Invention of the Enemy*, Philadelphia, 2s 6d.
Bancroft, H.H., *History of the Pacific States of North America*, Vol. 11: Texas, Vol. 2, 1801–1809, San Francisco, 24s.
Bates, J.W., *A Nameless Wrestler*, Philadelphia, 2s 6d and 5s.
Bixby, J.T., *Religion and Science Allies*, Chicago, 2s.
Blackstock, E.F., *The Land of the Viking and the Empire of the Czar*, New York, 6s.
Bolton, C.K., *Famous Men of Science*, New York, 7s 6d.
Caspar, C.N., *General Directory of the American Book, News, and Stationery Trade*, Milwaukee, 63s.
Smith, Huntington (ed.), *Century of American Literature*, New York, 9s.
Chambers, H.E., *A Higher History of the United States for Schools and Academies*, New Orleans, 6s.
Chenery, E., *Alcohol Inside Out from Bottom Principles*, Boston, 7s 6d.
Clarke, Mrs A., *The Ideal Cookery Book*, Chicago, 7s 6d.
Clayton, G., *Wheat and Tares, A Novel*, Philadelphia, 6s.
Constitutional History of the United States, New York, 12s 6d.
Curtis, G.T., *John Charaxes: a Tale of the Civil War in America*, Philadelphia, 6s.
Day, H.N., *Elements of Mental Science*, New York, 5s.
Durny, V., *A History of France*, New York, 10s 6d.

Elson, L.C., *History of German Song*, Boston, 6s.
Errett, I., *Evenings with the Bible: New Testament Studies*, Vol. 3, Cincinnati, 7s 6d.
Farmer, L.H., *The French Revolution*, New York, 7s 6d.
Fawcett, E., *Agnosticism and Other Essays*, Chicago, 7s 6d.
Fawcett, E., *Solarion: a Romance*, Philadelphia, 2s 6d.
Froebel, F., *Autobiography*, Syracuse, 7s 6d.
Gibson, L.H., *Convenient Houses and How To Build Them*, New York, 12s 6d.
Goodloe, D.R., *The Birth of the Republic*, New York, 10s 6d.
Goss, W.L., *Jed: a Boy's Adventures in the Army of '61–65*, New York, 7s 6d.
Harris, C.A., *Principles and Practice of Dentistry*, Philadelphia, 35s.
Hawthorne, N., *Mosses from an Old Manse*, Boston, 2s 6d.
Hildreth, C.L., *Adventures in Orbello Land*, Chicago, 7s 6d.
Hutchinson, W.F., *Practical Electro-Therapeutics*, Philadelphia 7s 6d.
Jackman, J.S., *Fatima: a Dream of Passion*, New York, 5s.
Johnson, L.W., *Eight Hundred Miles in an Ambulance*, Philadelphia, 4s.
Klemm, L.R., *European Schools*, New York, 7s 6d.
Luce, R., *Writing for the Press*, Boston, 5s.
McNaughton, J.L., *Onnalinda: A Romance*, Caledonia, 15s and 21s.
Nelson, W., *Five Years in Panama*, Chicago, 7s 6d.
Parvin, T., *Obstetric Nursing*, Philadelphia, 4s.
Peattie, Mrs E.W., *The Story of America*, Chicago, 24s.
Phelps, E.S., *The Story of Avis: a Novel*, Boston, 2s 6d.
Purinton, D.B., *Christian Theism*, New York, 9s.
Ranney, A.L., *Lectures on Nervous Diseases*, Philadelphia, 28s.
Richardson, L., *Lord Dunmersey: a Novel*, New York, 2s 6d.
Saltus, E., *The Pace that Kills*, Chicago, 2s 6d.
Schenck, Mrs E.H., *The History of Fairfield, Fairfield County, Connecticut*, Washington, 25s.
Tillman, S.E., *Elementary Lessons in Heat*, Philadelphia, 10s.
Tolstoi, L.N., *War and Peace*, New York, 15s.

Wall, E.J., *A Dictionary of Photography*, New York, 7s 6d.
West, N., *Studies in Eschatology*, New York, 10s 6d.
Witham, J.M., *Steam Engine Design for the Use of Mechanical Engineers, Students, and Draughtsmen*, New York, 30s.
Whitman, Walt, *November Boughs*, Philadelphia, 6s.
Winter, W., *The Press and the Stage*, New York, 7s 6d.
Winter, W., *Wanderers: a Collection of Poems*, Boston, 5s.
Woodlard, M.C., *The Hon. Geoffrey Wiley: a Philosophical Novel*, Chicago, 2s. 6d.

The American Copyright Act of 1891 had no effect on this trade. A manufacturing clause excluded books printed in Britain from American copyright, but the reciprocity required under the Act was not true reciprocity and accepted British conduct under the Berne Convention (to which the United States did not subscribe) as sufficient to entitle British authors to protection in the United States. Thus protection of American authors' rights in Britain derived from international agreement, not from British law, and it did not exclude completely manufactured copies of books. This anomaly was taken up later by American publishers when they were forced to comply with the requirements of British copyright law.

The *Publishers' Weekly* reported in August 1891:

> The literary 'American invasion' of England is making headway sure enough. A few weeks ago we counted in the bibliographic list of the London *Publishers' circular* twenty books by American authors out of sixty recorded for one week. During the week ending August 3rd the London correspondent of the New York *Evening Post* reports that 'seven novels have been published by English houses, and three out of the seven are by American authors. They comprise Maurice Thompson's *Alice of Old Vincennes*, Theodore Dreiser's *Sister Carrie*, and Will Payne's *Story of Eva*. J.M. Mowbray's *A Journey to Nature* and Hugh McHugh's *John Henry* have also been published in London this week. And these bring up the leaven of American books in the departments of fiction and *belles lettres* to 50 per cent. Furthermore, four out of the five American books I have

instanced are by common consent far and away the best books which have been published during the week.' And yet there are still some Englishmen left who seriously wonder 'who reads an American book?'

The old taunt which the Rev. Sydney Smith had made in the pages of the *Edinburgh Review* in 1818 was still remembered, and still rankled.

American bibliography after the 1880s

The origins of American book trade bibliography have already been described. The most significant event in the bibliographical control of American imprints after this was the reorganisation of the Library of Congress under A.R. Spofford, who was Librarian in Chief from 1864 to 1897. A result of this reorganisation was that in 1870 the Library of Congress was given entire responsibility for the administration of copyright; registration of copyright had prior to that been done by local courts. This meant, of course, that the new catalogues of the Library of Congress collections initiated by Spofford would eventually become the prime bibliography of American imprints, but it was not until the great expansion of the collections that occurred under the administration of Herbert Putnam, cousin of the publishing Putnams, and Librarian of Congress, 1899–1939, that this aspiration even approached reality. A relatively late start to a national library from its original function as a legislative reference library had made the Library of Congress only one among several other major American collections. Among these were Lenox's at the New York Public Library, the John Carter Brown Library in Providence, and a number of other state, university, civic and private libraries that had received collections of Americana, often of regional or specialist significance, for example the Arents tobacco collection, the books of H.H. Bancroft, the Californian historian, or the collection of works on American history assembled by Robert Clarke, the Cincinnati publisher.

Thus it was not until the establishment of the National Union Catalogue in 1968 that Spofford's aspirations actually became reality.

In retrospective bibliography the major work of the twentieth century has been the *American Bibliography* of Charles Evans which appeared in print between 1903 and 1959. Like Sabin, Evans did not live to complete his work, which was intended to be a bibliography of American imprints up to 1820, and it was continued by Clifford K. Shipton under the auspices of the American Antiquarian Society. Imprints from 1800 to 1820 were later added by Ralph R. Shaw and Richard H. Shoemaker.

Commercial publishing stimulated further development: in 1939 Albert P. Boni had started a company called Readex to publish works in opaque microprint, and after the war it began the long project of publishing in this form all the works listed in Evans' *Bibliography*. In conjunction with this enterprise, the American Antiquarian Society published a volume of additions to Evans compiled by Roger P. Bristol, and an author index to Evans, the *National Index of American Imprints Through 1800: The Short-Title Evans*, (1969), by Clifford K. Shipton and James E. Mooney.

Another firm that became a major force in bibliographic publishing, the H.W. Wilson Company, started the *Book Review Digest* in 1905, and the *Cumulative Book Index* in 1928. These two publications did not confine their scope to American imprints or Americana.

Richard Garnett and the cultural duty of the British Museum

An Englishman who did not agree with Sydney Smith's rhetorical question was Richard Garnett, an Assistant Keeper of Printed Books of the British Museum in the 1880s, and appointed Keeper in 1890. He was in a less dramatic way as significant in library history as Panizzi, but it was Panizzi's reforms that had paved the way for the emergence of professional librarians like Garnett. While not a confidant of statesmen as Panizzi had been – a role that had been necessary in the transition of the British Museum from a country-house library to a national library – Garnett was well known to the scholars and librarians of his time.

His standing is confirmed in R.R. Bowker's charming account of library and bookish circles in Britain, contained in two articles he published in the *Library Journal* in 1886, accounts coloured by nostalgia, no doubt, as they referred to his two and a half years in Britain between 1880 and 1883. Garnett was at the time Superintendent of the Reading Room. Bowker met the ubiquitous Henry Stevens, Nicholas Trübner the bookseller, whose friends included George Eliot and Bret Harte, Bernard Quaritch, who described himself as the Bismarck of booksellers, Sampson Low, agent for Harpers and other American publishers, E.B. Nicholson, Bodley's Librarian (ie the librarian of Oxford University), Henry Bradshaw of Cambridge University Library, Louis Fagan, biographer of Panizzi, and, at the centre desk of the British Museum Reading Room, 'the head spider in his great web', Richard Garnett.

Not least among Garnett's contributions to librarianship was a conception of the cultural role of libraries which was to give his own library a duty towards the rising literary culture of the United States. During his second year in Britain, Bowker heard Garnett explain to the annual meeting of the Library Association the relationship between libraries and literature; 'his usual happy speech: libraries owed their existence to literature and literature its stability to libraries'. Garnett was himself a prolific contributor to literature, writing about libraries, the book trade and the history of printing, and he also wrote a biography of Ralph Waldo Emerson (1888). He was not well known as a poet, but a tongue-in-cheek sonnet, 'To America; after reading some ungenerous criticisms', shows, behind the poetic expression and, especially when one notes his sympathy towards Emerson, that he had high expectations of American culture:

> What though thy Muse the singer's art essay
> With lip now over-loud, now over-low?

'Tis but the augury that makes her so
Of the high things she hath in charge to say.
How shall the giantess of gold and clay,
Girt with two oceans, crowned with Arctic snow,
Sandalled with shining seas of Mexico,
Be pared to trim proportion in a day?
Thou art too great! Thy million-billowed surge
Of life bewilders speech, as shoreless sea
Confounds the ranging eye from verge to verge
With mazy strife or smooth immensity.
Not soon or easily shall thence emerge
A Homer or a Shakespeare worthy thee.

Copyright deposit of American books

In 1886, the year of Henry Stevens' death, an opportunity arose for the Library to discharge the duty which Garnett might have considered it owed to American literature. A series of events occurred that enabled the Library to add to its American collection without either the need for funds or an American agent. On 16 April Edward Stanford, a map publisher of Charing Cross Road in London, wrote to the Principal Librarian of the British Museum, requesting the return of a copy of *Scribner's Statistical Atlas* that had been inadvertently sent to the Museum as if it was a British book subject to copyright deposit. The book had been published in New York and the Museum had purchased a copy in the course of its own acquisitions. Stanford had imported one hundred copies for sale in Britain and had had his own name added to the title page of those one hundred copies only as was the custom of the time. But he had no copyright in the work, which was copyrighted only under American law. The initial opinion of the Museum's solicitor to whom the request was referred was that Stanford should be treated merely as an agent for the sale of the book, which was certainly correct in fact. But a discussion had already taken place between Stanford and Richard Garnett, the subject being raised, according to

Stanford, by himself, and the Museum Trustees decided on 8 May to refer the matter, with several others, to the Treasury Solicitor, the Government's lawyer. The matter fell again into Garnett's hands when the Keeper of Printed Books, George Bullen, was absent through illness, and the opinion of the Treasury Solicitor was given that the Museum could lay claim to free copies of such books even when no British copyright was claimed. Garnett was able on 16 September 1886 to report progress on the enforcement of the new interpretation of the law.

While Edward Stanford had said that he cheerfully accepted the decision of the Treasury Solicitor, the specialist American importers did not, and three years later in 1889, Sampson Low and Co. was still protesting against the ruling. By this time, as well as the Copyright Act of 1842, the Licensing Act of 1662 had been invoked in support of the Library's claim, the latter being a law that had been designed to *prevent* the printing and importing of treasonable books!

What really irritated the Americans was that after depositing with the British Museum, they also had to supply copies, if requested, to the libraries of Oxford and Cambridge Universities, Trinity College, Dublin, and the Faculty of Advocates in Edinburgh (who exercised the former right of the Scottish universities). The librarians of these, while sympathising with the distributors of American books, believed nonetheless that they had a duty to use the privilege that the law gave them, and actively pursued those copies of American books that they wanted for their libraries. The distributors and publishers of American books, on the other hand, felt that each free book that they sent to the university libraries, as it had to be specifically requested and was thus a book that had been selected for acquisition in any case, was a lost sale. Furthermore no library in the United States other than the Library of Congress had this right, not Harvard, Princeton, or Yale, nor any state library, and it was inconceivable that they should ever be given it. But American publishers and distributors could do nothing but comply with the law. Thus the list of titles quoted above (page 71–3) of American books imported by Sampson Low and advertised in September 1889 could have required the firm to deposit 250 volumes, all of them books that the importer paid for and thus to be covered by his sales in Britain. It says much for the anglophilia of the American publishers that they did not persist in disputing this interpretation of the law; they could, after all, have pressed for the law itself to be changed.

One of the most notable steps in the making of the modern British Library has been acknowledged to have been Panizzi's enforcement of copyright deposit, which had required a clarification of the law in 1842 and had, from the 1850s, begun to swell the numbers of British books received. This had brought in, particularly after the 1870s, those American works of fiction whose authors had fulfilled the conditions for obtaining British copyright under British law, ie they had been printed in Britain while the author was on British soil. These acquisitions were not great in terms of numbers of titles although they were of books that sold a great many copies in Britain. I.R. Brussel listed 285 published between 1827 and 1914. (*Anglo-American First Editions. Part Two: West to East 1936*). The dates of publication and the number by each author are given in the table which follows.

Louisa May Alcott	1	1872
Ambrose Bierce	5	1872–1874
Mark Twain	18	1871–1903
James Fennimore Cooper	30	1827–1850
Ralph Waldo Emerson	9	1841–1884
Harold Frederick	4	1890–1896
Bret Harte	63	1872–1914
Nathaniel Hawthorne	8	1857–1872
Oliver Wendell Holmes	4	1846–1887
Washington Irving	6	1824–1835

Henry James	81	1878–1928
Henry Wadsworth Longfellow	13	1851–1883
James Russell Lowell	12	1861–1888
Herman Melville	6	1847–1857
Joaquin Miller	9	1871–1878
Edgar Allen Poe	1	1846
James Whitcomb Riley	2	1888–1896
Frank R. Stockton	1	1895
Harriet Beecher Stowe	2	1863–1865
James McNeill Whistler	9	1878–1899
John Greenleaf Whittier	1	1884

These books which came to the Library by copyright deposit were predominantly fiction by well-established authors, and might have been expected to be bestsellers in Britain. They were joined after 1886 by imported and reprinted books, many of them non-fiction and by unknown authors, and which could be expected to sell only a few dozen copies in Britain. But the lesser-selling books accounted for a greater number of titles and this method of acquisition, as Anglo-American book importing continued, came to dominate the American collections of the British Library, and is still an important source of American books. It remains to consider how this change has affected the composition of the American collections.

The death of Henry Stevens in 1886 was a break with the old order, and although the firm, managed by his son Henry Newton Stevens, continued to supply American periodicals to the Library, no agency of the kind that Henry Stevens had received from Panizzi was used again. The last substantial purchase of Americana for virtually seventy years was made at the sale of Henry Stevens' American stock on 1 and 2 July 1886; £115 was spent and among the books bought were *A*

Journal of the Proceedings in the Detection of the Conspiracy Formed by Some White People in Conjunction with Negro and other Slaves for Burning the City of New York (The New York Conspiracy, 1744), a very rare book, and a copy of Jefferson's *Notes on the State of Virginia* (1787) with manuscript notes by the author.

Effect of copyright deposit on the American collections after 1886

The effect of copyright deposit must be measured against an overall decline in the acquisition of American imprints from the level of 1861–1870. The table below gives the numbers of American imprints in the sample of books pressmarked 8175 to 8177 arranged by the decades in which they were acquired:

1861–1870	1374	1901–1910	189
1871–1880	578	1911–1920	234
1881–1890	185	1921–1930	195
1891–1900	277	1931–1940	45
		1941–1950	199

The budget of the Department of Printed Books does not appear to be the main reason for this decline: £92,675 was available for purchasing books in the decade 1881–1890, and £81,500 in the following decade, and yet the acquisition of American imprints showed an increase of 50%. (The number of pamphlets acquired in each decade was much the same, so the Spanish-American War does not seem to have affected the reliability of the sample.)

But the funds available for book purchasing did decline after 1896, and until 1939 were only about half what they had been in the best years of the nineteenth century.

The effect of the new interpretation of the copyright law in 1886 can be seen in the increase in the proportion received by copyright deposit, which overtook the proportion purchased after 1910.

Method of acquisition of American imprints

	By copyright deposit (per cent)	By purchase (per cent)	By donation (per cent)
1881–1890	0.5	73.5	25
1891–1900	17	52	30
1901–1910	40	38	20
1911–1920	50	25	25
1921–1930	67	18	15
1931–1940	76	24	0
1941–1950	55	28	17

(The discrepancies are accounted for by a small number acquired by exchange.)

British books relating to America were of course also added to the collection by copyright deposit; in the group of books selected for analysis, about 10 per cent were British, a proportion that remained constant from 1870 onwards.

The first and most obvious consequence of acquisition by copyright deposit was that only current publications were received in this manner. Retrospective acquisition, ie gap filling, measured by the numbers of books acquired more than two years after publication, declined in the years covered by the sample to almost nothing during the depression decade, and accounted for, at its best, barely a quarter of all acquisitions.

Pamphlets are less likely to come by copyright deposit than monographs. Twice as many pamphlets as monographs were acquired in the decade 1881–1890, but this proportion was reversed in the early years of the twentieth century and, by the decade 1941–1950, six times as many monographs as pamphlets were acquired.

Compared with the Stevens period, acquisitions of American books evened out from year to year after the 1890s, although the process had begun earlier, and the last single year of large acquisitions was 1875.

The fluctuations in acquisitions, shown in the sample, did not correspond with any trends in American publishing, but as acquisition by copyright deposit provided only those books that were expected to have a British market, there is no reason why they should have. In the decade 1931–1940, 25 per cent more titles were published in the United States than in the previous decade, yet there was a substantial decline in the number of American books acquired by the British Museum Library.

Another trend, more difficult to measure in its effect on acquisition, was the westward movement in American publishing after the Civil War. Of current American monographs received by the Library, 95 per cent of those received in 1861–1870 were published in the eastern states; the figure declined to 80 per cent in the decade 1891–1900, then rose again to 90 per cent in 1941–1950. It must be concluded that the Library's acquisitions did not pick up the westward trend. The first five places of publication of all American imprints in the sample, acquired between the 1850s and 1950s, was, in order of rank: New York, Boston, Washington, Philadelphia and Chicago. But, of these, the proportion published in Chicago was substantially smaller than for those published in Philadelphia – less than one third – and about a twentieth of the number published in New York.

The imprints of seventy-five American publishers are recorded on deposited books in the sample; the full list is given in Appendix IV. This number included seventeen American university presses. Many of these books, of course, also had printed or stamped British imprints. Not every book published by these firms was deposited, of course; only those that they or their agents expected to sell in Britain.

Purchasing, although it declined after the 1890s, still remained important, and it apparently compensated to some extent for the weaknesses of copyright deposit. Two hundred and ninety-seven publishers are recorded on books purchased and there is, even within that number, less concentration on a few firms, and indeed on New York imprints.

The ten publishers in the left hand list, who are ranked in order of the number of books they supplied to the British Library between 1850 and 1950, accounted together for 61 per cent of the total number of American books deposited; the ten on the right hand side accounted for 6 per cent of the total number purchased.

First ten publishers of monographs deposited	First ten publishers of monographs purchased
Macmillan	Putnam
Putnam	Scribner
Harper	Harper
Appleton	Houghton Mifflin
Longmans	Little Brown
Princeton University Press	Appleton
Century	Doubleday
Columbia University Press	Lippincott
McGraw Hill	Henry Holt
Scribner	Knopf

Donation was an important method of acquiring pamphlets; one quarter of all pamphlets acquired between the 1850s and 1950s were given to the Library.

It must be noted that in three categories acquisition remained strong after the 1890s: serial publications, the publications of learned societies and universities (in addition to the commercial university presses) and official publications acquired by exchange.

Ever since Parliament had voted funds to keep the serials in the Banks collection up to date, the Library had been disinclined to cancel subscriptions, even when funds were short, and thus periodicals and 'works in progress' continued to arrive, in some cases as the result of arrangements for purchase, exchange or donation made originally by Henry Stevens. Many such publications were deposited, especially those of universities, but it is common to see all the modes of acquisition in use at different times for the same periodical, and also for books published in series. The transactions of learned societies have come to the collections largely through donation.

In fiction the overwhelming method of acquisition of American imprints has been copyright deposit. This brought into the collection of American fiction not only the works of those writers whose books were sufficiently sure of a British sale to be printed by British publishers, but a large number that were printed in America for American sale and have either a rubber-stamped London imprint or even none at all. 17,700 single works of American fiction, almost all of them American imprints, were acquired between 1850 and 1950, and the collection must therefore descend to works of a fairly minor character. In addition to single works collected editions of American authors were frequently published in the United States. These, if they were distributed in Britain, were liable for copyright deposit even if only one of the works included was missing from the British Museum's shelves.

The works of well-known American authors, both those received with critical acclaim and bestsellers, continued to be published in Britain even though prior publication to establish copyright declined after 1891. The reason for this was that the informal 'rights' market that had come to exist continued to be useful to publishers even after it had no legal necessity. These British editions often differed sufficiently from the American to count as new editions rather than reprints, and were thus liable to deposit. But even when they didn't, British publishers usually deposited such books as a matter of course.

Character of American acquisitions since the 1850s

Some comment might now be made in evaluation of the American collection acquired after the 1850s, that is the period of routine acquisition which followed Henry Stevens' special efforts between 1846 and 1849. Comparison of the figure of 99,000 books in American classes in the shelving system with the total output of American publishing between the 1850s and 1950s is not realistic because most of the output of American publishing was not Americana, and there are thus American imprints in classes where the country of origin is of no significance. There are also, one assumes, a considerable number of American books in the library that cannot be identified by such a rough and ready method as counting the numbers in the American sections of the classified shelves. It is possible to say, though, that the American collection was increased at least tenfold between the 1850s and the 1950s, which is also, coincidentally, the factor by which the output of American books published each year increased during the same period. In the sample of 5033 books examined, two hundred and fifty-two places of publication were recorded in forty-two states. In spite of the concentrating effect that copyright deposit had after the 1890s, it was ameliorated to some extent by purchasing.

Because acquisition was primarily of current publications and because it remained relatively constant after the 1890s except for the drop during the depression, it must have reduced in relation to all American publishing, but it might nevertheless have remained fairly representative. It is possible that about a third of all books in all subjects published in the United States between 1850 and 1950 have been acquired by the British Library by the various means available; but if only those books relating to American politics are considered, a proportion of possibly 10 per cent before 1890 dropped to about 3 per cent between 1890 and 1950. This suggests something that seems quite obvious, that the British Library's collection is strongest in American imprints that do not relate particularly to American subjects, that is, in the Library's own terms, in American books rather than in Americana.

Increase in American acquisitions in the 1960s

The inadequacy of an acquisition policy that relied too much on copyright deposit was recognised within the Library in the 1960s, and greater emphasis was given to the purchase of American books. Two overlapping areas attended to were privately-printed works and fine printing; the latter, because it often consists of reprints of well-known works, did not generally come by copyright deposit. Purchasing has risen in recent years to equal copyright deposit in importance, but because the decisions to purchase have been, since the 1960s, based on factors similar to those that cause books to come by deposit, purchasing has tended to reinforce the trend established by the importers of American books. The emphasis had been on books of academic interest, particularly those published by university presses, and otherwise books of fairly general interest – trade books mostly, that is books that are sold through bookshops; science, technology, law, medicine and other specialist subjects have been left for the special and academic librarians in other libraries to collect. But there are, among the books published in these specialised subjects, many that are of wider interest which ought to be in a national collection. Fiction has not been well served in recent years; acquisition has continued to rely on copyright deposit. Apart from books missed altogether, because they were neither issued by a British publisher, nor imported by a sole agent with a British imprint, American editions of the books of major authors have not been available in the British Library. There are innumerable examples of textual differences (other than of mere spelling) between American and British editions of the same work, and a copyright library is the most obvious place where one might expect to be able to compare editions.

Many books are not distributed through the book trade and their titles do not appear in the trade bibliographies that are used in the selection process at the British Library. Thus pamphlets, the publications of political parties, of professional organisations, of companies not primarily concerned with publishing, and so on – publications, that is, not issued by conventional trade publishers – have not recently been acquired to any extent. Yet publications of this kind made up a large part of the books supplied by Henry Stevens until the 1860s, and are acknowledged to be one of the strengths of the early collection.

The American Trust for the British Library

The deficiency in the collections of the British Library, which extends from the 1860s to the present, is being remedied by the American Trust for the British Library which, since 1980, has been supplying American publications missed in the acquisition process between the 1880s and 1950s. The money for these books is raised in the United States, and thus donation is becoming once again an important means for the acquisition of Americana. Stimulated by the activity of the Trust, the Library has used its own funds to purchase similar material outside the dates that limit the Trust's operations. One might expect that this retrospective acquisition will eventually have an effect on the method used for current selection, so that the problem is not continuously created almost as quickly as it can be remedied.

The classification system that had been used by the Library until the 1950s was partially abandoned for publications received after then, because of the great increase in the number of British books that arrived by copyright deposit. The new shelving system (pressmarks preceded by 'X') did not concentrate books on American subjects to quite the same extent.

Part Two
LOCATING AMERICANA

4.
The Catalogues

The General Catalogue

The fact that an author catalogue is now found in almost every library is largely due to the success of the British Museum catalogue. The decision to make the author the point of entry in the main catalogue was not inevitable; it was made at a time, the mid-nineteenth century, when classed catalogues which were based on the Renaissance idea of logical divisions of knowledge were generally in favour. When Panizzi became Keeper of Printed Books in 1837, the existing catalogue of printed books was inadequate. In the following year, when the Library moved from Montague House to the newly-constructed parts of the present building, there were about 160,000 volumes, but Panizzi and his staff knew that they were on the threshold of a great expansion brought about first by the enforcement of copyright deposit, then, after 1846, by a greatly increased annual book purchase grant. The opportunity existed for the last time, so it might have seemed, to reform the cataloguing system. A committee which included Panizzi's two immediate successors, John Winter Jones and Thomas Watts, prepared ninety-one rules for a catalogue which, although arranged primarily by author – stemming from the philosophy of Italian humanism rather than the rationalism of the classed catalogues – did nonetheless contain some convenient elements of classed catalogues. Furthermore, the new shelving system that had been introduced produced what was in fact a classed catalogue if the fourth copies of the catalogue title slips were arranged by shelfmark.

The major principles of the General Catalogue changed very little between 1839 and 1968; the Anglo-American cataloguing rules have been used for books catalogued since then. The rules of alphabetisation and so on used in the General Catalogue are given in *Readers Guide No. 7, How to Use the Catalogue,* by R.S. Pine-Coffin and R.A. Christophers.

Two aspects of the catalogue, both modifications of the basic author rules, are particularly useful to Americanists: cross references and the retention of several classes. Biographies are cross-referenced under the name of the author, and literary criticism is cross-referenced under the name of the author under discussion; these are called 'cross references of the third kind' in the *Rules for Compiling the Catalogue.* Such cross references note the fact that a book includes a portrait of the subject. Joint authors, collaborators, translators, editors, writers of prefaces and introductions if they are substantial, illustrators and the authors of manuscript notes in the Library's copy of the book are cross-referenced under this rule.

The following classes are retained in the General Catalogue:

Bible, including its constituent parts, cross references to commentaries and books of which the Bible is the subject, and in an appendix to the main entry commentaries by anonymous authors.

Congresses, that is reports and publications of congresses and conferences. But this class is incomplete and reports of conferences of particular organisations are often entered under the name of the organisation, or a conference might be entered under the country and town where it took place. Prodeedings of annual conferences are entered as a serial under the name of the body organising them.

Ephemerides, including almanacs and calendars although both might be entered under author or illustrator.

Directories, a particularly useful class for Americanists as it is divided by country, then subdivided by place, profession, trade association and so on.

Encyclopedias

Dictionaries

Catalogues, of public and private collections, exhibitions and sales. This class contains only anonymous catalogues and is otherwise incomplete.

Liturgies, some hymns are entered in a separate class.

Hymnals and metrical psalms such as the *Bay Psalm Book* are entered under Bibles.

Academies, an old class, which contained the publications of learned societies, universities and so on, has ceased to exist except as a prefix to shelf marks.

Where the works in these classes have authors or editors named on the title page, they are cross-referenced under the name of the author. A separate class, *Periodical Publications*, contains periodicals which are entered alphabetically by title under the place, ie town of publication; it is not divided by country. This class does not include 'academic' journals – publications of learned societies, universities and other such institutions – but consists mainly of popular publications, such as monthly magazines and even some weeklies which are not kept in the Newspaper Library at Colindale. There are also a few annual publications. 'Academic' journals are entered under the name of the publishing body, which in turn is entered under the town in which it is situated. But some bodies publishing journals might also be found under the name of the state. Generally the publications of national institutions are entered under state, followed by the title of the issuing institution, while local institutions are entered under town. There is fortunately an index to sub-headings for the 'United States' entry in the General Catalogue.

Periodicals are cross-referenced under their title alphabetically in the General Catalogue which is usually the best way to find them, but the cross reference does not give the shelf mark. Of course titles as well as places of publication change, and such changes are often not noted in the Catalogue. Resort must then be made to other finding aids: BUCOP – the *British Union Catalogue of Periodicals* – is out of date, but it is still the most useful way to trace a periodical; the *National Union Catalogue* records dates and changes in title under title entries, and the *Union List of American Serials in Britain*, (ed.) Dr C. Deering, gives details of British Library holdings but not the shelf marks. The British Library's purchase records, which are not available to readers but can be consulted by the staff at the enquiry desk, can also be used to trace periodicals. As a general guide, periodicals not entered under title in the General Catalogue will be found in the Periodical Publications section.

The rules for anonymous works are given in *Readers Guide No. 7*. The most distinctive aspect is that there is an element of subject cataloguing, as with biographies and literary criticism, in that where the subject of the work is represented by a proper noun in the title, the work is catalogued as an appendix to the entries under that heading. Thus there are a number of works catalogued under United States: appendix, and under Washington, George: appendix.

Where there is no proper noun in the title, the first substantive, or alternatively an adjectival expression, is used in preference to the first word (articles excepted) occurring in the title, in order to catalogue the work.

Publications of governments and laws are entered in the General Catalogue under the name of the government or department. The publications of the American state governments and of states and cities are not so voluminous as to cause any difficulty, but federal publications pose their own problems. Many official publications were not recognised as such by early cataloguers, and are catalogued and shelved as publications of authors or as anonymous publications. Commentaries on laws and official reports by acknowledged authors are catalogued under the names of the authors and cross-referenced. The cataloguing of American official publications tends to be inconsistent and incomplete and therefore other finding aids must be used. The *National Union Catalogue* is again useful, but much enterprise and resourcefulness is needed.

When there is more than one author with the same name, epithets are added to the name. The author then remains saddled with an epithet which might be idiosyncratic; thus Alexander Hamilton, political philosopher and founding father, is described as 'general of the United States army'.

Notes of two kinds are added to the entry by the cataloguers. The first consist of information not given on the title page – that the book contains portraits, plans or plates, for example – and the second consist of information relating to the particular copy catalogued – for example that it contains manuscript notes or has belonged to an eminent person. Cataloguers have often given other information such as attributions of authorship where the work is anonymous, pseudonymous or fictitiously or falsely attributed on the title page.

Panizzi's catalogue was a long time in gestation, and printing was not introduced until 1880, the manuscript catalogue slips being pasted in the guard books kept in the Reading Room. From 1880 the catalogue slips of accessions were printed and shortly afterwards the catalogue was published. This catalogue is known within the Library as GKI. Incorporation of new entries was made by pasting into the guard books until 1931 when a new edition, GKII, began publication. This edition was at first intended to be fully revised but by 1955 it became obvious that it could not be completed according to its original design and a short cut was made of merging the revised entries, some unrevised entries and entries from the printed supplement into new columns. This edition, GKIII, with pasted additions from 1956 to 1970, constitutes the present Reading Room Catalogue. Additions since 1970, published in supplementary volumes, have been printed on blue pages and inserted at the back of each of the Reading Room guard book volumes. Marc works published after 1975 are printed on microfiche in the current Marc catalogue.

Publications with imprints before 1971 but catalogued after 1975 are also pasted into the main part of the guard books. Such books catalogued after 1983 are entered in a special microfiche supplement and not in the current microfiche catalogue. Most works published since 1971 can be found in the microfiche catalogue, but there are some 1970–1975 imprints accessible only in the 'blue pages'. A further group of catalogue entries are the 'quick copy' cards, which apply to publications that were not incorporated into either the General Catalogue or the microfiche (Marc) catalogue between 1968 and 1982. They include publications of all kinds: periodicals, ephemera, works duplicated from typescript, and a number are American in origin. The cards are kept in a cabinet marked '...books not at present entered in the main catalogue', and are in a single alphabetical sequence following the cataloguing rules.

To summarise: American books might be located in
1. main sequence in guard books
2. blue pages
3. pre-1971 microfiche
4. microfiche (Marc) catalogue
5. 'quick copy' cards

A new consolidated edition of the General Catalogue, the last no doubt that will appear in printed form, is published by K.G. Saur.

The Subject Catalogue

In spite of the success of Panizzi's author catalogue, the need for a subject catalogue to supplement it was recognised in the 1880s; alphabetical institutional catalogues had been published in France and the United States, the best known American one being the *Index-Catalogue of the Library of the Surgeon-General's Office* which began publication in 1880. There were also precedents in Britain: *Bibliotheca Britannica: a General Index to British and Foreign Literature* compiled by Robert Watt and published 1819–1824 combined an author-dictionary and a subject-index referring to 40,000 books; but it was apparently almost unknown in the nineteenth century. George Knottesford Fortescue had the responsibility for classifying and shelving books for several years before he was appointed Superintendent of the Reading Room in 1884 and was thus familiar with the problems of classification when he was set the task of devising a subject catalogue.

There are two forms of subject catalogue, one based on a logical classification of knowledge, like the shelving system was, and the other an alphabetical index like Watts' *Bibliotheca Britannica*. Fortescue chose the latter. He explained his choice using the example of books on the horse which in his subject index appear under the heading 'Horse' with several cross references, whereas in Brunet's *Table Méthodique*, a standard

The Catalogues

class catalogue, such books would appear in two places: under the sub-sub-heading 'Veterinary Science' and the sub-heading 'Gymnastic Exercises'. It is fair to assume that Fortescue's choice represented British resistance to French rationalism; thus the subject index had no logical sequence but derived from the titles or where necessary the contents of the books themselves. Sub-division could therefore multiply in subjects where titles proliferated and books could be listed separately under several headings. Furthermore, by not aiming to be a complete classification of knowledge, the subject catalogue could omit those categories that were served by the General Catalogue. The difference between the two systems is shown by comparing the sub-divisions for the entry under United States of America, in the *Subject Index of the Modern Works Added to the Library of the British Museum in the Years 1881–1900*, ed. G.K. Fortescue, with the ten classes of the shelving scheme. These were: theology; jurisprudence; natural history and medicine; archaeology and arts; philosophy; history; geography; biography; belles lettres; philology. The sub-divisions used in the subject index, rather than being derived from these abstract categories of knowledge, have been uniquely adapted to the main heading, 'United States'.

Army
Churches and Religious Bodies
Civil Service
Constitution
 History
 General Works
 Congress: Elections
 Presidency
History
 Bibliography
 General History
 Colonial History
 War of Independence to the Civil War, 1773–1860
 Civil War, General
  Biographies

>   Confederate States
>   Separate Campaigns, Battles etc.
>   Regimental Histories
>   Naval History of the Civil War
>   Relations with Great Britain
>   Prisoners of War
>   Poems and Ballads
>   1865 to the Present Time
>   War with Spain, 1898
> Immigration
> Law
> Navy
> Politics
>   General
>   History of Political Parties
>   Municipal Politics
>   Pamphlets
>   Foreign
>   Monroe Doctrine, etc.
> Protestant Episcopal Church
> Public Domain
> Social Life
> Southern States
> Statistics
> Topography
>   Geography, Guide Books, etc.
>   Travels, etc.
> Trade and Finance
>   Tariffs and Taxation
>   Trade and Manufactures
> Western States

Cross references are given to several other main headings: America, Indians, the names of several of the states, land tenures, American literature, English literature, poetry, and the names of various churches. The subject index entries use a shortened form of title, but they include the place of publication, so that American imprints can be identified in subjects that are not subdivided by country – for example 'military science'. All subjects in which the nature of the subject and the titles of the books allow have sections subdivided by country, 'mineralogy' and 'medicine' for example. The quinquennial volumes of the subject index up to 1900 indexing 262,651 titles were afterwards combined into a three-volume alphabetical sequence and followed by quinquennial cumulations in published volumes until 1970. These are followed by a microfiche catalogue which has been published in book form by K.G. Saur.

A reversal of Fortescue's policy was necessary when it was desired to produce a subject index that could be searched by computer. This required a return to the philosophy of the class catalogue containing categories that could be divided and subdivided, thus allowing a computer search to narrow down to a single, or a small number of titles. This new subject catalogue, *Precis*, is available in the Reading Room on microfiche and can also be searched online through the British Library's automated information service, *Blaise*. An illustration of the analytical way the computer subject index works is given in the subject 'environment' under the main heading, 'United States'.

    United States: Environment, Conservation –
        Proposals
        Attitude of Negroes
        Law – Bibliographies
            Effects on land
            use planning
            National Environment
            Policy Act 1969
        Participation of Public
        Planning
    Economic Aspects
    Law
    Policies of Government – Decision making –
                      Application of
                      mathematical models

Economic Aspects –
Mathematical
models
Pollution – Control measures – Policies
of government
Taxation
Planning – State of the art reviews
Information sources
Mathematical models
By local authorities

5.
Microfilm Collections

Three kinds of material which are particularly important when using American material at the British Library are not particularly well served by the two catalogues: microfilm research collections, pictorial material and official publications of the Federal Government.

Microform is used at the British Library, as it is in other libraries, to preserve the texts of fragile material; therefore the items in the Burney Collection of Newspapers, for example, are produced for readers in this form. Periodicals and newspapers are often acquired in microform for convenience of storage; and some individual books not available in print are acquired in microform as an alternative to not having them at all – thus many of the titles destroyed during the Second World War when a section of the book stacks was set alight by an incendiary bomb have been restored to the collection by microfilm; part of this has been paid for by the American Trust for the British Library.

There is another function that can be performed only by microform: the creation in one place of collections whose components are otherwise dispersed. No single library has a collection of all the titles in Charles Evans' *American Bibliography* in their original form but all these titles are available on microcard in the Readex edition *Early American Imprints*. 'Impossible' collections in original form have been created by microfilm publishers, usually based on a well known bibliography, or one, or a number, of existing collections. These collections make the texts available, and, unless there are limitations of copyright, copies can be made from the film.

The research collections of this kind acquired by the British Library often overlap with titles in the original collection. The Library has original copies of the *Liberator*, William Lloyd

Garrison's abolitionist newspaper; being a weekly, it is kept at Colindale. The *Liberator* is also in the research collection, *American Periodicals 1741–1900*, available at Bloomsbury. The individual titles in these collections are not entered in the catalogue, although there are some exceptions; the whole collection is catalogued under the title of the micropublication. But it is not possible to know what particular titles the microfilm publication contains from the catalogue. In some cases the bibliography on which a collection is based is shelved with the Reading Room reference collection, but the title and author of a book can be known without the knowledge that it appears in a particular bibliography or that all the works in the bibliography have been filmed, or that the resulting collection is available in the British Library. The only perfect solution is to catalogue all the individual items in microfilm research collections in the Library; a less laborious compromise has been made with the compilation of a guide to the microfilm research collections available in the Reading Room.

The publication based on the bibliography of Evans and his successors, Shaw and Shoemaker, (ie *Early American Imprints*, Series I and II) is the most important single microform collection of Americana. It is ordered by the shelfmarks Series I, 1639–1800, Cup. 901.a.1/(Series I, 1639–1800), and Cup. 901.a.10/(Series II, 1801–1819). The oblique stroke is followed by the Evans or Shaw-Shoemaker number which is obtained from the printed bibliographies shelved in the Reading Room (2037a, 2037aa).

The following microform collections also contain Americana: *American Fiction* (Mic.A.4281–4453, 5133–5142, 5926) contains all the works listed in Volume I of Lyle H. Wright's *American Fiction: A Contribution Toward a Bibliography* (1939) (BB.G.a.1.). Volume I covers the years 1774–1850; the Library's existing collections 1850–1900 were considered adequate without acquiring the rest of the collection. It is ordered by shelfmark and Wright numbers given in the index kept in the Reading Room (BB.G.a.1).

The *American Periodicals 1741–1900* collection is in three series:

Microfilm Collections

Series 1	18th Century	shelfmark Mic. A. 130–162
Series 2	1800–1850	
	reel nos. 1–253	Mic. A. 163–416
	254–845	Mic.A.3621–4212
	846–1966	Mic.B.604/846–1966
Series 3	1850–1900	Mic.B.606/1–771

An index to the collection is available at the Enquiry Desk. Series 1 contains 88 periodicals, Series 2, 923, and Series 3, 110, so the collection is by no means complete. But it ranges from popular magazines to publications of learned societies and, what is most useful, the index has subject and editor as well as title access. It also has notes of varying length on some, but not all of the titles.

Perhaps a third of the titles are also available in original form and are thus entered in the catalogue. But these files are often incomplete and the microfilm collection must be used to fill the gaps. The original copies are useful if copies of illustrations are required for reproduction.

The Publishers' Trade List Annual, which began publication in 1873 as the *Uniform Trade Lists Annual* reproducing publishers' lists for each year, is one of the major components of American book-trade bibliography, and the microfiche edition published by Meckler Publishing has the advantage of a comprehensive index. It is ordered by the shelfmark Mic.F.181 and year. The printed index arranged in alphabetical order of publisher is available in the Reading Room reference collection (2169a).

Several microfilm collections of British material contain Americana:

British Publishers Archives, published by Chadwyck-Healey, contains the archives, complete or partial, of

George Allen and Co.	Mic.B.53/1–27
Index	2169 a
George Routledge and Co. (1853	
–1902)	Mic.B.53/28–33

Kegan Paul, Trench, Trübner, and Henry S. King (1851–1912)	Mic.B.53/71–97
Index	2169 a
Routledge and Kegan Paul (since 1912)	Mic.B.53/71–97
Handlist	2719.gg.98
Swan Sonnenschein and Co. (1876–1911)	Mic.B.53/34–58
Index	2169 a
Elkin Mathews (1871–1938)	Mic.B.53/59
Cambridge University Press (1696–1902)	Mic.B.53/60–70
Index and Guide	2169 a
Richard Bentley and Son (1829–1898)	Mic.B.53/99–214 and Mic.F.123/1–55
Indexes	2169 a

A number of American authors were published by these firms. *Early English Books, 1475–1640* (Mic.B.57/1–1536, Indexes NL 4c and Reading Room enquiry desk) contains titles selected from the *Short Title Catalogue* by Pollard and Redgrave, some of which relate to America.

English Cartoons and Satirical Prints, 1320–1832, in the British Museum (Mic.B.78/1–21), published by Chadwyck-Healey, contains the satirical prints listed in the *Catalogue of Prints and Drawings in the British Museum, Division I: Political and Personal Satires*, by F.G. Stevens and M.D. George (2083.d.e) and includes prints relating indirectly to American history.

Three Centuries of English and American Plays (Cup.700.1.1/5) contains 250 American plays, being all but eight of the titles in Frank Pierce Hill's *American Plays Printed Before 1830* (1934). There is a printed checklist in the Reading Room (AAG.c).

This survey by no means exhausts the quantity of Americana available in microfilm collections. Recent acquisitions have included county histories, city directories, census schedules and historic buildings surveys. There is a catalogue in the Official Publications Library to the microfilm collection (mainly politics and social science) held there, but there is no microfilm catalogue for the Department of Printed Books and enquiry must be made in the Reading Room.

6.
Picture Research

Picture research in Britain must begin with *The Picture Researcher's Handbook* by Hilary and Mary Evans and Andra Nelki (Reading Room enquiry desk), and, if American pictures in particular are required, *Picture Searching – Techniques and Tools* by Renata Shaw (Reading Room enquiry desk). The first, after a brief survey of illustrations, is an international directory of library and commercial picture research collections; the second is a bibliography. Also useful are Helmut Gernsheim, *The History of Photography* (1969), which has chapters on photography in America, and Mick Gidley, *American Photography* (1983).

Pictures are often required as historical documents rather than for their aesthetic qualities; it is good of course if one can combine both. The portraits available of General Sir Frederick Haldimand, a Swiss mercenary who was the British military commander in North America on the eve of the Revolution and whose papers are in the British Library, are all unattractive, but that fact alone seems to attest to their authenticity – the fault was with the sitter.

The quickest way to find a portrait in the British Library is to look up the cross reference in the General Catalogue, under the name of the person required. This will direct the reader to the main entry (under the author) and so to any biography that might have been published; the main entry will note if the book contains a portrait. One can assume that the biographer has selected a flattering picture, but the picture credits in the book will often lead to others which might be less well known or otherwise more suitable, and which will very likely have been copied from periodicals.

McClure's Magazine, the 'muckraking' journal, began in its first issue (1893) a feature, 'Human Documents: portraits of distinguished people of different ages', which consisted of half-tones made from photographs. 'Here are', said Sarah Orne Jewett in her introduction, 'the impersonal baby face; the domineering glance of the schoolboy, lord of his dog and gun; the wan-visaged student who is just beginning to confront the serried ranks of those successes which conspired to hinder him from his duty and the fulfilment of his dreams; here is the mature man, with grave reticence of look and a proved sense of achievement; and at last the older and vaguer face, blurred and pitifully conscious of fast waning powers.' The promise is fulfilled: thus the Octover 1893 issue contains seven pictures of George Washington Cable, author of *Old Creole Tales* and the historical romance *The Grandissimes*, and four of Bill Nye, the satirist. Other articles and other magazines besides *McClure's* provide portraits and biographical pictures such as those of homes and families. These can be located by using Poole's *Index to Periodical Literature* and the other indexes to periodicals shelved with it.

The authenticity of magazine illustration is usually satisfactory. As well as the use of half-tones made from photographs, most wood or metal engraving since the mid-nineteenth century has been copied from photographs. But the quality both aesthetically and for reproduction is often not good. Half-tones tend to make poor reproductions, and the early half-tones themselves are often poor. Both wood and steel engraving continued after the invention of photo-mechanical processes because of their clarity of detail which makes them especially good for architectural and technological illustration, and also because early photographs were usually posed, and were therefore not good for illustrations of action. Until the invention of the Kodak in 1888, there was rarely a camera in the right place at the right time. Thus Mathew Brady's photographs of the Civil War are perfect within their limitations, but engravings, such as those reproduced in *Harper's Weekly,* must be used for the scenes where no photographer was, nor could have been, present. *Poole's Index* is far from perfect and in any case does not index illustrations specifically or index advertisements which are a fruitful source of pictures. Illustrated advertisements on the other hand are quite easy to find because, once blocks were made, they were used again and again, and thus no specific reference is necessary.

Political caricature is found predominantly in magazines and, more recently, in newspapers. It has a distinctive character in the United States and has been an important mode of political communication since the eighteenth-century propagandist in Thomas Nast's cartoons of Boss Tweed; giving a cosy feeling of identity in the social in-jokes of the *New Yorker*. Its most elegant form was reached in the lithographs in *Puck* (1877–1918. The British Library does not have, unfortunately, a complete file.). The best examples of cartoons have been collected into books, often under the name of the artist, and one can thus find them in the General Catalogue. These books can also be located through the Subject Index which contains a section on caricature, as can also more general books such as Allan Nevins and Frank Weitenkampf, *A Century of Political Cartoons: Caricature in the United States 1800–1900*. The Department of Prints and Drawings of the British Museum, not a part of the British Library, contains a large collection of caricatures which can be located through the published *Catalogue of Political and Personal Satires in the Department of Prints and Drawings in the British Museum*. The subjects are mostly British, but a number of Englishmen are included who were significant in American history, George III and Lord North for example.

Elegance in design and reproduction is important in fashion pictures and also in giving a sense of period. This is certainly found in *Puck* and most notably in Charles Dana Gibson's pictures in *Life* and other magazines. Advertisements are also a source for fashion, a major one perhaps. Through copyright deposit, the Newspaper Library has acquired a number of Butterick pattern books from the 1930s to the 1950s, and there are several journals concerned with the clothing trade entered in the Newspaper Library Catalogue under New York and Chicago.

Illustrations of machinery – domestic, agricultural and

Picture Research

industrial – are most likely to be found in advertisements, and *Poole's Index* can be used to locate articles on mining, railways and so on. There are also specialist scientific and technological journals, the *Scientific American* being the best known. These did not have a high priority in the British Museum during the late nineteenth and early twentieth centuries, and after 1973 scientific and technical publications went to the Science Reference Library which did not aim to keep material that was not of use to contemporary science. But, fortunately, an important collection came to the British Library from the British Patent Office, and this included several American technical and industrial journals. Pictures of places such as city views at different periods and pictures of the West can be located through *Poole's Index* and so can pictures related to historic events.

Book illustrations are harder to trace; most illustrated books are fiction and the illustrations of fiction are not usually useful to the picture researcher. But there are some notable books used as picture sources. Theodore Bolton's *American Book Illustrations: bibliographic checklists of 123 artists*, provides one way to locate pictures in books. Illustrators tend to specialise in a particular type of subject: pictures by Frederic Remington can be located in *The Virginian* by Owen Wister, and Will James drew only cowboys; Bolton lists locations of his pictures in both books and magazines. As well as checklists, Bolton gives references to more extensive bibliographies of the illustrators' works.

Bolton is also the most convenient way to locate the profusely illustrated general histories of the United States that were usually issued originally as part-works, and were each illustrated by several artists. These can be used to illustrate almost any event in the history of the United States. Thus *Battles and Leaders of the Civil War* 'for the most part' by former Union and Confederate officers and edited by R.U. Johnson and C.C. Buell is listed under both of its chief artists Winslow Homer and Joseph Pennell. It was issued as a part-work beginning in 1884 and is a much quicker way of illustrating a person, place or event in the Civil War than, for example, looking through the file of *Harper's Weekly*, and it complements the photographs, many of them by Brady, published in *The Photographic History of the Civil War*.

Pennell is most famous for his pictures of European cathedrals, many of them published in a series of articles in *Century Magazine*, but he also drew many scenes from American cities, Philadelphia, New Orleans, New York and San Francisco among them. *New England Bygones* by E.H. Arr [Ellen Chapman], and *A History of the United States* by Horace E. Scudder, are other works illustrated by several artists.

The names of photographers are less likely to appear as authors or in the titles of collections and thus the General Catalogue is of little assistance in locating them. The subject catalogue can be used, but unlike the General Catalogue, it doesn't indicate whether or not a book is illustrated unless the fact appears in the title. Thus *The Photographic History of the Civil War*, edited by Francis Trevelyan Miller, published in 1911–1912 in ten volumes, is listed under 'United States: Civil War – General History' in the volume for the years 1911–1915. But one would be lucky to find it just by looking through the list; 7,000 other books about the Civil War had been published by 1911. Fortunately a more select bibliography appears in the *Harvard Guide to American History*, Revised Edition, ed. Frank Freidel, under 'Civil War: Pictorial History', with eighteen other titles. The *Harvard Guide* has similar sections on Indian life (ten titles), World War I (five titles), and World War II (four titles). Other specialised subject bibliographies can be used in the same way. Academic books are not usually good sources of illustrations, but it is surprisingly easy to guess the likelihood of illustration from the title.

The Photographic History of the Civil War contains reproductions of several thousand photographs by a number of photographers working from both sides. Mathew Brady was an Irishman who had emigrated to New York as a boy; he visited Daguerre's studio in Paris in 1838 and a few years later set up his own studio on Broadway. He was present at the first battle of Bull Run, but got caught up in the action and had to return to New York for more equipment. Later Brady and the others fitted out mobile studios to process their 8 × 10 inch glass plates and followed the armies throughout the war. A.D. Lyte, of Baton Rouge, realised the military potential of photography and made pictures for the Confederate secret service, the first 'camera spy'. There is a large collection of Brady photographs in the Library of Congress, but his own negatives were taken in default of a debt in the 1870s and after changing hands several times became the nucleus of the collection on which the *Photographic History* is based.

Reproductions can be ordered from the original source, which can often be found from the picture credit, but are more usually taken from the book or magazine in which they appear. Pictures are subject to copyright if they are at all recent, and in any case, the owner of the book can charge a fee for reproduction. Thus it is necessary to state when ordering a photograph if it is to be used for publication.

Photographs solve the problem of authenticity which must always be suspect to some degree when etchings are used, but the quality of reproduction suffers if it is done from half-tones which until about 1912 were the only way photographs could be printed simultaneously with type. Since March 1880 when the New York *Daily Graphic* printed the first newspaper photograph, the half-tone process has been the usual way of reproducing photographs in newspapers; but more recently in books and in high quality pictorial magazines, photographs have often been printed by photogravure or collotype, both of which reproduce better.

The advantage of reproducing again from existing illustrations in books and magazines is that it enables great resources to be used which would not otherwise be conveniently available or indeed available at all. Thus panoramic or 'birdseye' views of cities, a genre which flourished in America between the 1820s and 1880s, and not available in original form in the British Library, become available in the form of book illustrations if one can accept some loss of quality.

7.
American Maps

Mapping early Americana

Most of what has been said about printed books in the American collections applies also to maps, although since 1867 maps have been kept separately from the other collections, first as a distinct department of the British Museum, and after the removal of most of the manuscript maps to the Manuscript Department in 1892, as a branch of the Department of Printed Books. In 1985 the Map Library became part of Special Collections.

The publication of early maps of the New World was closely related to printed books, maps being printed as part of or in association with books; with the later publication of atlases, map publication remained dependent on the book trade.

Bibliographers of early Americana were interested equally in maps and text, thus both Henry Harrisse and Henry Stevens collected maps and included them in the canon of early Americana. But there are ways in which maps and plans of towns and fortifications are bibliographically distinct from books, and both Harrisse and Stevens listed them separately. With maps the distinction between the value of the information conveyed and the aesthetic value as an object is not as clear as it is in books. Two consequences of this are that the interests of collectors and scholars have diverged further in the case of maps than of books, influencing the composition of private collections; and that the production of manuscript maps of importance, often also objects of great beauty, survived in the print era. Such maps were often intended for display and are not the equivalent of confidential memoranda which continue in manuscript in the twentieth century.

Otherwise maps relating to America followed the same course of development as printed books, having their origins in

Spain, Portugal, Italy, France and Germany, and later England; the earliest surviving map showing America was that of Juan de la Cosa, dated 1500. After the slow displacement of Ptolemaic geography from European knowledge the configuration of the eastern coast of North and South America was established, and by the middle of the sixteenth century the exploration of the interior had begun.

Drawing and publication of maps was not confined to the explorers themselves. From the beginning stay-at-home cartographers had relied on information provided by others, the travellers and explorers who might have later supervised the production of the maps, and indirectly they made use of the knowledge possessed by the indigenous inhabitants. As might be expected, the geographical knowledge acquired during the later part of the sixteenth century related chiefly to colonisation, and the attempts to find a route to the east. The culmination of sixteenth-century cartography was the Wright-Molyneux map of 1599, which is the map referred to in *Twelfth Night*: 'he does smile his face into more lines than is in the new Map. . .'

During the seventeenth century, the expeditions of the French in the north of the continent – the penetration of the Great Lakes and the upper Mississippi – balanced the exploration by the Spanish in the south east and south west, while the English, from their colonies on the east coast, explored their hinterlands as far as the mountains.

Two geographical fallacies persisted in the seventeenth century: the existence of an inland sea – the Sea of Verrazano, linked to the Pacific – appeared on a map as late as 1651 (John Farrar's 'A mapp of Virginia discouered to ye falls', published in the third edition of Edward William, *Virgo Triumphans: or Virginia Richly and Truly Valued*), and California was occasionally drawn as an island until 1747 when Ferdinand VI of Spain decreed that this was to be done no longer.

In addition to topographical mapping, settlement created the need for plats, or plans showing titles to land. The plantations of Virginia, the manors of New York and the seigneuries of New France appeared on maps from the seventeenth century.

War provided an additional and powerful motive for mapmaking in the eighteenth century. The first map published in America had accompanied William Hubbard's *A Narrative of the Troubles in New England with the Indians (Indian Wars, 1677)*. During the eighteenth century, five wars between the colonial powers, the last being the Revolutionary War, were fought on American soil.

The French and Indian War (the Seven Years War) began with the incursion of colonial surveyors, George Washington and William Gerard DeBrahm among them, into the Ohio valley, and during its course the Ohio valley was mapped and numerous plans drawn of forts and roads along the frontier from Ticonderoga to Fort Pitt. The accurate charting by Captain James Cook of the St Lawrence, the charts of which were published in 1760, was also the result of military necessity.

The culmination of eighteenth-century map-making might be considered to be the maps delineating the boundaries of the United States itself, not, as it turned out, unambiguously; the 'Red-line Map', the annotated version of the Mitchell Map used by the Peace Commissioners at Paris in 1783, is in the Manuscripts Department of the British Library. But this would be to undervalue the detailed maps of localities frequently published in atlases and which were the result of accurate surveys. From the 1770s, maps of this kind had in their detail, typography and colouring, a distinctly modern appearance.

Administration was also a generator of maps: the Proclamation Line of 1763 gave a geographical expression of the British determination to administer the colonies with vigour after the conclusion of the French and Indian War. The political expression of the same intention was the creation of an American department in Whitehall.

Contemporary accounts and the early histories of the Revolution usually contained maps or plans, quite often of fortifications and battles; these were often large and elaborate fold-out plans.

Pilot books produced to serve growing intercolonial trade contained navigational charts and plans of harbours. *The New*

American Practical Navigator published by Nathaniel Bowditch in 1802 replaced the previous British sailing manuals and became the standard American authority.

These early maps, like the printed topographical accounts of the American colonies that they often accompanied, were primarily intended to put forward or to correct information, or, in some cases, to establish claims to sovereignty or title. For all these reasons it was usually necessary to repeat the information; thus there are some maps, mother maps, from which a number of others are derived; sometimes the existence of such earlier maps has been hypothesised and they have been subsequently discovered. This was the case with the 'Contarini' map, now in the British Library, 'A Map of the World' made by Giovanni Matteo Contarini and Francesco Roselli in 1506, the existence of which was predicted by Henry Harrisse, who had also predicted, in a similar fashion, the existence of the Columbus 'Spanish letter'.

American maps in the British Library

There is no single map collection anywhere within which one can find copies of all these key maps in the evolution of the cartography of early America; some are manuscript, and some printed maps survive only in a single copy. But the foundation collections of the British Library were rich in manuscript maps, and the King's Library contained 50,000 maps and charts including many important contemporary manuscript surveys of the American colonies and the theatres of war in North America. The library of Thomas Grenville which passed to the British Museum in 1847 was also strong in American maps. Thus the strength of the British Library's collection of maps of early America, as with the collection of early books, stems from its being a composite of several great private collections. But the acquisition of early maps did not stop with the foundation collections and both separate maps and map collections have been acquired since. The map collection of the Royal United Services Institution, purchased in 1968, included the map collection of Lord Amherst who held military and civil offices in North America between 1758 and 1763.

Manuscript maps have continued to come into the collections by donation and purchase as do written manuscripts, but the greatest accessions of maps in recent years have been of printed maps. It was an atlas, *Scribner's Statistical Atlas of New York*, that was the occasion of the first application of copyright deposit to an American printed book; maps came also as official publications by exchange. Thus county atlases, meteorological, geological and other thematic maps, navigational charts and so on, published in the United States, although not necessarily concerned with American subjects, have been acquired by the Library in the same way as printed books.

Unlike official publications, printed maps are not entered in the General Catalogue, although the presence of a map in a printed book, especially an early one, is noted, but there is a separate catalogue of printed maps. Manuscript maps which are in the custody of the Department of Manuscripts are listed in the catalogues of that department. The Map Room of the British Library contains related printed books and periodicals.

The following printed catalogues of maps are available in the British Library:

Catalogue of Maps, Prints, Drawings etc. forming the Geographical and Topographical Collection attached to the Library of King George III, (King's Library) 1829.

Catalogue of the Manuscript Maps, Charts and Plans and of the Topographical Drawings in the British Museum (3 vols. 1844–1861, repr. 1962).

After 1861 manuscript maps are entered in the Catalogue of Additional Manuscripts, printed by the Manuscript Department.

Catalogue of the Printed Maps, Charts and Plans in the British Museum to 1964 (15 vols. 1967).

Most of the early printed maps are listed in the *Catalogue of American Maps in the Library of the British Museum*, issued by Henry Stevens with his *Catalogue of American Books,* 1866.

8.
American Music

Music is dealt with at the British Library in the same way as maps; manuscript music is in the custody of the Manuscript Department and is listed in their catalogues, and printed music is not included in the General Catalogue of Printed Books, but in a separate music catalogue.

The Music Library has twenty-two items of music published in America before 1801, and a reasonably good representation of American music from the nineteenth century, including about 1,250 hymn and psalm books containing music (those without music form part of the general collections of printed books). For the twentieth century the collection is less good. Current policy is to acquire the works of major American composers and the important works at least of lesser composers.

Because of the international nature of much music publishing, a large number of American scores are received by copyright deposit in the same way as printed books.

'Secondary' music (mainly light and popular music) is not entered in the music catalogue, but stored in ten-year sequences alphabetically by composer for instrumental music and by title for vocal music – a slip index for vocal music arranged alphabetically by composer is also maintained.

The *Catalogue of Printed Music in the British Library to 1980*, published by K.G. Saur (1981–1987) is, like the General Catalogue, an author catalogue, with the consequence that American music cannot be directly located in it. Bibliographies such as those in Claire R. Reis, *Composers in America* (1977), Clifford McCarty, *Film Composers in America* (1953) and the *New Grove Dictionary of American Music* (1986) must be referred to.

Some indication of the scope of the holdings of American

music is given by the following survey of the Library's holdings of separate works of individual composers:

Milton Babbit	21
Samuel Barber	50
William Bergsma	20
Marc Blitzstein	7
Elliott Carter	38
Aaron Copland	86
Henry Cowell	44
Arthur Farwell	45
Lukas Foss	12
George Gershwin	80
Rubin Goldmark	12
Morton Gould	47
Charles T. Griffes	22
Roy Harris	46
Charles Ives	90
Edward MacDowell	48
Daniel Gregory Mason	34
Gian Carlo Menotti	19
Douglas Moore	16
Horatio Parker	90
Walter Piston	31
Wallingford Riegger	37
Carl Ruggles	8
Gunther Schuller	29
William Schuman	33
Roger Sessions	32
Randall Thompson	6
Virgil Thomson	81
Edgar Varese	12
Kurt Weill	40
Stepan Walpe	15

9.
Americana in Languages other than English

Publications in oriental languages, which are taken to include Yiddish and Hebrew, are kept by the Department of Oriental Manuscripts and Printed Books, and, although some American Judaica has been purchased recently with the help of the American Trust for the British Library, it is likely that the number of works relating to America is quite small – books about America by Chinese such as travel diaries, for example, or general works on Chinese foreign policy. It has generally been the policy in foreign language acquisitions to concentrate on works relating to the countries themselves.

The same has tended to be true of works in European languages, whether published in Europe or America; but there are in the collection, because of its strength in early printed works, important books in the languages of early printing. Thus, of books printed before 1600 and listed in Alden's *European Americana*, the British Library holds 781 in Latin, 148 in German, 311 in Italian, 36 in Dutch, 264 in French, 25 in Portuguese, 205 in English, 5 in Polish, and 200 in Spanish. The countries of origin of these are:

Italy	473	Belgium	183
France	343	Switzerland	179
Germany	306	Holland	41
England	217	Portugal	25
Spain	194	other	14

Spanish printing began in the Americas before English, and was introduced into the United States as former Spanish colonies were added to its territories: the first Louisiana, which had been a Spanish colony from 1765 until 1803, and in which the first Spanish-American newspaper was printed in 1808.

Printing began in Texas and California while they were still parts of Mexico; a press was set up in Monterey by Augustin Zamorano in 1834 and it continued printing after the Treaty of Guadalupe Hidalgo in which Mexico ceded its northern territories to the United States. The treaty put a large number of Spanish speakers, the Chicanos, or Mexican Americans, under the political authority of the United States, and its bilingual clause encouraged the publication of newspapers in Spanish; more than a hundred were published in California between 1848 and 1942. Migration since the treaty has dominated the ethos of the Chicano community and its press.

Puerto Ricans have migrated to the continental United States since they became citizens in 1917, and Cubans, Haitians and other Latin Americans have migrated for much the same reasons as the European immigrants who preceded them. Works concerning these communities, ie books, periodicals and bibliographies in Spanish and English, published in the United States and in Latin America, have been acquired by the British Library in recent years (for example, publications by Cuban exiles in Miami).

Early books printed in Spanish, or printed in Spain, can be identified in Alden's *European Americana*. More recent works, and American imprints in Spanish, must be identified in scholarly bibliographies such as Frank Pino, *Mexican Americans, a Research Bibliography* (1974); the *Chicano Periodical Index,* published by G.K. Hall; Ester B. Gonzales, *Annotated Bibliography on Cubans in the United States, 1960–1976*; ed., Diane Herrera *Puerto Ricans and Other Minority Groups in the Continental United States: an Annotated Bibliography* (1973).

Works about the Portuguese in the United States are listed in a bibliography by Leo Pap, *The Portuguese in the United States* (1976). There are also several guides to Latin-American history and literature which include works relating to early American history and to the relationship between Latin-American countries and the United States. Among them are: Curtis W. Wilgus, *Historiography of Latin America: A Guide to Historical Writing, 1500–1800* (1975), David F. Trask,

Michael C. Mayer and Roger R. Trask, *A Bibliography of United States – Latin American Relations since 1810* (Supplement by Michael C. Mayer, 1979). The Hispanic Division of the Library of Congress has published as a series since 1936, *Handbook of Latin American Studies*. Academic periodicals also publish occasional bibliographies. It should be noted that all these academic works are concerned with their subjects and not specifically with publishing or with American imprints.

German printing flourished in the American colonies at Germantown, Pennsylvania, from 1728 at the press of Christopher Sower (Saur): he issued in 1743 a German edition of the Bible, the first American Bible since Eliot's *Indian Bible*. His son of the same name continued the business until his death in 1784, and Christopher Sower 3rd, who, like many other Germans in America, supported the British side during the Revolution, settled afterwards in Canada where he continued printing. American imprints in German can be identified in Oswald Seidensticker, *The First Century of German Printing in America, 1728–1830* (1893), Karl J.R. Arnt and May E. Olson, *The German Language Press of America*, and in a forthcoming bibliography by Helmut Vogt. The *Eighteenth Century Short Title Catalogue* recorded in 1982 twenty-five American imprints in German held by the British Library.

Like the holdings of German Americana, those of French and Italian can also be assumed to be good: French books include the works of Cartier and Champlain and of Father Hennepin, the first European to set eyes on the Falls of Saint Antony at the headwaters of the Mississippi. The bibliographer, Henry Harrisse, published a bibliography of New France, and French works can also be identified in Charles Leclerc, *Bibliotheca Americana* (1867), and in the *Catalogue de l'Histoire de L'Amérique* of the Bibliothèque Nationale. The *Eighteenth Century Short Title Catalogue* recorded in 1982 twenty American imprints in French held by the British Library.

The Library also has a substantial holding of Russian and slavonic Americana, and collects works published by the

American Institute of the Soviet Academy of Sciences, and by the Russian community in the United States. Ukranian, Hungarian and Armenian works are likewise acquired. Acquisition of Scandinavian Americana has in recent years been largely confined to works concerned with the life of Scandinavian communities in America, although it includes, as do the collections in other languages, earlier works concerning discovery and settlement.

While they cannot be regarded as Americana, many books written by Americans are published in Europe: books in English on all subjects are published in Holland, and Americans have often been the authors of books on art and classical archaeology published in Italy, Greece and Germany.

10.
Official Publications

The publications of governments and other public bodies are termed 'official publications' at the British Library, and, although they are entered in the General Catalogue along with other printed books, they are distinctively pressmarked (prefix AS in the case of American publications) and are at present consulted in a special reading room. Publications of the Federal Government and its agencies are found in the catalogue under the heading United States, and the subheading of the department or agency in which they originated. There are indexes to the titles and subheadings of the United States entry in the General Catalogue. The publications of quasi-official bodies and other national institutions are entered in a miscellaneous section that follows the main entry. Publications by named authors are cross-referenced under the author's name. The same pattern is followed for the publications of states and towns.

Federal publications

The publications of the Federal Government are so large in number that the catalogue is not usually a sufficient means of finding one's way amongst them; they reached a peak of just over 24,000 a year in 1961. A large proportion have been acquired by the Library under the terms of an exchange arrangement made in 1883.

The publications of the Federal Government fall into two categories. The first are the printed records of the regular proceedings of government – of the legislative, executive and judicial branches. These are, of course, serial publications and there is a single pressmark for each series. But some series,

House Documents and *Senate Documents* for example, include reports and papers that should really be regarded as single publications. These can be identified in the *Monthly Catalog of United States Government Publications*, which has been published since 1895. It contains an annual index in the December issue, decennial indexes and there are two consolidated indexes, 1895–1899 and 1900–1971. Also useful are: a 'dictionary' catalogue, the *Catalog of Public Documents 1893–1940* (25 vols, 1896–1945. Usually cited as the *Document Catalog*), and J.G. Ames, *A Comprehensive Index to the Publications of the United States Government 1881–1893* (1905). Earlier publications can be identified in *A Checklist of United States Public Documents 1789–1970* (1971). John L. Andriot, *Guide to United States Government Publications*, is issued in two volumes: volume one, *Current Agencies*, is published annually, and volume two, *Non-Current Agencies*, every five years. There are many privately compiled and published guides to either the whole body or particular parts of the Federal Government's publications. A useful selection is listed in the *Harvard Guide To American History*, but the primary bibliographic record is the *Monthly Catalog*. Publications marked with a dot in the *Monthly Catalog* are received on exchange by the British Library; these are the publications selected for deposit in designated libraries within the United States, and, although comprehensive, the selection excludes much that will interest historians. Fortunately the most important of the excluded items have been published on microfilm and are available in the Official Publications Library. Among them are: *Congressional Committee Prints, 1829–1970* (there is a printed guide), *Congressional Committee Hearings 1839–1969* (printed index), *United States Government Publications (Non-Depository) 1975–*. Other microfilm collections contain documents that were produced for the internal use of the government such as United States Consular Despatches (from British countries only) 1790–1906, and the series of presidential papers. There is a card catalogue to these microfilm collections which is added to as further items are acquired.

The second category of government publications consists of

single publications of agencies of government or of national institutions such as libraries and museums. These seldom relate to the proceedings of government. They might be produced by a government agency to give information to the public – the health risks to smoking or safety at work, for example – or they might be catalogues of libraries, monographs by staff members of national museums, catalogues of exhibitions and so on. Many of these come by exchange and will thus be marked in the *Monthly Catalog*, but it is often easier to find them initially in the General Catalogue. The printing of laws and proclamations began in the colonial era and records of the formal proceedings (ie journals) of public institutions were sometimes printed. More detailed reports of debates and votes appeared in newspapers and pamphlets, particularly during the Revolutionary crisis, for example the *Votes and Proceedings of the American Continental Congress* (Philadelphia, 1774). But no legal requirement for the printing of the proceedings of the United States Congress existed until 1831 when a bill was enacted to provide for the printing of 750 copies of the surviving documents of the first fourteen Congresses. This was compiled by General William Hickey, chief clerk in the office of the secretary of the Senate and printed by Gales and Seaton, Washington, between 1832 and 1861.

Commercial publishing was, and still is, an important part of the means of dissemination of government information. The debates in Congress have only been officially published since 1874; they were privately published as the *Register of Debates in Congress* 1824–1837, and the *Congressional Globe* 1833–1873. A popular compendium of laws, *Corpus Juris Secundum*, has been commercially published since 1936.

State and local publications

The records of colonial governments are, of course, British state papers, and the originals are found in the Public Record Office – mostly in the class C.O.5. There is a set of the lists and indexes to the Public Record Office on the shelves of the

Official Publications Library. An attempt at a quasi-official (ie published under the authority of an act of Congress) printed archive of colonial documents was made by the historian Peter Force. Only two series, the 4th and 5th of the projected compilation, were finally published (1837–1853) covering the period from 7 March 1774 to the end of 1776.

Colonial records are the predecessors of the records of state governments, not of the federal system. They are therefore included in the *States Records Microfilm Project* which produced 1800 reels of microfilm between 1941 and 1950. The printing of the records of state legislatures was not universal; in the late nineteenth century the records of some states were still kept in manuscript. In 1936 William S. Jenkins began travelling round the states collecting state records – this led eventually to the microfilm project. The present Library holding of this series is not complete, but it is being added to.

A movement began in the 1840s which led to the placing of a number of the publications of state governments in the Library. (Nicolas) Allexandre Vattemare, a French ventriloquist and impersonator, went to the United States in 1839 to perform at the Park Theatre in New York. He used local libraries to prepare the historical impersonations for his show and he devised an idea while in the United States for library exchanges. These were to consist of any serious books, not just official publications. He had some success in promoting exchanges within the United States and to a more limited extent with France. Limited exchange of state publications, particularly laws, had in fact already begun, but the enthusiasm that Vattemare's scheme generated led to an increase in the printing of official records as well as to more exchange.

These years – 1848–1855 – were also the years when Henry Stevens was making his greatest additions to the American collections of the British Museum Library and he was able to exploit the growing interest in state publications. Stevens purchased some state records for the Library, and he was also able to make private exchange arrangements or else to have state publications donated to the Library without cost. These arrangements sometimes extended to towns, quasi-official

Official Publications

bodies and societies, but they were largely confined to New England. Neither exchange nor donation are satisfactory methods for the regular acquisition of serial publications, and the holdings of these early state records are therefore patchy. State records have since been supplemented by microfilm collections such as the compilation of the records of *State Constitutional Conventions 1776–1976*, but town and county records have seldom been added to. The list of items recorded in the General Catalogue for the Massachusetts town of Lowell shows the typical pattern of such local holdings.

> Catalogue of the Library of the Middlesex Mechanic Association, 1840.
> Lowell Five Cent Savings Bank, Officers, Act of Incorporation, By Laws etc. 1869.
> Contributions of the Old Residents' Historical Association, 1873–1876.
> Proceedings of the city of Lowell at the semi-centennial celebration of the incorporation of the Town of Lowell, 1876.
> Revised charter and ordinances of the city of Lowell, 1876.
> List of Members, Old Residents' Historical Association, 1880.
> South Congregational Society, semi-centennial anniversary, 1880.
> Merchants' Collecting Agency's Philatelic Blue Book, 1898.
> American Correspondence School of Textiles, Instruction Papers, 1898–1902.
> Bulletin of the City Library, no. 18 (Special list on gardening), 1903.

For most towns and counties in the United States, however, the British Library holds nothing. This lack is ameliorated to some extent in the case of counties by 'county histories'. These are a fairly standard kind of publication produced in the late nineteenth and early twentieth centuries by specialist publishers who contracted with the county authorities. The Library acquired quite a large number at the time of publication and has since purchased more on microfilm. They vary in length from a few hundred to several thousand pages and are not usually regarded as very reliable scholarly sources, but they do extend the uses of the British Library's collections in an area in which they would otherwise be very weak. Volumes of similar format were published for some towns, and towns are also served by a microfilm collection of city directories. There are, of course, many town and state histories and travel guides, acquired as a part of the general collections, but these are not official publications. They are listed under the names of their authors in the General Catalogue and are not, unless anonymous, cross-referenced under the name of the state or town. Record commissions and state and local historical societies have produced compilations of state records for many states – such as that for the state of New York edited by E.B. O'Callaghan. The Library's holdings of these are in general good, and missing series have been acquired retrospectively. Often the most reliable sources for the proceedings of state and local governments are the local newspapers. As state capitals and county seats are often small towns, the newspapers required are not likely to be available at the British Library.

One major source of local information is the series of census records. The Library has microfilm of the United States manuscript census schedules (the enumerators' reports) from 1850. (Records for the earlier censuses are held by the British Library of Political and Economic Science – the London School of Economics library).

For librarians, the particular difficulties that arise in selecting, acquiring and cataloguing the publications of governments have led to the source rather than the subject of such publications being the characteristic that marks them off from the general collections. But for the user the distinction is not important, and it is a strength of the system in operation at the British Library that government publications are merged with the other general collections in the Catalogue.

11.
Newspapers and Periodicals

The Newspaper Library

The distinction between a newspaper and a periodical is not a clear one, and it would be unimportant except that at the British Library the two are physically separated. The definition of a newspaper used is the simple one of frequency of issue: that it is issued at an interval of no longer than two weeks. Those newspapers so defined are held at the Newspaper Library at Colindale in north London. There are some anomalies in the case of American publications which result in early American weekly or fortnightly publications being as likely to be held at Bloomsbury as at Colindale. Such publications held at Bloomsbury are entered in the General Catalogue under Periodical Publications by the name of the town in which they were published. Those held at Colindale are entered in the newspaper catalogue only. The principal cause of this confusion is that the microfilm collection *American Periodicals 1741–1900* is held at Bloomsbury and the titles it contains are entered individually in the General Catalogue. Many of them are weeklies or fortnightlies, as indeed were most eighteenth-century American newspapers. But, in many cases, original publications duplicated by the microfilm collection were in any case kept at Bloomsbury and entered in the General Catalogue.

The Burney Collection of Early Newspapers, formed by the collector Dr Charles Burney, is also kept at Bloomsbury. A list of the American newspapers it contains is given in Appendix V.

The Bloomsbury Library also contains two volumes of early American newspapers which were purchased from Richard Kennett, the London bookseller, in 1841. These were never transferred to Colindale and are catalogued under Periodical Publications in the General Catalogue. A list also appears in Appendix V.

The remaining American newspapers are kept in the Newspaper Library at Colindale. A list of the Colindale holdings of original American newspapers published before 1820, ie 'Brigham' newspapers (listed by Clarence Brigham in his *Bibliography of American Newspapers)*, is given in Appendix V. The titles in the microfilm collection *Early American Newspapers,* which is kept at Colindale, are not included in this list.

This confusion in the collection of American newspapers is most marked in the case of early publications, but is less noticeable if one considers original publications alone. But some newspapers can be found in both collections, and it is essential therefore to check both catalogues.

The main newspaper collection of the British Library has been housed separately from the book collections since 1903, and between 1903 and 1932 no direct access to newspapers was provided for readers, although copies could, with some delay, be produced in the Reading Room. The great volume of newspapers received by copyright deposit was the chief reason for 'outhousing' them, but it is difficult not to believe that the diminished reputation that the press in Britain acquired after the rise of mass-circulation newspapers after the 1880s, borrowing as they did from the American sensational press, was not also a cause. Newspapers had been objects of collection in America and Britain in the eighteenth and early nineteenth centuries and the British Museum had acquired quite a respectable collection of colonial and early American newspapers, but Victorian scholarship stressed sources close to the centre of political power, such as public documents. London newspapers, at least until Northcliffe took over *The Times*, might just be permitted as reputable sources of information, but the ephemeral character of daily publications put British provincial newspapers, and indeed any foreign ones published outside capital cities, beyond the academic pale. In 1900 the early newspapers in the British Library were threatened with dispersal or even destruction. But during the 1920s, as part of the general shift in political attitudes, the histories of radicalism, of the Labour movement, and of social life in general, became respectable subjects even within the universities, and newspapers became prime historical material. Thus in 1932 a reading room was opened at the previously inaccessible newspaper repository at north London.

A separate catalogue of the Colindale Newspaper Library is still maintained, but a copy of it is kept with the General Catalogue. A title index on cards lists all newspapers alphabetically but the main catalogue is arranged by place of publication ie by country and town. So American newspapers are, unlike printed books, catalogued together, but, unfortunately, they are arranged under an alphabetical sequence of the names of towns, and not subdivided by state.

As arrangement by state is usual in the bibliography of American newspapers, it is often necessary to consult one of the various bibliographies of American newspapers before using the catalogue. As printed books these bibliographies are normally placed with the Bloomsbury collection. A reference library has been established in the reading room at Colindale, but many works on the history of newspapers in America must still be at Bloomsbury.

Bibliography of American newspapers

Newspaper collecting was hampered in the nineteenth century by a lack of good bibliographers. Isaiah Thomas had included newspapers in his *History of Printing in America*, published in 1810, but this is seldom referred to. In 1913, Clarence Brigham, who was librarian of the American Antiquarian Society at Worcester, Massachusetts, and thus curator of Thomas's own collection, began to compile a systematic bibliography of American newspapers as a parallel to Charles Evans' *American Bibliography*. As it progressed it was published in parts in the American Antiquarian Society's *Proceedings*, and then as a book after the parts were completed

– *History and Bibliography of American Newspapers, 1690 to 1820* (1927). The standard guide after 1820 is Winifred Gregory, *American Newspapers, 1821 to 1936: a Union List of Files Available in the United States and Canada* (1937). Rowell's and Ayer's current trade directories of American newspapers and popular periodicals have existed since 1869 and were eventually merged into *Ayer's Annual Directory of Newspapers and Periodicals* which still continues. These trade directories were not intended as systematic bibliography and are not complete, but they have an immense amount of useful information – circulation, ownership, editor, political persuasion and so on. The Library of Congress publication, *Newspapers in Microfilm*, which is cumulative and supplements the *National Union Catalog*, is another useful bibliographic aid. State and subject newspaper bibliographies have proliferated in recent years, often in conjunction with projects to locate and preserve local newspapers, and it has become usual to list newspapers separately in bibliographies of works of scholarship. A guide to American newspapers in the British Library is given in D.K. Adams, *American Newspaper Holdings in British and Irish Libraries* (1974), published by the British Association for American Studies.

History of the American press

The first attempt to publish a newspaper in the American colonies was made by Benjamin Harris in Boston, 25 September 1690. Called *Public Occurrences*, only one issue was published and of that only one copy survives, located in the Public Record Office at Kew. Harris began a newspaper in England in 1679 but fled to Massachusetts from London in 1686 to avoid arrest for publishing pamphlets hostile to the government. In 1695 he returned to England, and *Public Occurrences* is hardly part of the history of the American press. This had its real beginning with the publication of the *Boston Newsletter* by John Campbell, Postmaster of Boston, on 24 April 1704. It had no rival until 1719 when William Brooker, who superseded Campbell as Postmaster in that year, started the *Boston Gazette* with James Franklin, the brother of Benjamin, as its printer. Both these newspapers printed the words 'published by authority' under their titles, more in imitation perhaps of the British *London Gazette* than through necessity, as there was no authority to license newspapers in the colonies. The first non-establishment newspaper was the *New England Courant* (Burney Collection) started by James Franklin on 7 August 1726 when he lost the printing of the *Gazette* after a change of postmasters. Benjamin Franklin published his first piece in the *Courant*, the Silas Dogood letters, sent in anonymously while he was a printing apprentice to his brother.

Newspaper controversy began in America at the same time as the press proliferated, during the Boston smallpox epidemic of 1721. The *Newsletter* and the *Gazette*, the two existing newspapers, took different sides on the question of the desirability of inoculation; inoculators were accused of spreading the disease. The controversy continued when James Franklin's *New England Courant* was published and inoculation was attacked on the front page of the first issue. The second issue suggested with savage irony that an army of inoculators be sent among the Indians, the origin, perhaps, of a long surviving legend.

Outside New England, the *American Weekly Mercury* began in Philadelphia in 1728, the *New York Gazette* on 18 November 1726, *Pennsylvania Gazette*, December 1728, the *Maryland Gazette*, 1727, *Virginia Gazette*, 1736, *South Carolina Weekly Journal*, 1730, *Rhode Island Gazette*, 1732. The second paper in New York and the first 'opposition' newspaper in America was the *New York Weekly Journal*, first issued on 5 November 1733. It was no more radical than the *New England Courant*, which it imitated in raiding the British opposition press – *Cato's Letters* and the *Spectator* – for copy, but it was embroiled in faction and on 17 November 1734, Peter Zenger, the printer, was arrested and tried for seditious libel. His acquittal is usually cited as the foundation of the freedom of the press in America.

Partisanship flourished during the Revolutionary controversy: this can be traced in John B. Hench and Bernard Bailyn, eds., *The Press in the American Revolution* (1976), and in the bibliography of Loyalist newspapers 1763–1784 by Timothy M. Barnes printed in Gregory Palmer, ed., *Bibliography of Loyalist Source Material in the United States, Canada and Great Britain* (1982).

But it was in the nineteenth century that partisanship came, one might almost say, to dominate the American press and to pose a problem in judging the quality of newspapers. There is a dilemma for librarians in that everyone is agreed on the various criteria of quality in a newspaper – objectivity, honesty, coverage of national and international affairs – but the newspapers most useful to historians are often those that disregard all of these. This is nowhere more true than in the United States. Because of the dispersal of much of the population into separate and often isolated communities with a tenuous connection with national political institutions, newspapers were the nervous system if not the sinews of national party organisation. Thus the 'bad' instead of the 'good' newspapers must often be selected, and partisan newspapers must also be collected in twos and threes rather than singly. A similar problem confronts the selector of special-interest newspapers such as the black native American, women's, ethnic, anarchist, labour, religious and trade press.

The Stevens Newspaper Collection

The Newspaper Library has a unique, if partial, solution to the dilemma in the collection of 780 single issues of American newspapers published in spring 1858. These newspapers are present in the British Library, as is so much of its American collection, through the offices of Henry Stevens. He got them during his book-buying trip to the United States in 1858 from the offices of the *New York Tribune* and the *New York Herald*, the newspapers of Horace Greeley and James Gordon Bennett Jr respectively. They were exchange copies.

Newspapers and Periodicals

In 1858 the telegraph was becoming the major medium for the transmission of news, but the posts still went by train, stage, steamer and pony express, and with the posts went copies of newspapers exchanged by the editors in order to reprint each other's news. The system was highly organised; the convention was that the articles copied would be acknowledged and could be reprinted free of charge except that in some cases a scale of prices was charged for the actual exchange copies, to eliminate the disproportion that would arise for example in the exchange of a daily for a weekly. The penalty for breach of the convention was exposure, but the convenience of the system was sufficient to enforce the rules. Telegraphed news went mostly outwards from Washington – one Washington correspondent could serve a number of papers – but who knew where the next steam-boat, or political crisis might blow up; no newspaper in the 1850s could maintain a national network of correspondents. Western news was in demand in the eastern newspapers, particularly Greeley's, and the exchange system was the best way to get it. Thus the *Herald* and the *Tribune*, competing newspapers, both exchanged with a network of other papers throughout the United States, and almost all the newspapers in the Stevens' collection are marked 'Herald' or 'Tribune' and often as well 'please exchange' or 'please X'. Articles are frequently marked for copying and in several cases have been cut out, and the space repaired. Stevens apparently tried to get copies that were not mutilated; thus the issues he collected are not all of the same date.

Without anticipating the uses the collection can be put to, several areas of interest are obvious, such as the structure of the press itself – the exchange system, prices, subscription terms and subscribers' clubs. One can see the alliances led by the two great New York papers. Some newspapers unashamedly professed their party allegiances, while others were coy or attempted to be neutral; the motto of the *Warren Telegraph* of Rhode Island claimed with good Augustan rhetoric, 'No party pledge or discipline we own, but freely to follow truth alone'. The non-partisan papers exchanged with both the *Herald* and

Tribune, but the editorial comment and the items reprinted from the New York papers show that beyond the openly partisan there were relatively coherent groups of opinion corresponding roughly to the positions of the *Herald* or the *Tribune*. The reformist and faddist papers such as those on abolition, dress reform, Fourierism and spiritualism were connected with the political alliances, although they were not rigidly partisan, and the papers of the immigrant groups, where they were concerned with American politics and not European, also fall in partially with these constellations of opinion.

The newsworthy events of spring 1858 were the three contending Kansas constitutional conventions, the entry of a United States army into Utah, a filibuster raid into Nicaragua and a religious revival in New York. All these issues were reported nationally by means of the exchange system, then further disseminated into the local network.

Advertisements carry a great deal of information: on transport and communication (the railway, steamboat and stage advertisements), on prices and commerce and indirectly, on many aspects of social history. An example of the latter can be found in the frequent advertisements for female pills directed to 'married ladies' – the pills should not be used during pregnancy 'as a miscarriage would certainly result therefrom'.

Above all else, this collection provides a kind of index to the American press that is not provided by the *Union List* or by the contemporary directories. Special interests and political connections cannot always be discerned without looking through the papers themselves: the titles of the *American Commercial and Chemical Journal* (druggists), *The Musical World* (which carries an article on the cure of dyspepsia by music), or the *Spiritual Telegraph*, convey some information about the likely contents, but the interests of the *Southern Vineyard* (a Los Angeles local paper), *Type of the Times* (spelling reform), or *Mountain Messenger* (the local paper of La Porte, California) are not so easily identified from their titles.

The 780 exchange newspapers were presented to the Library by Henry Stevens along with a proposal that the Library subscribe to some of them, but his suggestion was turned down, along with much else of what Stevens offered at the same time.

Newspapers on microfilm

Thus the Library did not acquire in original form the nineteenth-century newspaper collection that it might have had and has had to resort in recent years to microfilm. The microfilm acquisitions have in general been complete files of the major newspapers from the largest states, and of quality newspapers; but there has also been a policy of completing when possible fragmentary files of original newspapers held, which if it were extended to the single issues of the Stevens' collection, would provide a very extensive nineteenth-century collection indeed. As microfilm acquisition is a continuous process, and is being supported at the present time by the American Trust for the British Library, it is not readily amenable to bibliography. Thus the notes on aspects of the American press which follow refer to materials that are being actively acquired. These describe the character of the American press, not the present holdings of the Library, although all the titles mentioned might be expected to become available as microfilm acquisition proceeds.

The Black Press

The black press has been a major fact of American city life for 150 years. The first black newspaper, a weekly, was *Freedom's Journal*, the first issue of which appeared in New York City on 16 March 1827, three years before the founding of the *Liberator*. It lasted for two years, had a circulation probably equal to that of most other political weeklies of its time, (ie less than 1,000), and had agents from Portland, Maine, to

Washington, D.C. Its editors were Samuel Cornish, a pastor in the African Presbyterian Church, and John Russwarm, a Jamaican educated at Bowdoin College. 'We wish to plead our own cause', they said in the first issue. That they would oppose slavery, abolished in New York by an Act of 1827, was obvious, but the issue of colonisation, the settlement of free blacks in Africa, was more difficult. The newspaper was initially opposed to colonisation, although it published the views of supporters, but in 1829 it changed sides, opposing the opinions of most of its readers, and Russwarm, by then the sole editor, was forced to resign. He was succeeded by the other founder, Cornish, who after a short delay republished the paper with a new title, *Rights of All*. But it ran for only six issues until 9 October 1829, and, in spite of reaching a fairly respectable circulation of 800, left the editor out of pocket.

The negro readership was kept in existence by the *Liberator*, founded by William Lloyd Garrison in Boston on 1 January 1831: although it was a white paper, eighty per cent of its first subscribers were black. But as it grew its readership became predominantly white and fewer negro news items were carried.

In 1837 Cornish started the *Coloured American* in New York, and between then and 1865 about 50 other black newspapers were started, including Frederick Douglas's *North Star*. Most of these were established, like the *North Star*, specifically to attack slavery and few survived long.

After the Civil War the black press flourished – 1,200 new newspapers began between 1865 and 1905, most of them small and most in the South. But several reached a circulation of more than 5,000, and six survived into the mid-twentieth century: the *Philadelphia Tribune*, 1885, the *Baltimore Afro-American*, 1892, the *Houston Informer*, 1892, the *Dallas Express*, 1892, the *New Iowa Bystander*, 1894, and the *Indianapolis Recorder*, 1895. Other successful black papers of the period were the *New York Age*, the *Boston Guardian*, the *Washington Bee*, and the *San Francisco Elevator*.

What in retrospect appears to be a major event in the history of the black press was the founding of the *Chicago Defender* in 1905 by Robert S. Abbott, who became the first black newspaper millionaire. Chicago had a black population of more than 40,000 in 1905 and had had several black newspapers since the founding of the first in 1874, but they had been typical of the post-Civil War papers, ie race conscious and largely concerned with Republican party politics.

The *Defender* introduced the staple of mass-circulation newspapers, crime reporting – 'Chops Wife to Pieces with Ax' was a headline in the *Defender* of 17 March 1924 – and in 1921 it had reached a circulation of 250,000, made possible by the massive migration of blacks to the northern industrial cities in the early decades of the twentieth century. Other papers, mostly published in big cities, achieved large circulations and were able to extend from their home cities towards a national readership. These papers continued to 'plead our own cause', against segregation for example, which increased in the northern cities as the black population grew, and against the way negroes were portrayed in the white press. But although their appeal was to a wide section of the population, the successful papers became big businesses by mid-century, catering for the black middle class whose interests increasingly coincided with those of the white. As the major city newspapers began increasingly to carry news of the whole community, the potential market for predominantly black newspapers, and therefore also their numbers, declined.

The native American press

The *Cherokee Phoenix*, if not actually the first, has been the most famous of the American Indian newspapers; the British Library has an almost complete original file. The *Phoenix*, later renamed *The Cherokee Phoenix and Indian's Advocate*, began in New Echota, Georgia, with the issue of 21 February 1828 and appeared weekly with occasional gaps for more than six years. It was bilingual in English and Cherokee using an 86 character syllabary invented by a member of the tribe. The difficulties of publication are illustrated by an apology printed in the issue of 11 March 1829:

We are extremely sorry to inform our patrons that our last papers, a few hours after leaving this place, were nearly lost. It appears that the post rider, in attempting to cross the Holly Creek, fell from his horse and dropt the mail bags. The rider escaped with difficulty and the bags were not obtained until seven hours after. The Post Master of Springplace writes, that 'the papers are all injured, and the directions on the bundles which held together are defaced – in short the whole mail is in a miserable situation. I will however open them and dry them as well as I can, and send them on.'

There was some conflict of purpose at the newspaper's foundation. It was sponsored by the Cherokee National Council and the American Board of Commissioners for Foreign Missions, and the controversy which developed in its columns over the removal of the Indians to reservations led to the decline of the paper and to the retirement and murder of its first editor, Elias Boudinot. In 1832 the *Phoenix* was taken over by the Georgia authorities and used to promote migration to the Oklahoma territory and it ceased publication on 31 May 1834. But it was the forerunner of a vigorous native American press; 250 newspaper titles in the Indian territory have been listed for the nineteenth century and a further 320 were established in the first decade of the twentieth century. As well as the healthy growth in newspaper publishing, twenty native magazines also began publication before 1900. Since the 1930s, when economic pressure and government policy have encouraged Indians to move from the reservations to towns, newspapers have developed to serve the urban native community. A useful guide is Daniel F. Littlefield Jr, and James W. Parins, *American Indian and Alaskan Native Newspapers and Periodicals, 1826–1924*, (1984).

Spanish newspapers

Languages other than English and those native to America have been represented in the American press. Newspapers in

Spanish are a distinct group. The first news-sheet in the Americas was in Spanish, printed in Mexico City in 1542, but these remained sporadic, as they were at that time in Europe, until the publication of *Gaceta de Mexico* in Mexico City in 1722 which carried the usual legend, 'published by authority'. The phase had more significance in Mexico than in New England, however, as censorship was stringent; the editor of the *Gaceta* was a canon of the cathedral and the news was largely religious; the Feast of the Circumcision, the preservation of the bones of a former archbishop, and, the staple of the irregular news-sheets, the arrival of a fleet.

The Mexican press is the direct ancestor of the Spanish press in the United States. Printing was taken to the northern territories of Mexico in the nineteenth century; a weekly newspaper, *El Crepusculo de la Libertad*, was published in Taos, New Mexico, in 1835. The press continued to serve those Mexicans who stayed put after the territory was annexed by the United States. This was partly because the Treaty of Guadalupe Hidalgo provided for bilingualism, and therefore Spanish printing was subsidised in order to print laws and public notices. The Mexican population of the United States did not become entirely cut off from Mexico; northward migration continued after the War of 1846–1848. Between 1900 and 1930 the composition of the Chicano population was changed by mass migration, largely of agricultural workers, and the Spanish language press lost the subservience it had had during the nineteenth century. *El Clamor Publico*, the most notable radical paper, was founded in Los Angeles in 1855, and in the twentieth century newspapers such as *El Heraldo de Mexico* were established to serve the working-class immigrants.

Between 1848 and 1942, 350 Spanish language newspapers were established in the United States, 36 each in Los Angeles and El Paso, 26 in San Antonio and 21 in San Francisco. San Francisco is an unusual case; four papers were published there in 1878 because it was the major sea-port of the west coast, and its newspapers have always been concerned more with Latin America than the Chicano papers have.

In recent years Chicanos have migrated from the borderlands to the cities further north, and, with immigrants from other Spanish-speaking countries, particularly Puerto Rico, have created Spanish-language communities in most large American cities. These are served by about 100 Spanish newspapers today.

German and French newspapers also served old-established communities, the German press becoming increasingly important in the nineteenth century, as German immigration continued. It was joined during the nineteenth and twentieth centuries by most of the languages of Europe, including Yiddish, and several of Asia. There is also an English-language press catering for Scottish, Irish and English immigrants. Unlike the Spanish press, that of the other non-English groups has a history of constant decline through lack of continued immigration, and through economic success, which has encouraged its readers to assimilate into the main stream of American life. American Yiddish newspapers on microfilm are at present being acquired by the Library with the help of a grant from the American Trust.

The Woman's press

A fairly substantial female readership was recognised by colonial magazines and newspapers; this is evident from the advertisements, the poetry and the selection of the fiction published, but they seldom addressed themselves to issues concerning women's rights and the position of women in society; the *Pennsylvania Magazine* edited by Thomas Paine is a rare exception. The reform movements of the nineteenth century gave the real impetus to the emergence of a women's press and the abolitionist and temperance press took up the women's cause. *The Lily* was originally a temperance magazine until its editor, Amelia Bloomer, made it an advocate of female suffrage and dress reform – freedom from the encumbering garments that most women then wore. *Today's Lady's Book, The Lowell Offering* and *The Woman's Advocate* were wholly or largely written, printed, and published by women.

Female suffrage came near to being achieved before the Civil War, but it was then pushed aside by the issues of the war and its aftermath. In 1868 Elizabeth Stanton and Susan B. Anthony founded *The Revolution,* a sixteen-page weekly originally financed by an eccentric (and male) millionaire; its famous motto was 'Men, their rights and nothing more; women, their rights and nothing less'. *The Revolution* lasted only until 1870, bringing about its own demise through its advocacy of a number of radical causes, which upset conservatives, and through its opposition to the Fifteenth Amendment, which would have franchised negro men before women, white or black, had the vote. This upset the former abolitionists still associated with the women's movement, who founded the American Woman Suffrage Association and the *Woman's Journal.* The *Woman's Journal* confined its advocacy more narrowly, but not entirely, to the franchise, believing other kinds of equality would follow; it survived until 1931, twelve years after the passage of the Nineteenth Amendment, which provided for women's suffrage.

Labour, political and trade press

Anarchist, Fourierist, socialist and labour newspapers have flourished since the *Peaceful Revolutionist,* an anarchist weekly, was founded by Josiah Warren in Cincinnati in January 1833. The most fertile period was from the 1880s until the American entry into the First World War in 1917, when a number of newspapers were suppressed.

Labour and trade papers are present in the collection of the British Library, but not as complete files or, in general, in long runs; indeed, most are scattered single issues. But there are several sequences that extend over one or more years, some in original form and some on microfilm. This suggests that they have been acquired either by donation or in response to readers' requests. One such acquisition came with the library of the British Patent Office. The industries represented by these longer sequences are predominantly mining and chemicals and there are some railway periodicals. The scattered issues of trade publications are catalogued under the town where they were published and must thus be located by town; since most of those in the Library's collection have come from New York City, the task is relatively easy. As might be expected, a number of these publications (in Chicago as well as in New York) related to the fashion industry. While the present division of the Library into humanities and science sections persists, the acquisition of more historical files of trade periodicals is unlikely. But the same limitation should not apply to the radical and labour press, which is, because much of it is becoming available on microfilm, an area of likely acquisition.

As well as clipping news from other papers, editors of early American newspapers filled out their columns with poetry, short stories, serialised novels and travel or humorous sketches. There is hardly a figure in nineteenth-century American literature who did not write for, or even edit a newspaper. These papers were generally weeklies and were largely superseded by the growth of literary magazines and the rise of subscription publishing in the mid-West, which made books more easily accessible. The practice flourished particularly in the colonial era and in the Whig papers on the frontier which in the first half of the nineteenth century made their appeal to a self-perceived educated minority; thus an issue of the *Commercial Advertiser* published in Apalachicola, Florida, in 1838 contained a short story, three original poems, a list of the contents of the latest *Edinburgh Review* and also of the *London Quarterly Review* which it particularly commended to its readers.

British-American press

The collection of American newspapers and periodicals published in Britain, while being relatively small, is a particularly valuable part of the Newspaper Library's holdings, and is, indeed, unique to the Library. The oldest of these, *The*

American Gazette, was published between 1768 and 1770, and was later issued in a single volume. It reprinted speeches, letters and so on relating to the crisis in Anglo-American relations which followed the imposition of the 'Townshend duties'. *The American Magazine* was a literary monthly published from 1851 to 1852 and having among its contributors Longfellow, Poe, James Russell Lowell and James Fennimore Cooper. A political weekly, *The London American*, was founded in 1860 and continued to 1863. The same title was used between 1895 and 1902 for a social magazine designed to serve the American community in Europe. *The Anglo American Times*, a weekly, ran from 1865 to 1896. It was joined in the 1870s by *The American Settler, The American Herald, The American Register, The American Traveller, The American News*, and in the 1880s by *America, The American Visitor, The American Eagle, American Humorist and Storyteller* and *The American and Colonial Gazette*. Of these, only the *Settler* (1872–1892), the *Register* (1873–1909) and the *Traveller* (1875–1890), all weeklies, outlasted the decade of their founding. Between the 1890s and the beginning of the First World War, the American community and British citizens intending to emigrate or to invest in the United States could turn to *America Abroad, American Society in Europe, The American Visitors' News and Register and Colonial Gazette, The Anglo-Californian, American Referee and Cycle Trade Journal, The Anglo-Colorado Mining and Milling Guide, The Anglo-Saxon, The American Trade Review, The Anglo-American Traveller, The Anglo-American and Continental Courier* and *The Anglo-American Illustrated News*, as well as the older, longer-running weeklies. The American YMCA published a daily news-sheet for servicemen between July 1918 and March 1919, *American Home News*. Social news of the American community in London has continued to be disseminated from 1925 to the present by the *American Women's Club Magazine*. Although there is no file of it in the British Library, it is available, with the other titles listed above, on microfilm (published by World Microfilm Publications, London).

The titles of these publications generally give a good

impression of their contents. Their proliferation between 1890 and the First World War shows the size and liveliness of the American 'colony' in London; the shift in emphasis from literature and literary humour to trade, commerce and social jottings shows the changing character of the colony during these years.

General periodicals and magazines

The history of general periodical and magazine publishing in the United States and the American colonies is described in great detail in Frank Luther Mott, *History of American Magazines*; five volumes were published (1930–1968) covering the years 1741 to 1930. As well as chapters on the general background to magazine publishing, the volumes contain essays on each of the most important periodicals in the periods covered and therefore serve as bibliographies.

The 'core' American periodical is the *North American Review*, which was published from 1815 to 1940. It was founded in Boston by a circle with Harvard connections and literary and historical interests who, although they admired England, wished to elevate American culture. The first editor, William Tudor, was also a founder of the Boston Athenaeum and was active in the affairs of the Massachusetts Historical Society. The second was Jared Sparks who served two terms, 1817–1818, and 1824–1830, and was a member of the founding board. Edward Everett, afterwards American Minister in London, James Russell Lowell, Charles Eliot Norton and Henry Adams were all editors before the *North American* moved to New York in 1878. It became more 'popular' after leaving Boston and eventually began publishing fiction, although of a fairly highbrow kind; *The Ambassadors* was its first serialised novel. The circulation, which had been of the order of two or three thousand in the early Boston days, reached a peak of 76,000 in 1891. The *North American* was stuffy and represented the views of the elite. It ignored authors like Poe and Melville and loathed the transcendentalists. It was schizophrenic in its attitude to American culture; Edward Everett, when editor in the 1820s, wrote to Sparks: 'American books are too poor to praise, and to abuse them will not do.' But it provides some reference through its indexes to almost everything of importance that was going on in the United States or in Anglo-American relations for more than a century, and it is therefore the most useful means of entry into the American periodical culture.

The *Atlantic Monthly*, also founded in Boston, in 1857, appealed to a similar intellectual set as the *North American*. Its first editor was James Russell Lowell, and it was edited by William Dean Howells from 1871 to 1881. *Harper's Weekly*, also established in 1857, provides a source of more popular material as do *McClure's Magazine* and the others mentioned in the section on picture research. *Harper's Monthly Magazine*, founded in 1850, serialised both British and American authors. *Century* (1881–1930, superseded by *Scribner's*) carried the first publication in 1899–1900 of *Sailing Alone Around the World*, by Joshua Slocum, a descendant of a Loyalist refugee of the American Revolution and the pioneer not only of such voyages but also of the literary genre that has sprung from them.

A more enterprising literary magazine was *The Literary World* (1847–1853), published by Evert A. and George C. Duyckinck. It was the first American journal to review currently published books. Political radicalism survived in *The Nation*, founded in 1865, whose second editor, Wendell Phillips Garrison, was a son of William Lloyd Garrison – it has been regarded as a successor to the latter's *Liberator*. A satirical magazine, *Puck*, appears to have been modelled on the London *Punch*, but it was in fact first published in German and was based on a similar type of magazine published in Germany. It became notable for its elegant lithographs. (The British Library has only two years, 1915–1917, and one issue from 1891.)

The American magazine tradition did not spring forth fully-formed in the nineteenth century, but had American antecedents as well as English examples. The two great early American publishers, Mathew Carey and Isaiah Thomas, each started magazines after the Revolution: Carey, *The American Museum* (1787-1792) in Philadelphia, and Thomas, *The Massachusetts Magazine* (1789-1797). Noah Webster launched *The American Magazine* in New York in 1787, but it ran for only twelve issues.

These early magazines were less original in their contents than those of the later nineteenth century and had much smaller circulations. They were produced, like most eighteenth-century periodicals, by their proprietor editors and relied greatly on reprinting material; pamphlets of the Revolutionary controversy, for example, were reprinted in the 1780s and 1790s. This older tradition was continued in the nineteenth century by *Nile's Weekly Register* (1811-1849), and it still persisted in the mid-twentieth century in *I.F. Stone's Weekly* (1953-1972).

The British Library's collection of general periodicals is good. There are complete files of all mentioned here (except for *Puck*) either in original form or microfilm. The microfilm research collection, *American Periodicals 1741-1900*, described in Chapter IV, supplements (and indeed duplicates parts of) the Library's own collection. There is a printed guide to this collection, although the titles are also entered separately in the Catalogue. *Poole's Index to Periodical Literature 1802-1906* provides a subject and names index to the contents of magazines and general periodicals in the nineteenth century, and the *Readers' Guide to Periodical Literature* (1900-) and the *Social Science and Humanities Index* (1916-) continue the same in the twentieth century. C. Deering, *Union List of American Serials in Britain,* gives library holdings of periodicals of all types, but unfortunately the holdings indicated for the British Library are not complete (the fault is with the British Library, not Deering).

Academic periodicals

Deering includes academic journals as well as general periodicals. The British Library's holdings of American academic journals, transactions of learned societies and other such publications, are good. Subscriptions have generally been kept up even during lean times, and what gaps have occurred have generally been the result of accident and have been remedied when they have been discovered. It is generally possible in London to use specialist libraries, ie those of the British learned societies, institutions or colleges, the American counterparts of which published the periodicals in the first place.

12.
American Manuscripts in the British Library

Introduction

Manuscripts of American interest in the British Library, while considerable in number, make up only a small proportion of the whole and to list them gives a rather distorted impression of the real richness of the collections. This is particularly true of the group of large antiquarian collections that came to the Library at its foundation or shortly afterwards. Those that contain American manuscripts are the Cottonian, Harleian, Royal and Sloane, ie the foundation collections, and the Lansdowne, Stowe, King's, Hargrave and Egerton collections which were acquired later; with the Egerton collection came a bequest to be used for further acquisition.

These early collections had been used by scholars while in the possession of their original owners and had been arranged in volumes, and were mostly already listed or catalogued in some form when they came to the Museum. They were retained in their original arrangement and not merged into a single collection as were the collections of printed books. When new catalogues were made and published, the foundation and early collections were therefore catalogued separately. Between 1753 and 1782 about five hundred volumes of additional manuscripts were acquired by the Museum (in addition, that is, to the foundation collections). The series of numbers used for the Sloane catalogue was continued for these Additional Manuscripts. Only a small number of the manuscripts had been purchased; most were gifts and bequests or were deposited by the government; a regular grant for purchasing manuscripts (or books) did not become available until the 1840s.

The Catalogue of the Sloane and Additional Manuscripts,

published by Samuel Ayscough in 1782, departed from the principle of giving serial numbers to manuscripts by arranging its entries under subject classifications, but its example was not followed, and a cut and pasted re-arrangement of the Ayscough catalogue was produced (and served until the twentieth century). The Additional Manuscripts series was continued and volumes published for manuscripts acquired 1836–1840 (1843), 1783–1835 (index only 1849) and 1841–1845 (1850). These continued as a regular published series with non-cumulative indexes for groups of years; parallel series of Additional Charters and Egerton Manuscripts were included in the same volumes. Volumes of the catalogues of the separate collections were published: Cotton 1802, Royal and Kings 1921, Lansdowne 1812–19, Stowe 1895–96, Harley 1808–12, Hargrave 1818, and an index to the Sloane Manuscripts in 1904.

Each of these collections was separately indexed, but the indexes to all the manuscript collections and series list only direct references to America or to American places, persons and subjects. The compilers of the early guides to Americana, Professor Andrews and his associates, (these guides are described in the next section) realised the inadequacy of the indexes in respect to American references, and searched through the catalogue entries themselves and sometimes (but infrequently) consulted the original manuscripts.

Their research was thorough, but they were limited in general to what the cataloguers had reported. They dealt with this obvious limitation by a caveat in each introduction. The guides have been available to scholars for eighty years, and the documents listed are now well known and have in many cases been transcribed in printed compilations. Future scholarship is therefore more likely to make use of the British Library collections by tracing the background to American affairs – colonial policy, taxation, trade, British politics and European diplomacy, all of which are well represented.

A brief and general survey will be given here of the documents held by the British Library, and individual manuscripts will be listed only to illustrate the type of material to be found in the collections, and not as an attempt at an exhaustive list.

American history and British documents

The revolution in historical writing which occurred in England in the seventeenth century had a counterpart in the American colonies in the eighteenth, in that the apocalyptic history of Cotton Mather and the New England divines, and the special pleading of John Smith and Fernando Gorges were replaced by the urbane histories of men of power such as William Smith of New York and Thomas Hutchinson of Massachusetts.

The first British History of America in this style was by George Chalmers – *Political Annals of the United Colonies* (1781) – but it was a tendentious work, and its successor, *Introduction to the History of the Revolt of the Colonies*, which supported the general drift of British colonial policy, was suppressed by the author when, at the moment of publication, Lord North's ministry fell. Chalmers was rewarded for his judiciousness with a position at the Board of Trade in 1786.

Narrative history written with direct reference to public documents was used in Whitehall as an aid to decision-making. John Pownall, an official of the American Department of the British government, had written a long memorandum, 'State of the disorders, confusion, and misgovernment which have lately prevailed, and do still continue to prevail in His Majesty's province of Massachusetts Bay' (Public Record Office, CO5/759), for the American Secretary, Lord Hillsborough in 1770, and, as the crisis developed, further narratives were commissioned before major decisions were taken. No regular public access to state papers was provided for at that time, but in the circles of American Loyalists in London with which Chalmers was connected, the general gist of such documents was apparently known and applications for extracts to be made from the records were attended to, although this was at the discretion of the Secretary of State and information was withheld from the extracts when it was considered to be possibly detrimental to the reputation of the present or previous governments. But original official documents, indeed, passed into the library of George Chalmers. The

Public Record Office Act of 1838 opened up the opportunity for historians of the American colonies to use official records and the considerable quantity of printed information that the public records contained. The opportunity was not taken up immediately, however, and the earliest recorded use of American records was by the descendant of a Loyalist claimant pursuing remuneration he believed to be due to him. As the works of J.A. Froude became known in the United States, the possibilities of the British Public Records, and those also of other repositories in Britain and Europe, became apparent.

George Bancroft, while American Minister to Britain from 1846 to 1849, was able from his position of influence to initiate transcription on a considerable scale of British records relating to American history. The most ambitious enterprise, however, was that of Benjamin Franklin Stevens, who began in the 1860s to transcribe records from the Public Record Office relating to New Jersey and other states that offered commissions. This led him to begin on his own initiative a catalogue and selective transcription of all documents in the archives of Europe relating to the origins of the United States, a project that he hoped would become eventually the beginning of an American national archive. His dream was not fulfilled; Congress proved parsimonious when proposals were made to take over Stevens' work, and after his death, the index alone was acquired for the Library of Congress. The full transcripts were presented to the British Museum several years later by the firm of Stevens and Brown. Stevens' skill in tracing and cataloguing documents was acknowledged by others, if not by the American government, and he catalogued the Dartmouth papers for the Royal Commission on Historical Manuscripts, some Loyalist papers (which were also transcribed) for the New York Public Library, Board of Trade records for the Pennsylvania Historical Society, and records relating to the state of New Hampshire. Between 1888 and 1898 he published a facsimile edition of selected documents from European archives, which threw new light on several aspects of the American Revolution, especially the alliance with France, espionage, and the Carlisle peace commission of 1778.

The Carnegie guides to American manuscripts

In 1899, J. Franklin Jameson, who has achieved lasting fame in American historiography as the author of *The American Revolution Considered as a Social Movement*, and who was, at the time, Professor of History at Brown University, conceived the idea of a guide to manuscripts relating to American history in London archives, and persuaded the American Antiquarian Society to support it. In 1903 the project was passed on to the Carnegie Institution, which had just been founded with an endowment of ten million dollars, and in 1905, while the project was under way, Jameson became the Institution's Director of Historical Research. The Public Record Office and the British Museum which had been the main repositories used by Stevens were the first whose holdings were investigated. They were surveyed by Charles Andrews, and, after he returned to America, Edith Moodie, who had been secretary to Benjamin Franklin Stevens, assisted in preparing the guide for publication. Andrews had requested that the initial survey should extend only to 1783, and documents relating to the United States after independence were thus included in a subsequent volume. The two volumes, which remain the primary guides to American manuscripts in the British Library, are: Charles M. Andrews and Frances G. Davenport, *Guide to the Manuscript Materials for the History of the United States to 1783, in the British Museum, and in Minor London Archives, and in the Libraries of Oxford and Cambridge* (1908) and Charles O. Paullin and Frederic L. Paxson, *Guide to the Materials in London Archives for the History of the United States since 1783* (1914). The publication of the guide to the Public Record Office, by Andrews alone, was delayed by a change in classification which had taken place in the repository, and it appeared in two volumes in 1912 and 1914. A supplement to the Carnegie guides was published in 1961 under the auspices of the British Association for American Studies: B. Crick and M. Alman, *Guide to Manuscripts Relating to America in Great Britain and Ireland*, and a substantial revision of this work, by John W. Raimo, was published by Meckler Publishing Corporation in 1979.

The British Library catalogues

The Manuscript Department's own catalogues also identify many American documents but, particularly in the early catalogues, only direct references to America have generally been indexed, and many British political and commercial papers that contain material relating to American affairs have not been identified. It is often necessary, therefore, to look thoroughly at those parts of the collection that might be expected to contain the material being sought. They can often be located by using the *Index to Manuscripts in the British Library* (twelve volumes, 1984–1985) published by Chadwyck-Healey of Cambridge. As well as the periodic indexes in the catalogues of accessions, there is also a classed catalogue which is indexed in the first two volumes.

13.
The Manuscript Collections

Although the foundation and early subsequent collections of the Library contained a relatively small number of American documents, their contents more than make up in interest what they lack in quantity. They consist mainly of grants of territories, charters of colonies, papers of the Board of Trade and its predecessor Councils, scattered memoranda and reports on the affairs of the settlements, journals of expeditions on sea and land, and a few manuscript books. As distinction was seldom made by the early colonial officials between public and private affairs (a situation that not infrequently led to scandal), so the scattered manuscripts that related to colonial administration before the 1750s also in general make no such distinction. During the late 1740s the position began to change as colonial administration became more sophisticated, a fact that can be noted in the increase in the number of administrative documents surviving from these years in the papers of the Duke of Newcastle.

As the nature of colonial administration changed, so has the character of the American manuscript collection of the British Library. The most extensive section is the series formed by several large collections covering the military and political affairs of the American colonies and the early years of the United States from the 1740s to about 1810. These are the Newcastle, Hardwicke, Bouquet, Haldimand, Hutchinson, Auckland, Liverpool and Grenville collections and the Stevens' Transcripts. From then until the 1860s the large political collections of Peel, Aberdeen and Gladstone, supplemented by several smaller groups of papers, provide originals or copies of official documents concerning British policy towards the United States. Throughout the century covered by both of these series, there are diaries and letters by British travellers and emigrants to the United States and letters from Americans to persons in Britain, most of which for later years do not relate in any direct sense to the history of the United States. As with printed books, any letter originating in America in the seventeenth century might be considered an American document, but a twentieth-century letter from an academic author to an English publisher would hardly be considered to be so.

The summary of the American manuscript collection that follows takes this change in historical value into account, and is thus more sketchy as the documents become more recent.

Cottonian manuscripts

These were part of the foundation collection of the British Museum in 1753, and, as the Cottonian Library, had existed as a quasi-public library before then. When the Cottonian Library was acquired by the British Museum the printed books were merged with those of the other collections, but the Cottonian manuscripts have been kept together. The collection had been assembled by Sir Robert Cotton, 1571–1631, and was added to by his son and grandson. Sir Robert (who added the second Christian name Bruce in honour of his descent from the Scottish kings) was associated in 1589 with a proposal by the Society of Antiquaries to form a state or national library to be known as the Queen Elizabeth Library and to succeed the existing Royal Library. The proposal failed, but subsequently Cotton formed a private library of such repute that he was consulted on matters of precedent even, in 1600, by Queen Anne's advisers. After the accession of James I to the throne of England, Cotton entered public life. He became a Member of Parliament in 1604, and in 1608 and again in 1613 was commissioned by the crown to investigate the administration of the navy. In 1611 he was consulted by the King on the matter of increasing the royal revenue. The papers accumulated by Cotton in pursuit of his public duties were added to his collection, and it is among these manuscripts that papers relating to America are to be found. Several direct references are identified in the catalogue compiled by J. Planta and printed in 1802. These were transcribed by Professor Andrews in his *Guide*, but no further reference to the documents was apparently made.

Among these direct references are: a map of the northern hemisphere which shows the east coast of North America, made by John Dee for Queen Elizabeth in 1580 (Augustus I i 1), and a chart of the James River (Augustus I ii 46) both of which were contained in two volumes of maps in the original collection. (The sections of the Cottonian manuscripts take their names from busts of the twelve Caesars which, together with those of Cleopatra and Faustina, stood on the bookcases in the original library.) There is also a chart by John Dee, 1580, of the north-west passage and there are a number of papers concerning voyages of exploration, 1574–1582, by Frobisher, Drake, Raleigh, Hawkins and others (Otho E viii). But while direct references to the Americas are few, there are papers concerning shipping, customs revenues, and state papers relating largely to diplomacy with Spain distributed throughout the collection. It is here that information bearing indirectly on American affairs might be found. The relevant volumes are identified in the catalogue as papers and tracts concerning naval and financial affaris but, although the catalogue is extensive, there is not a catalogue reference to every single document that might make up what is described in the catalogue as a tract.

The contents of Cotton's library played a part in his fall from favour in 1629 and he was deprived of its use for the remainder of his life. Considerable use might be made of the Cottonian manuscripts in the study of the exploration and trade of early America; to list only the direct references, as the Carnegie Institution Guides did, misrepresents the collection, but it was of course impossible for the compilers to anticipate at that stage in the development of American historiography the wider reference that would be made by later scholars.

Harleian manuscripts

The printed books in the library founded by Robert Harley, 1st Earl of Oxford, 1661–1724, were dispersed by sale, but the manuscript collection remained intact through its purchase by the government (for £10,000) in 1753. The Harleian Library was a much later foundation than the Cottonian; Harley purchased his first books in 1705, and it thus post-dated the antiquarian enterprise of restoring to secure custody the manuscripts that had been dispersed by the dissolution of the monasteries. A large part of it consists of the same kind of antiquarian documents as are found in the Cottonian and of heraldic, historical and genealogical papers derived from them. But manuscripts that were more or less contemporary with Cotton were already antique and thus collectible to Harley and even more so to his son Edward, the 2nd Earl, who added to the collection. Harley was very much involved in public affairs over a period of almost forty years; he held the highest offices of state: Commissioner for the Public Accounts, 1691–1697, Treasury Commissioner and Chancellor of the Exchequer, 1710–1711, and Lord High Treasurer, 1711–1714; he was effectively prime minister before the office was known as such. Thus, like Cotton's library, Harley's included important state and economic papers, but the latter are to be found in greater numbers because Harley had occupied higher office. Many of the papers concerning economic affairs and revenues came to Harley as an official of the Treasury and would have in later years become part of the public records; some do in fact duplicate papers in the Public Record Office.

It is among these political and economic papers that material for new research is likely to be found; the catalogue (although not the index) lists a number of direct references to America. The most notable of these are the following:

> Collection of tracts and papers relating to sea matters, customs etc.
> a manual of navigation tr. from Spanish.
> notes by...

voyages, trade, customs, receipts.
notes on New England by Simonds D'Ewes.

    167

Frobisher NW Passage 1577.

    168

Two journals kept on the voyage and other papers concerning a voyage to Virginia, 1690–1691, in the Woolff, Capt. George Purvis.

    466–467

A volume of tracts and papers containing Charter by James I for the planting of New Foundland, 1610.

    589

A book consisting of legal tracts containing an abstract of the laws of New England in reign of Charles I 'bearing a great analogy to the Laws of Moses.'

    829

A tract, 1661, concerning the loss of the North American trade to other countries and the threatened destruction thereby of the 'nursery of seamen'.

    1223

Printed and ms papers concerning the maintenance of the monopoly of American tobacco, 1626–1694.

    1238

A manuscript book containing extracts about the Antilles, the Incas and Florida.

    1589

Charts and maps drawn by John Martines, 1578, which includes the coast of North America.

    3450, 3489

The Manuscript Collections

Documents regarding appointment of Alexander Murray, Rector of Ware, Virginia, as Bishop of Virginia, 1672–1673.

3790

Book of maps and charts of the west coast of America from California to the Straits of Magellan, surveyed by order of the King of Spain, 1669.

4034

Instructions to Capt. Bartholomew Valegas for sailing from Acapulco to California. Seventeenth century.

4225

'Account of an an famous and Rediculous Action and Dispute that happened in New England about the year 1633, whether the Red Cross in the Banner of England was an Idol or no, with the argument urged on both sides.'

4888

Command from the council of Virginia to the College of Heralds to record the names and orders of rank of a colonial aristocracy, 1609.

6067

Letter from Robert Quary to the Board of Trade concerning New York, 1703.

6273

Commonplace books with notes on Newfoundland, New England and Virginia.

6494

List of persons executed after Bacon's Rebellion in Virginia.

6845

Papers relating to New Jersey, 1672–1677.

7001

Letter from Charles II to the Corporation of Rhode Island, 12 February 1679.

7006

Letter from Robert Tindall, Jamestown, to Prince Henry, 1607.

7007

Journal of a voyage to Virginia, 1610.
Letter of the Governor and Council of Virginia to the Virginia Company, 1610.

7009

Papers concerning the settlement by Governor Robert Hunter of German Palatines in New York in 1710.

7021

Printed order of Governor and Assembly of New York, 1691.

7310

Royal Manuscripts

These manuscripts made up the greatest part of the old Royal Library which had been formed between the reigns of Henry VIII and George II and was one of the foundation collections of the British Museum. While rich in medieval documents, it contains relatively little relating to America, but does contain maps and manuscript books relating to navigation. The following direct references to America are made in the Catalogue:

Drake's voyage to the West Indies and Virginia, 1585.

7 C xvi Art 36

Sketch of the known world including west coast of North America, c. 1525–1550.

14 Cv 7

John Rolfe's 'A True Relation of the State of Virginia,' 1616–1617.

18 A xi

John Rotz, 'Book of Hydrography' (1542) with charts of the coast of the North Atlantic coasts of Labrador and Newfoundland, West Indies and Florida.

20 E ix

King's Manuscripts

The catalogue of the Royal Manuscripts continues in volume III with the King's Manuscripts, which is the manuscript section of the library formed by King George III to replace the Royal Library. Apart from some printed material in a collection of papers concerning the history of Antwerp (King's 178), the American material consists mainly of military papers that came into the possession of the King.

The American papers are found in volumes 201–213 and contain correspondence of Rev. Myles Cooper, a Loyalist who left America in 1775, with Benjamin Franklin, Thomas Pownall and others between 1769 and 1775; official reports on the American colonies 1766–1721; a report by De Brahm of a survey of the Southern District, 1764; a journal kept by an officer on Braddock's Campaign, 1755; a journal of travels in the American colonies in 1764–1765.

The King's Library contained a great many maps, plans and charts, and these are separately catalogued. Those parts of the catalogue relating to America have been transcribed in Paullin and Paxson, *Guide to the Materials in London Archives for the History of the United States since 1783*, pp. 511–517.

Lansdowne Manuscripts

These were purchased by the British Museum in 1807. They are from the library of Lord Shelburne who had been Secretary of State for the Southern Department and thus had responsibility for American affairs from 1766 to 1768. He then spoke generally in opposition to the government on American affairs until the fall of Lord North's administration in 1782 when he served as Prime Minister for a few months. Shelburne began collecting manuscripts in 1764. His library contained three major collections: those of Lord Burghley (William Cecil, 1520–1598), who served as a minister to Henry VIII and Queen Elizabeth; of Sir Julius Caesar, 1558–1636, an admiralty judge and Master of the Rolls in the reigns of Elizabeth, James I and Charles I; and the papers of White Kennett, 1660–1728, Bishop and a founder of the Society for the Propagation of the Gospel. The divisions of these papers can be seen in the list of the most prominent American material that follows. The Burghley papers occupy volumes 1–122 and are followed by the Caesar and then the Kennett papers. The remainder consists of small collections acquired by Lord Shelburne and individual manuscripts of antiquarian interest:

Martin Frobisher's three voyages in search of a North West passage, 1581.
31

Letter from John Davis to Sir Francis Walsingham concerning discovery of North West passage.
46

References to Drake, Raleigh, Hawkins.
52

Agreement between Drake and merchants, 1586.
56

Papers relating to a controversy in the church at Hartford, Connecticut, 1656–1659.
93

Drake's circumnavigation, 1577–1578.

122

Proposal for a seven year monopoly to be granted for the import of tobacco, 1620.

162

'A Relation of New England.'

209

Papers relating to the tobacco trade, 1752–1760.

681

Papers relating to the Philipse estates in New York, 1766.

707

Paper relating to the Choctaw Indians in South Carolina, 1753.

809

Oglethorpe's campaign in Florida during the War of Jenkin's Ear, 1741.

820, 861

Papers concerning colonial administration and trade, eighteenth century.

846

Board of Trade papers, 1697–1710.

849

Treasury papers: New England expedition against the fort of Louisbourg, Cape Breton Island, 1747. Payments to clergymen and presents to Indians.

885

An Account of the Society for the Propagation of the Gospel in Foreign Parts established by the Royal Charter of King William III, London, 1706, by White Kennett; also *A Collection of*

Papers printed by order of the Society, London 1706. Author's interleaved and annotated copies.

1012

Commonplace book of White Kennett into which are copied extracts from books and papers. Treatise on the Virginia Company.
White Kennett's account of America.

1032

An index of books and pamphlets relating to trade, many of them referring to the administration and trade of the American colonies, 1608–1761.

1049

Papers relating to the claims of the Mohegan Indians to lands in Connecticut.

1052

Indian testimony concerning the possibility of an overland route to the Pacific.
Papers relating to the American Revolution.

1219

Hargrave Manuscripts

Francis Hargrave, 1741–1821, was a lawyer and antiquarian. He was involved in the case of James Sommersett in 1772 in which slavery was ruled to be illegal in England and wrote a pamphlet supporting Lord Mansfield's judgement. His library of legal books and manuscripts was bought by the government in 1813 and deposited in the British Museum. It contains legal opinions on American cases in volumes 141, 231, 275, 493 and 494.

Egerton Manuscripts

This was the collection of Francis Henry Egerton, Earl of Bridgewater, 1756–1829, an eccentric scholar, who left his manuscripts to the British Museum at his death, with a bequest of £12,000 for their custody and augmentation. The original collection contained a number of documents of American interest and others have been purchased from the fund. They are catalogued in a separate open series, which is bound and indexed in the same volumes as the Additional Manuscripts. The papers of the family of Thomas Hutchinson (Governor of Massachusetts, 1769–1774, afterwards a Loyalist refugee in London) make up part of the collection (2659–2675), but apart from documents bearing directly on American affairs, the most notable of which are listed below, there are other political, commercial or miscellaneous collections of indirect American interest. As with the earlier collections, the indexes to the catalogue are inadequate for American material. The guides to American manuscripts cover the following sections of the collection: Andrews and Davenport, manuscripts before 1783 up to Eg 2861; Paullin and Paxson, manuscripts after 1783 up to Eg. 2889, and before 1783, Eg 2861–2889; Raimo, Eg 2900 onwards, covers all periods, but lists only a few references. For material relating indirectly to American history, resort must be made, even when using these guides, to the numerical catalogue series. The list that follows of some of the major items is intended to provide some guidance, in particular to accumulations of papers that are likely to contain American material.

Trade with Newfoundland and Virginia, 1705–1708.
921

Proposal to establish a colony on the Kennebec River, 1705.
Petition from Nathanial Byfield to be governor of Massachusetts and New Hampshire.
Defeat of Braddock, 1755.
929

Drawings and natural history of birds in Georgia by John Abbot, 1804
1337–1338

Russian exploration in Alaska, 1764.
1717

Papers relating to California and Texas, 1748–1815.
1798–1801

Papers relating to the American Revolution: British military operations, 1776–1778; Loyalist papers, 1775–1785.
2135

Papers relating to the Penns, 1714, 1734.
2168

Journals of the voyage of James Cook to the Pacific Coast of America, 1776–1779.
2177–2179, 2591

Papers of Thomas Povey, a seventeenth century merchant. There are several documents relating to the early history of Virginia, New York and New England.
2395

Journal of a visit to North Carolina, 1775.
2423

Papers of members of the Barrington family which included several letters from New England, 1621–1645.
2643–2650

Papers of the Hutchinson family, 1741–1880. These include papers of Thomas Hutchinson, and Peter Oliver, Chief Justice of Massachusetts, 1771–1774; Andrew Hutchinson; and diaries and letters of several members of the family especially during the Revolutionary period. Included also is the manuscript of Peter Oliver's 'Origin and progress of the rebellion in America', not published until 1961. The collection was used by P.O. Hutchinson for *The Diary and Letters of...Thomas Hutchinson*, (1884–1888) and many of the papers are annotated with his comments.

Manuscript book: William Hubbard's 'History of New England,' (not published until 1815).

2659–2675

Papers relating to the French in America, 1750–1760.

2694

Maps showing North America.

2803, 2854, 2856, 2860

Letters of Mark Twain to his publishers, Chatto and Windus, 1881–1892.

2952

Letters of J. Crampton, British Minister to the United States, 1853–1854.

2972

Notes on the charter of the Virginia Company, 1624.

2978

Letters from American musicians, 1902–1903.

3090–3097

Letters from James Russell Lowell, Ezra Pound, Walt Whitman

3247–3248

Letters from American musicians, 1902–1929.

3301–3306

Leeds Papers, 3324–3508; papers of the Osborne family, Dukes of Leeds, from Hornby Castle. Papers relating to America described in the Historical Manuscripts Commission Report XI were not acquired by the British Museum in 1947 when the original collection was sold. The part of the collection that came to the Museum includes the correspondence and papers of the first Duke of Leeds: New York, 1670; New England, 1675–1692; Virginia, 1691–1692.

3340

Stowe Manuscripts

These are papers formerly belonging to the Grenville family, and they include papers of George Grenville relating to the Stamp and Sugar Acts. Only a part of the original collection was acquired by the British Museum, by purchase, in 1883. The following are among the direct references to American affairs, but there is other material of indirect relevance noted in the catalogue.

American Episcopacy, 1777.

119

Specimen of stamps for use in America under the Stamp Act.

142

Letters from Sir John Digby in Madrid concerning Spanish antagonism to the British colony in Virginia, 1612–1613.

172–174

Correspondence of the Earl of Warwick with the Council of New England, New England and Virgina, 1646, 1648.

184

Papers relating to the War of the Spanish Succession (Queen Anne's War), 1711.

246

Transcripts and printed papers relating to the Stamp Act.

264, 265

Treatise on the North West passage, 1612.
301

Papers relating to customs revenue, 1679–1742.
316, 317, 318, 320, 323, 326

Account of the English sugar plantations. Accounts of the London Custom House, 1671–1694; and of customs in general, 1671–1723.
324

Notes on the Stamp Act crisis, 1766.
752

Oglethorpe's campaign in Georgia during the War of Jenkin's Ear, 1742.
792

Sloane Manuscripts

These were part of the library of Sir Hans Sloane and one of the foundation collections of the British Museum. The American material in the collection mainly concerns the description of the American settlements in the late-seventeenth and early-eighteenth centuries. The collection is strong in documents relating to the West Indies which Sloane had visited.

Early voyages to the Americas, 1568–1684.
42, 43, 45–49, 50, 54

William Penn's 'Frame of Government', 1682.
79

'Relation' of New England (1635–1638). See also 2505.
172

Correspondence between England and New England, 1633–1645.

 922

Account of Virginia in 1622 by Governor Nathaniel Butler.

 1039

Acts of the Assembly of Virginia, 1657.

 1378

Voyages to Virginia, 1667–1671.

 1426

William Strachey's 'Historie of Travaile Into Virginia...' containing De Bry's engravings and John Smith's map.

 1622

Tobacco imported from Virginia, 1685–1688.

 1815

Letter from John Winthrop, a professor at Harvard, to Sir Hans Sloane concerning American minerals, 1734.

 1968

Plants of Virginia.

 2202

Journal of a voyage to Maryland, 1705–1706.

 2291

'Description of American plants', English translation of Charles Plumier's work published in French in 1693.

 2337

Specimens of New England paper money, 1713, 1715.

 2375

Instructions to Martin Frobisher for a voyage to discover the North West passage, 1577.
2442

Patent of Hudson Bay Company.
2447

Journal of a voyage to New York, 1674–1675.
2448

Proposals for the improvement of the plantation in America.
2728

Notes on trade with the American colonies and on the affairs of New York, Pennsylvania, Maryland, Virginia and South Carolina, and the Indians of the Five Nations.
2902

Notes on botanical and other matters concerning America, 1689–1712.
3321, 3324, 3328, 3338–3340

Tobacco imports to London, 1682–1683.
3329

Abstract of the laws of New England.
3448

An account of the voyage to America in 1562 of Jean Ribault to establish a French protestant settlement.
3644

Note on the connection of George Calvert, the first Lord Baltimore, with the foundation of Virginia and Maryland, 1670.
3662

Journal of a voyage to America, 1670.
3833

Proposals for the improvement of the New England colony.
3962

Scheme for a colony in Georgia.
3985

Papers relating to the natural history of America.
4002, 4017, 4019, 4020, 4025

Letters to Sir Hans Sloane, a number of which are on scientific, medical and other matters concerning the American colonies.
4036–4070

Additional Charters

Andrews and Davenport discovered several charters relating to America in this series (see Andrews and Davenport, p. 71) and Raimo added a few more (Raimo, p. 82). There are of course many charters in the early separately catalogued collections. Andrews and his associates do not seem to have consulted the original volumes of patents, warrants and so on which might contain documents relating to the American colonies not identified as such in the catalogues.

Additional Manuscripts

This became the designation of the small collections and single manuscripts acquired by the Museum after 1753 which were catalogued together with the Sloane manuscripts in the Ayscough catalogue in 1782. Their serial numbers continued the numbers of the Sloane manuscripts.

The first group of these was the collection bequeathed to the British Museum in 1766 by Thomas Birch, historian and biographer, who had been Secretary of the Royal Society and a trustee of the Museum. These became Ad Ms 4101–4478. The papers of American interest were confined to two sections of this collection: some state papers of John Thurloe, Cromwell's Secretary of State (eg 'Declaration of the People of Virginia' signed by Nathaniel Bacon, 1676, Ad Ms 4159) which occupy volumes 4155–4159, and scientific papers of the Royal Society, (4432–4159), which contain several communications with Americans or which concern American phenomena, such as a journal of an expedition to western Virginia, 1671 (4432).

Although some collections, the Hargrave and Stowe for example, were separately catalogued during the nineteenth century, other quite large collections, such as that bequeathed by the Cambridge antiquary William Cole in 1782, were catalogued in the Additional Manuscripts series. But the series also contained single items, like the eight letters from George Washington, 1792–1797, bound in leather as a souvenir by Sir John Sinclair and presented to the Museum (5757), and a volume (9828) of American correspondence of Sir John Eardley Wilmot who had been a commissioner appointed to enquire into Loyalist claims for relief during the American Revolution.

In 1810 the Museum purchased the papers of Sir Andrew Mitchell, British Ambassador at Berlin from 1756 to 1770 (6804–6871). These contained papers concerning French claims to the Ohio Valley (6865) and other diplomatic papers of indirect relevance to American affairs. The papers of Sir Joseph Banks, naturalist and traveller, were bequeathed to the Museum on his death in 1820. They contain accounts of a number of voyages and expeditions, including the journals of Jonathon Carver of his expedition in the interior of North America in 1766–1767 (8949, 8950).

A large collection like that of William Cole might contain little of American interest other than a few scattered references, but a single volume, like that presented by Sir John Sinclair, can be entirely Americana. A good index is therefore essential to trace American material because, although it is feasible to look through the numerical catalogue series of Additional Manuscripts for the large collections, to trawl hopefully through the whole series is too daunting. The compilers of the Carnegie Institution guides to American manuscripts appear to have used a mixture of both methods. The indexes to the early catalogued separate collections and the Ayscough classed catalogue were not very good. But a better standard of indexing developed during the nineteenth century, and it can be seen in the index to the *Catalogue of Additions to the Manuscripts in the British Museum in the Years 1836–1840*, which was published in 1843. This volume was followed in 1849 by an index to Additional and Egerton manuscripts acquired between 1783–1835 (the catalogue remained in manuscript) and in 1850 by a catalogue and index in the one volume to manuscripts acquired 1841–1845. Further volumes followed for 1846–1847 and 1848–1853. A different form of publication was introduced for manuscripts acquired 1853–1875, a catalogue based on class (ie subject) headings, but the earlier system was returned to after 1875 and catalogue volumes covering Additional Manuscripts, Additional Charters and Egerton Manuscripts with non-cumulative indexes, were published for convenient groups of years of acquisition.

In recent years, 'rough registers' of acquisitions have been printed by the Lists and Indexes Society to fill the gaps until the volumes appear. These indexes, together with the Andrews and Davenport, Paullin and Paxson, and Raimo guides are the most effective means of locating direct American references. (American Loyalist papers in the British Library are listed on pp. 601–603 of Gregory Palmer, ed., *A Bibliography of Loyalist Source Material in the United States, Canada and Great Britain*.)

The Additional Manuscripts series continued in the nineteenth and twentieth centuries to follow the same pattern of large and small collections and single items listed in the same series. Copies of public documents which relate to American history, especially military, Board of Trade and treasury papers, are common among the papers of former officials. There are two volumes of Board of Trade papers, 1696–1786, 1710–1781, and a volume of maps, 1738–1764 and 1783, which belonged to the Loyalist George Chalmers and were purchased at the sale of his library in 1841–1842 (14034–14036).

Manuscripts of published books have been regularly

acquired by the British Library. These are usually literary and are infrequently by American authors; but Henry Stevens was interested in them. Thus a number of such American manuscripts written before c1880 appear in the Additional Manuscripts series; for example Samuel Drake's 'Chronicles of the Indians of North America', 1836 (25699), John Dutton's 'Atlas of the United States', 1814 (27368), Nathaniel Hawthorne's 'The Marble Faun' (44889–44890). Non-American manuscript books of American interest are John Miller's 'New York Considered and Improved', 1695 (15490); papers collected by Adam Anderson for *Origin of Commerce,* 1764 (17476); Joseph Hunters's *Early History of the Founders of New Plymouth,* 1849 (25446; the genealogical collections of Joseph Hunter, 24436–24630, might contain information on the origin of other American families); and notes for a biography of John Paul Jones by Richard Filkin (25893–25895). As well as miscellaneous literary manuscripts, maps, such as a plan of New York, 1665 (16371), and botanical drawings have always been valued by the Library. An American example of the latter are the manuscript drawings in the French botanist Charles Plumier's 'Nova Plantarum Americanum Genera', 1703, which followed voyages he made to America in 1693 and 1695.

Documents which might properly have been part of the separate collections are among the miscellaneous manuscripts in the series; a collection of maps which belonged to Sir Hans Sloane includes maps of North and South America, 1558, Massachusetts Bay, 1634, and Boston Harbour, 1694, (5414–5415); and some further papers of Sir Julius Caesar which were purchased separately from those in the Lansdowne manuscripts contain several papers concerning Virginia, 1622–1624 (12,496).

Three large collections contain almost exclusively American material. The first two are of military papers, the collections of two Swiss mercenary officers, Henry Bouquet and Sir Frederick Haldimand, who served with the British army in America in the eighteenth century. These collections were presented to the Museum in 1857 by a descendant of Haldimand's and were calendered by Douglas Brymner, a Canadian archivist (*Report on Canadian Archives*, 5 vols., 1884–1889. Both the collections have been published in microfilm by World Microfilms Publications, London). Bouquet served in the French and Indian War and commanded the British forces during Pontiac's Rebellion in 1763. Haldimand served in America from 1756 until 1784 and held high civil and military office in all parts of the colonies. The collections (Bouquet 21631–21660 and Haldimand 21661–21892) contain military and civil administrative papers: returns, warrants, accounts, orders, petitions from officers and civilians and other documents which touch on all matters of frontier life between 1756 and 1784. It is best when using them to make use of the Brymner calendar cited above as well as the catalogue of Additional Manuscripts.

The third collection, the Stevens Transcripts (42257–42496) consists of the transcripts and translations of documents from British and European archives relating to American history before 1784, made under the direction of Benjamin Franklin Stevens as part of the project described in the previous chapter. (This collection has also been published by World Microfilms Publications, London.)

A considerable number of the direct American references made in the index to the Additional Manuscripts are to the collections of political papers that make up a large part of the modern records in the British Library. These collections might also be supposed to contain material of indirect relevance. The papers of the Godolphin-Osborne family, Dukes of Leeds, seventeenth and eighteenth centuries (28040–28095), contain some direct references, eg correspondence of Gouverneur Morris, 1789–1790 (28069); papers relating to New England and Virginia in the seventeenth century (28089). The correspondence of John Wilkes (30868–30875) contains letters from John Adams, Dr Benjamin Church, Samuel Adams and Joseph Warren. The papers of the Duke of Newcastle (32686–33057) contain a great number of letters and papers relating to the government and military affairs of the American colonies dispersed throughout the collection. Volumes 33028–33030 contain papers relating to America and the West Indies, 1701–

1802. Other such collections are:
– Auckland Papers (34412–34471), the papers of William Eden, Secretary of State, 1772–1778, and a member of the Carlisle Commission appointed in 1778 to treat for peace with the American Congress. Eden had personal connections with the American colonies through his father and his wife. Most of the American papers in the collection are letters and despatches concerning the Revolution, 1777–1779. Many of those concerning the Peace Commission, 1778–1779 (Carlisle Commission), and intelligence matters were transcribed by Benjamin Franklin Stevens, and appear in both his 'transcripts' and 'facsimiles'.
– Hardwicke Papers (35349–36278). The American part of this collection consists of papers of the 1st and 2nd Earls of Hardwicke. The American papers of the first Earl, who was Lord Chancellor from 1737 to 1764, are mainly legal papers, many of them concerned with cases from the colonies brought before the Privy Council, and with the Stamp Act. Volume 35427 contains letters to the 2nd Earl from Thomas Hutchinson, 1774–1778. There are many miscellaneous documents concerning America throughout the collection.
– Papers of Caleb Whitefoord, Secretary to the British Peace Commissioners, 1782–1783 (36593–36596).
– Correspondence of George III with John Robinson, Secretary of the Treasury, 1770–1782 (37833–37835).
– Liverpool Papers (38190–38489), the papers of Charles Jenkinson, 1st Earl of Liverpool, Secretary of War in the government of Lord North; and of Robert Banks Jenkinson, 2nd Earl, who was Prime Minister, 1818–1827. (See N.S. Jucker, *The Jenkinson Papers*, 1949.) The American papers in this collection consist mainly of papers concerning colonial administration from the 1760s until 1783, papers concerning trade with the United States, 1786–1795, Jay's Treaty, and the War of 1812.
– Papers of William Huskisson, 1770–1830. Papers relating to American affairs, particularly trade, 1805–1828 (38734–38740).
– Papers of Austen Henry Layard (38931–39164), Under-Secretary for Foreign Affairs, 1852 and 1861–1866. Layard was

the chief spokesman for the government in the House of Commons during the American Civil War; most of the American papers in this collection therefore concern the Civil War and matters arising from it.

– Papers of Sir Robert Peel, 1788–1850 (40181–40616). There are a number of American documents, 1813–1846, dispersed throughout the collection.

– Correspondence, 1752–1785, of Josiah Martin, Governor of North Carolina, 1771–1776 (41361).

– Grenville Papers (42083–42088). This collection contains the political diary, 1761–1768, and other papers of George Grenville, Prime Minister, 1763–1765.

– Papers of George Hamilton Gordon (43039–43358), 4th Earl of Aberdeen, Foreign Secretary, 1841–1846, and Prime Minister, 1852–1855. It contains papers concerning the disputed boundaries of Oregon and Maine, copies of despatches from the Foreign Secretary to British ministers in America, 1841–1846, and other miscellaneous correspondence.

– Papers of John Bright (43390–43391). These volumes contain letters, 1861–1888, concerning the American Civil War and slavery.

– Papers of George Robinson, Marquis of Ripon (43510–43644). Miscellaneous American letters, 1871–1875, some of them concerned with the Treaty of Washington, 1871.

– Papers of Richard Cobden, 1804–1865 (43647–43678). Contains American letters, 1850s and 1860s, some concerning the Civil War.

– Diaries of Richard Cobden's visits to America, 1835 and 1859 (43807–43808).

– Correspondence of Sir Charles Dilke, 1843–1911, which includes letters from America (43909–43922).

– Papers of William Ewart Gladstone, 1809–1898 (44086–44835). The political correspondence in this collection contains papers concerned with American affairs, in particular the Civil War and its consequences. There is also private correspondence with a number of Americans from the 1850s to 1890s.

– Volumes of the papers of Charles James Fox, 1749–1806

(47561–47563), contain letters concerning the peace negotiations in Paris, 1782–1783.
– Papers of Lord Palmerston before 1850 (48417–48589). These contain Foreign Office correspondence concerning America, 1835–1841, 1846–1850.
– Correspondence of Arthur Balfour (49740–49742) with Sir Cecil Spring Rice, 1915–1917, Sir William Wiseman and Lord Reading, 1917–1919, and various American diplomats and politicians, 1888–1930.
– Archives of Macmillans, publishers (54786–56035). These contain numerous letters from American authors dispersed throughout the collection including: letterbooks from the Macmillan Company of America, 1891–1940 (55283–55315); letters from Henry James, 1878–1914 (54931); letters from Edith Wharton, 1901–1930 (54956–54957) and Gertrude Atherton, 1897–1907 (54967). There is a card index to the letterbooks.
– Correspondence of Marie Stopes (58585–58588) with Americans, 1915–1954, including Mary Ware Dennett, 1919–1940, and Margaret Sanger, 1915–1950.
– Correspondence of William Wyndham Grenville (58855–59494), Foreign Secretary, 1791–1801, and Prime Minister, 1806–1807. Historical Manuscripts Commission Reports, xviii (iii) and xlv (v) (Fortescue, Dropmore MSS). The collection contains papers concerning American Loyalists, Jay's Treaty and the abolition of the slave trade. Papers concerning the United States are found in particular in volumes 59049–59050 for the years 1794–1803, and in 59083–59092 for the years 1789–1809.
– Correpondence and diaries of Sir Evelyn Wrench, 1882–1966 (59541–59597), founder of the English Speaking Union.
– Bentley papers (59622–59651). Papers of the publishing firm of Richard Bentley. The numerous letters from Americans in this collection can be identified in the index to the microfilm edition of the collection which is kept with the collections of printed books.

Blenheim Papers

A catalogue of the Blenheim Papers (61101–61710), the papers of the Dukes of Marlborough, is published in a separate series of volumes (3 vols, 1985) but continuing the numeration of the Additional Manuscripts. The papers are largely military, and of the sixteenth and seventeenth centuries, and the index contains few references to America, but like other large collections, might contain material of indirect relevance.

Appendices I to V

Appendix I – Sample Catalogue Entries for Americana

The catalogue entries for many individual works illustrate the history of acquisition and its relationship to publishing and scholarship, the thirteen editions of Hubbard's *Indian Wars* providing a good example (see page 188). It was printed originally in Boston in 1677 by John Foster (Item I) who set up the first press in Boston, the authorisation of the General Court being 29 March. The next edition (II, III, and IV) was printed in London in the same year, the licence to publish being dated 27 June. The Boston edition contained a woodcut map, the first printed in America, with the north to the right as was the custom of the time. The map was printed in the London edition but re-engraved with a great many errors in place names. It was not reprinted in subsequent editions until a facsimile was printed in Samuel Drake's edition of 1864 (XII). The duplication of the early editions shows the method of the establishment of the British Library's collection. Item I came to the Library with the Grenville Library in 1847, and item IV is from the King's Library, the library of King George III which became part of the collection in 1827. The origins of II and III cannot be established with certainty but III has a rectangular stamp containing the words MVSEVM BRITANNICVM which was put on all books in the Old Royal Library, and was used only between 1757 and 1810. This book might therefore have been part of the Old Royal Library and was certainly in the collection by 1810, before which date few books were purchased. Item II does not carry the rectangular stamp, but, from its lower initial shelf number, was unlikely to have been acquired after III.

The third edition, substantially abridged, was by John Boyle of Boston in 1775 (V) and others followed: Worcester, 1801, (VIII) not as one might have hoped published by Isaiah

Appendix I

HUBBARD (WILLIAM) *Minister of Ipswich, Massachusetts.*

I —— A Narrative of the Troubles with the Indians in New-England, from the first planting thereof in the year 1607 to ... 1677. But chiefly ... in ... 1675 and 1676. To which is added a Discourse about the Warre with the Pequods in the year 1637. (A postscript, *etc.*) [With "A Map of New-England, being the first that ever was here cut."] 2 pt. *J. Foster:* *Boston* [*U.S.*], 1677. 4°. G. 7146.
The postscript and pt. 2 are each separately paged.

II —— [Another edition.] The Present State of New England, being a narrative of the troubles with the Indians in New England, *etc.* (A narrative of the troubles with the Indians in New England from Pascataqua to Pemmaquid.) 2 pt. *London,* 1677. 4°. C.32.e.28.

III —— [Another copy.] C. 32. e. 27.(1,2.)

IV —— [Another copy.] 278. f. 33.
Imperfect; wanting the map.

V —— A Narrative of the Indian Wars in New England, *etc.* pp. 288.
John Boyle: Boston [*Mass.*], 1775. 12°. 9602. a. 3.

VI —— [Another edition.] A Narrative of the Indian Wars in New-England, *etc. Norwich* [*Connecticut,* 1780?]. 12°.
This edition is without map. 1448. b.9.

VII —— [Another edition.] COPIOUS MS. NOTES AND ADDITIONS [by S. G. Drake]. [*Brattleborough*? 1785?] 8°.
9602. g. 3.
Cut up and remounted in 4°, with a new titlepage in MS. The MS. additions were probably made in 1815.

VIII —— [Another edition.] *Worcester* [*Massachusetts*], 1801. 12°.
1447. c. 18.

IX —— [Another edition.] *Stockbridge* [*Massachusetts*], 1803. 8°.
9604. bb. 12.

X —— [Another edition.] COPIOUS MS. NOTES [by C. G. Drake]. *Brattleborough,* 1814. 12°. 9602. aaa. 27.

XI —— [Another edition.] *See* KNAPP (S. L.) Library of American history, *etc.* vol. 2. [1839.] 4°.
9604. e. 6.

XII —— [Another edition.] The History of the Indian Wars in New England ... Carefully revised, and accompanied with an historical preface, life and pedigree of the author, and extensive notes by S. G. Drake. 2 vol. 1865. *See* WOODWARD (W. E.) Woodward's Historical Series. Nos. 3, 4. 1864, *etc.* 4°. 9602. ee. 17.

XIII —— [Another edition.] A Narrative, *etc. See* AMERICA. The People's History of America, *etc.* (Continental Edition.) 1875. 4°. 9603. g. 1.

The entries for Hubbard's *Indian Wars* in the General Catalogue.

Appendix I

Thomas but by Daniel Greenleaf; Norwich, 1802, (VI) published by John Trumbull; Stockbridge, in 1803, (IX); Danbury, 1803, the only edition the Library lacks; and Brattleborough, 1814, (X). These last five reprinted the abridged edition of 1775.

In 1834 the text of the 1775 edition was included by Samuel Knapp in a two volume publication reprinting several earlier works. It was cheaply printed in three columns in quarto and illustrated with a rather indifferent engraving. Item XI is the second edition of this publication.

In 1825 Samuel Drake, who was at that time a book auctioneer in Boston and who was later a founder of the New England Historic Genealogical Society, conceived the idea of a new edition of Hubbard; he was stimulated by the inadequacy of the Brattleborough 1814 edition which was 'as sorry a specimen of typography as could be found, even at that day'. Drake was lent a copy of the original Boston edition and he used it to correct his copy of the 1814 edition. Item X is the copy with Drake's manuscript corrections and interleaved notes. In 1857 Drake bought twenty or thirty copies of the Boston 1775 edition at an auction and these he cut up and pasted into a quarto notebook. This notebook is item VII but although it appears to have been intended for the printer, it is not the copy used for the two volume edition published by Drake in 1865 (XII). The most recent edition (XIII) in the British Library is another reprint of the abridged 1775 edition printed probably from the same stereotype as the inferior Knapp edition. The order of acquisition of the later editions is VIII 1846; VI 1848; XI 1860; VII 1862; X 1863; IX 1864; XII 1867; XIII 1875; V 1895. All were purchased and all but the last acquired through Henry Stevens; the last was purchased with several other American books from Dulau and Co, a London firm specialising in foreign books, and the invoice is initialled by Richard Garnett who was then Keeper of Printed Books.

There is a possibility that the Museum once had five copies of the 1677 edition of the *Indian Wars*, and disposed of a London edition as a duplicate: a copy recorded in the

University of Virginia in 1938 was said to have come there by way of the British Museum and Henry Stevens.

Hubbard's other major work, *A General History of New England*, shows another, but less common, pattern. The first version was not printed but transcribed 'fairly into a Booke' by an order of the General Court of Massachusetts of 1682. Like many other colonial manuscripts it first appeared in print in the *Collections of the Massachusetts Historical Society* (Second Series, Vols 5 and 6, 1815) but in an unedited form. In 1848 a scholarly edition was published by Charles Deane, contemporary and correspondent of Henry Stevens. These manuscript books were not always 'lost' manuscripts like Governor Bradford's *History of Plymouth Plantation*; they were written out in order to be 'more easily perused' and illustrate the survival of manuscript books alongside printed books in the American colonies. Charles Deane played a part in the discovery of Bradford's manuscript *History*, which was one of the works from which Hubbard drew much of the material for his own.

New editions of the *Indian Wars* have continued to be printed, but while Stevens acted on Panizzi's instructions to acquire all editions of a particular work, later policy excluded reprints and therefore in practice has tended also to exclude most new editions.

The nineteenth-century policy of acquiring all available editions of a single work is illustrated by the catalogue entry for *Uncle Tom's Cabin*. In this case a particular effort was made by Thomas Watts, a talented linguist on the staff of the Museum, to acquire copies in all the languages into which the book had been translated.

The entry for *Narrenschiff*, in English *The Ship of Fools*, an item of early European Americana, demonstrates the same principle.

The contents of a volume of tracts, seventeen of them published in Boston and all relating to smallpox which were bound together and came to the Museum from the library of Sir Hans Sloane, illustrates the nature of the collection of ephemera which have come usually from the libraries of private collectors.

Appendix I

List of titles of tracts concerning smallpox in a volume from the Library of Sir Hans Sloane.

1. Hactenus Inaudita or animadversions upon the new found way of curing the small pox, by Rev. George Stradling (?). London, 1663. 86pp.

2. A short but full account of the rise, nature and management of the small-pox and other putrid fevers, with their proper remedy, by T. Byfield, M.D. London, 1711. 20pp.

3. A Dissertation concerning inoculation of the small pox, by W[illiam] D[ouglas]. Boston, 1730. 28pp.

4. Some account of what is said of inoculating or transplanting the small pox, by the learned Dr Emanuel Timonious and Jacobus Pylarinus. Boston, 1721. 2p.

5. Several Reasons proving that inoculating or transplanting the small pox is a lawful practice, and that it has been blessed by God for the saving of many a life, by Increase Mather D.D. Boston, 1721. 2p.

6. Several Arguments proving that inoculating the small pox is not contained in the law of physick either natural or divine, and therefore unlawful. Together with a reply to two short pieces by the Rev. Increase Mather, and another by an anonymous author intituled sentiments on the small pox inoculated and also a short answer to a late letter in the New England Courant, by John Williams. 2nd Edition, Boston, 1721. 20pp. (printed by J. Franklin.)

Appendix I

7 Some observations on the new method of receiving the small-pox by ingrafting or inoculating, by Benjamin Colman. Boston, 1721. 16pp.

8 A Letter to a friend in the country attempting a solution of the scruples and objections of a conscientious or religious nature commonly made against the new way of receiving the small-pox, by a minister in Boston. Boston, 1721. 13pp.

9 A Letter from one in the country to his friend in the city: in relation to their distresses occasioned by the doubtful and prevailing practice of the inoculation of the small-pox. Boston, 1721. 8pp.

10 An answer to a late pamphlet intitled a letter to a friend in the country, attempting a solution of the scruples and objections of a conscientious or religious nature, commonly made against the new way of receiving the small pox, by a minister of Boston, by John Williams. Boston (J. Franklin, 1722). 20pp.

11 The imposition of inoculation as a duty religiously considered in a letter to a gentleman in the country inclin'd to admit it. Boston, 1721. 28pp.

12 Inoculation of the small pox as practised in Boston, consider'd in a letter to A- S- M.D. and F.R.S. in London. Boston, 1722 (printed by J. Franklin). 20pp.

13 A vindication of the Ministers of Boston from the abuses and scandals lately cast upon them in diverse printed papers, by some of their people. Boston, 1722. 14pp.

Appendix I

14 Some further account from London of the small-pox inoculated. The second edition, by Increase Mather. Boston, 1721. 8pp.

15 The abuses and scandals of some late pamphlets in favour of inoculation of the small pox modestly obviated and inoculation further considered in a latter to A-S- M.D. & F.R.S. in London. Boston, 1722 (printed by J. Franklin). 11pp.

16 A friendly debate or a dialogue between academicus and sawny & mundangus (William Douglas and John Williams) two eminent physicians, about some of their late performances. Boston, 1722. 24pp.

17 A friendly debate or a dialogue between Rusticus and Academicus about the late performance of Academicus. Boston, 1722 (printed by J. Franklin). 12pp.

18 Postscript to Abuses, etc., obviated. Being a short and modest answer to matters maliciously misrepresented in a late doggerel dialogue. [No place or date, but obviously Boston 1722.] 8pp.

19 An Essay on the small-pox; whether natural or inoculated. Philip Rose M.D. of the Royal College of Physicians. London, 1724. 83pp. [pro-inoculation]

20 An Essay on the small-pox. Second edition improved. Philip Rose M.D. London, 1727. Dedicated to Sir Hans Sloane. 92pp

21 A practical essay concerning the small pox by William Douglas M.D. Boston, 1730. 38pp.

22 A short view of the nature and cure of the small pox the usefulness of spirit of vitriol, opiates etc. with reflections on the common practice of bleeding in that distemper, by Richard Holland. London, 1730. 117pp. [anti-inoculation]

23 The Small-Pox. A poem in five cantos. Canto I, by Andrew Tripe, M.D. London 1748.

Appendix II – Books in the British Library Relating to America Published between 1493 and 1525.

1493
CARVAJAL, Bernadino Lopez de, Cardinal. Oratio super praestanda solemni obedientia sanctissimo Alexandro Papae. Rome.
COLOMBO, Cristoforo. Epistola Cristoforo Colom. de insulis Indie supra Gangem nuper inventis. Rome (Plannck)
— (Another edition) Rome (Plannck)
— (Another edition) Rome (Silber)
— (Another edition) De insulis inventis Epistola. Basel
DATI, Guiliano. Questa e la hystoria della inventione delle diese . . . Rome
— (Another edition) Rome
— (Another edition) La lettera dell isole . . . . Florence
ORTIZ, Alonso. Los tratados. Seville
SCHEDEL, Hartmann. Liber chronicarum (Nuremburg Chronicle). Nuremberg

1494
BRANT, Sebastian. Das Narren Schyff. Nuremberg
CAROLUS VERARDUS (Verardi, Carlo). In laudem serenissimi Ferdinandi Hispaniarum regis . . . et de insulis in Mari Indico . . . (includes Columbus letter) Basel
— (Another copy)

1496
LILIUS, Zaccaria, Bp. De originie & laudibus scientiarum . . . Florence

Appendix II

1497
BRANT, Sebastian. Dat narren schyp. Lübeck
— La nef des folz du monde. Paris
— Stultifera navis. Basel
— (Another edition. Counterfeiting preceding) Basel (ie, Nuremberg)
— (Another edition) Augsburg
— (Another edition) Strasburg
COLOMBO, Cristoforo. Eyn schön hübsch lesen von etlichen insslen. (The Columbus letter) Strassburg.

1498
BRANT, Sebastian. Das neü narren schiff. Augsburg.
— Salutifera [!] navis. Lyon, 1488 (ie. 1498)
— Stultifera navis. Paris.
LEBRIJA, Elio Antonio. In Cosmographiae libros introductorium . . . Salamanca.
MELA, Pomponius. Cosmographia. Salamanca.
SACRO BOSCO, Joannes de. Uberrimum sphere mundi . . . Paris

1499
BRANT, Sebastian. La grant nef des folz. Lyon.
VAGAD, Gauberte Fabricio de. Coronica de Aragon. Saragossa.

1500
DATI, Giuliano (Bishop of S. Leone). Questa e la hystoria della inventione delle diese . . . (Brescia)
MARINEO, Lucio, siculo. De Hispaniae laudibus. Burgos.

1501
ALPHARABIUS, Jacobus. Panaegyricus in divi Ludovici Regis. Rome?

1503

FORESTI, Jacopo Filippo, da Bergamo. Novissime hystoriarum omnium repercussiones, . . . Venice

ORDEN DE SANTIAGO. Compilacion de los establecimientos . . . Seville

POLO, Marco. Cosmographia . . . . Seville

VESPUCCI, Amerigo. Petri Francesci de Medicis Salutem plurimam (Mundus Novus). Paris

1504

VESPUCCI, Amerigo. Mundus novus. Venice

1505

EMMANUEL I (King of Portugal). Copia de una lettera del Re di Portugallo . . . Rome

SACRO BOSCO, Joannes de. Opus sphaericum. Cologne.

VESPUCCI, Amerigo. (Mundus novus). De ora antarctica . . . Strasbourg

— Epistola Albericij. (Rostock)

— Lettera . . . della isole nuovamente trovate. Florence.

— Von der neü gefunden Region. Basel.

— (Another edition) Von der neuw gefunden . . . (Augsburg).

1506

FORESTI, Jacobo Philippo. Noviter historiarum omnium repercussiones . . Venice

MAFFEI, Raffaele. Commentariorum urbanorum liber i[-xxxviii] Rome

PICO DELLA MIRANDOLA, Giovanni Francesco. De rerum praenotione libri novem. Strassburg

VESPUCCI, Amerigo. Mundus novus. [Paris]

— (Another edition) [Paris]

— Von den newen Insulen und landen. Leipzig

— (Another edition) Von der new gefunnden . . . (Nuremberg)

1507
FRANCANZANO DA MONTALBODDO, Fracan. Paesi novamenti retrovati . . . Vicenza
— (Another edition).
— (Another edition).
LUD, Gualtherus. Speculi orbis . . . declaratio. Strassburg
PETRARCA, Francesco. Chronica delle vite de pontefici . . . Venice
PICO DELLA MIRANDOLA, Giovanni Francesco. Hymni heroici tres ad sanctissimam . . . Milan
WALDSEEMÜLLER, Martin (Hylacomulus). Cosmographiae introductio . . . St. Die
— (Another edition) St. Die
WELLENDARFER, Virgilius. Decalogium . . . . . Leipzig

1508
DIONYSIUS PERIEGETES. Situs orbis . . . . . Ruffo Avieno interprete. Vienna
FRANCANZANO DA MONTALBODDO, Fracan. Itinerarium Portugallensium e Lusitania . . . (Milan)
— Newe unbekanthe landte und ein newe weldte . . . Nuremburg
— Paesi nuovamente retrovati. Milan
PTOLEMAEUS, Claudius. Geographiae . . . Rome
REISCH, Gregorius. Margarita philosophica . . . Basel
— (Another edition) Strassburg
SACRO BOSCO, Joannes de. Opus sphericum. Cologne
SPRINGER, Balthasar. Die reyse van Lissebone . . . Antwerp
STAMLER, Joannes. Dyalogus . . . de diversarum gencium . . . Augsburg

1509
BRANT, Sebastian. Narrenschiff. Basel
— The shyp of folys of the worlde. London
FREGOSO, Battista. De dictis factisque . . . Milan
SIMONETTA, Bonifacio. De christiane fidei . . . Basel

VESPUCCI, Amerigo. Dis büchlin saget wei die zwen . . . Strassburg
WALDSEEMÜLLER, Martin. Cosmographie introductio . . . Strassburg
— (Another copy)

1510
ALBERTINI, Francesco. Opusculum de mirabilis novae & veteris . . . Rome
FORESTI, Jacopo Filippo, da Bergamo. Suma de todas las cronicas del mundo. Valencia
GEILER, Johannes, von Kaiserberg. Navicula, sive Speculum fatuorum . . . Strassburg

1511
ANGHIERA, Pietro Martire d' (Peter Martyr). Opera: Legatio babylonica, Oceani decas . . . Seville
— (Another edition) Seville
GEILER, Johannes, von Kaiserberg. Navicula, sive Speculum fatuorum. Strassburg
MAFFEI, Rafael. Commentariorum Urbanorum... Paris
PICO DELLA MIRANDOLA, Giovanni Francesco. Hymni heroici tres. Strassburg
PTOLOMAEUS, Claudius. Liber geographiae. Venice
WALDSEEMÜLLER, Martin. Instructio manuductionem . . . Strassburg

1512
BAPTISTA MANTUANUS, Spagnuoli. Joannis Corrunni . . . Enarrationes . . . Paris
BRANT, Sebastian. Das Narrenschiff. Strassburg
FRANCANZANO DA MONTALBODDO, Fracan. Paesi novamente retrovati. Milan
PICO DELLA MIRANDOLA, Giovanni Francesco. Staurostichon, hoc est Carmen . . . Tübingen
PRUDENTIUS CLEMENS, Aurelius. Opera. Logroño
REISCH, Gregorius. Margarita philosophica nova. Strassburg

1513

FORESTI, Jacopo Filippo, da Bergamo. Supplementum supplementi chronicarum... Venice

GEILER, Johannes, von Kaiserberg. Navicula, sive speculum fatuorum. Strassburg

PAULUS MIDDELBURGENSIS. De recta Paschae celebratione. Fossombrone

PTOLOMAEUS, Claudius. Geographiae opus novissima. Strassburg

1514

ALBERTUS MAGNUS (Saint Albert). De natura locorum. Vienna

CATANEO, Giovanni Maria. Genua. Roma

COPIA DER Newen Zeytung auss Presillg Landt. (Woodcut: seaport with ships) (Nuremberg)

— (Another edition) (Woodcut: arms of Portugal) Augsberg

PTOLOMAEUS, Claudius. Opere....Nova translatio.... Nuremberg

1515

AGRICOLA, Rudolf. Ad Joachimum Vadianum epistola. Vienna

ALBERTINI, Francesco. Opusculum de mirabilibus novae.... Rome

ALBERTUS MAGNUS, (Saint Albert), Bishop of Ratisbon. De natura locorum. Strassburg

FRANCANZANO DA MONTALBODDO. Sensuyt de Nouveau monde.... Paris

MACROBIUS, Ambrosius Aurelius Theodosius. Macrobius intiger... Paris

MAFFEI, Rafael. Commentarium Urbanorum... Paris

REISCH, Gregorius. Margarita philosophica nova. Strassburg

SCHÖNER, Johann. Luculentissima quaedam terrae.... Nuremberg

1516
ANGHIERA, Pietro Martire d'. De orbe novo....decades. Alcala de Henares
CORSALI, Andrea. Lettera...allo illustrissimo signore Duca Juliano de Medici... Florence
MAGNO, Marco Antonio. Oratio in funere Regis Catholici [Ferdinandi] Hispaniarum. Naples
MORE, Sir Thomas, Saint. Libellus...de optimo reip. statu,... [Louvain]

1517
FRANCANZANO DA MONTALBODDO. Paesi nuovamente ritrovati... Venice
ISOLANI, Isidoro. De imperio militantis ecclesiae. Milan
MORE, Sir Thomas, Saint. De optimo reipublicae statu . . . [Paris]
REISCH, Gregor. Margarita philosophica cum additionibus novis . . Basel
WALDSEEMÜLLER, Martin. Cosmographiae introductio . . . [Lyons]

1518
BAPTISTA, Mantuanus Spagnuoli. Fastorum libri duodecim. Strassburg
EUSEBIUS, Pamphili, Bishop of Caesarea. Chronicon. [Paris]
FREGOSO, Battista. De dictis factisque memorabilibus collectanea . . [Paris]
MELA, Pomponius. Libri de situ orbis tres . . . Vienna
MORE, Sir Thomas, Saint. De optimo repu. statu . . . Basel
— (Another issue) Basel
SACRO BOSCO, Joannes de. Introductorium compendiosum in tractarum sphere.. Strassburg
SCHÖNER, Johann. Appendices...in opusculum Globi... Nuremberg

1519
ALBERTINI, Francesco. Opusculum de mirabilibus novae... Basel

ENCISO, Martin Fernandez de. Suma de geographia que trata de todas ... Seville

FRANCANZANO DA MONTALBODDO. Paesi nuovamente retrovati... Milan

JAN ZE STROBNICY. Introductio in Ptolomei Cosmographiam. Cracow

MACROBIUS, Ambrosius Aurelius Theodosius. Macrobius Aurelius intiger...a Joanne Rivio... Paris

OVIEDO Y VALDES, Gonzalo Fernández de. Libro del muy esforçado y invencible cavallero.. Valencia

1520
ALBERTINI, Francesco. Mirabilia Rome... [Lyons]

ANGLIARA, Juan de. Die schiffung mitt dem Lanndt der Gulden Insel. [Augsburg]

— El viaggio. col paese de lisola del oro trovato. [Venice]

EIN AUSZUG ETTLICHER SENDBRIEFF DEM...Fürsten und Herren... Nuremberg

FORESTI, Jacopo Filipo, da Bergamo. Supplementum. Supplementi de le Chroniche... Venice

RASTELL, John. A new interlude and a mery of the nature of the elements. London

PICO DELLA MIRANDOLA, Giovanni Francesco. Examen vanitatis doctrinae gentium... Mirandola

PIGHIUS, Albertus. De aequinoctiorum solscticiorumque inventione. Paris

PTOLOMAEUS, Claudius. Ptolomaeus auctus restitutus... Strassburg

SOLINUS, Caius Julius. Joannis Camertis...in C. Julii Solini πολυιστωζα enarrationes. Vienne

SPAIN. Laws. Las pragmaticas del reyno. Seville

VARTHEMA, Lodovico de. Itinerario...Buelto de latin en romance... Seville

1521
ANGHIERA, Pietro Martire D'. De nuper sub D. Carolo repertis insulis . . . Basel
FRANCANZANO DA MONTALBODDO. Paesi novamente ritrovati per la navigatione di Spagna... Venice
PADILLA, Juan de. Los doce triumfos de los doce apostoles. Seville

1522
CORTÉS, Hernando. Carta de relacion embiada a su. S. Majestad... Seville
— Nove de le isole & terra ferma novamente . . . Milan
MELA, Pomponius. De orbis situ libri tres... Basel
PTOLOMAEUS, Claudius. Opus Geographiae noviter castigatum & emasculatum. Strassburg
SACRO BOSCO, Joannes de. Sphaericum opusculum... Cracow
EIN SCHÖNE NEWE ZEITUNG so Kayserlich Mayestet auss Indiat... [Augsburg]
SPRINGER, Balthasar. Of the newe landes and of ye people founde by the messengers of the kynge of Portygale.. [Antwerp]

1523
CORTÉS, Hernando. Carta de relacion embiada... Saragossa
— Carta tercera de relacion: . . . Seville
MAXIMILIANUS, Transylvanus. De Moluccis insulis . . . . Cologne
— [Another edition] Epistola, de admirabili & novissima Hispanorum in Orientem navigatione. Rome
PICO DELLA MIRANDOLA, Giovanni Francesco. Strix, sive de Ludificatione daemonum. Bologna
SCHÖNER, Johann. De nuper sub Castiliae ac Portugalliae regibus... Timiripae [ie Cologne?]
SPAIN. Cortes. Quaderno de las cortes que en Valladolid... Burgos

1524

ANGHIERA, Pietro Martire d'. De rebus, et insulis noviter repertis. Nuremberg

APIANUS, Petrus. Cosmographicus liber. Landshut

CORTÉS, Hernando. Praeclara...de nova maris Oceani. Nuremberg
— La preclara narratione . . . della nuova Hispagna. Venice
— (Another edition with cancel t.p.)
— Tertia . . . in nova maris Oceani Hyspania . . . Nuremburg

FORESTI, Jacopo Filippo, da Bergamo. Supplementum supplementi de le Chroniche... Venice
— (Another issue, with variant title omitting translator's name) Venice

HUTTEN, Ulrich von. De Guaiaci medicina et morbo gallico liber unus. Mainz

MAXIMILIANUS, Transylvanus. Epistola, de admirabili & novissima Hispanorum in Orientem navigatione. [Voyage of Magellan] Rome

MORE, Sir Thomas, Saint. Von der wunderbarlichen Innsel Utopia genant. Basel

PICO DELLA MIRANDOLA, Giovanni Francesco. Libro detto Strega, o Delle illusioni .... Bologna

1525

AVILA, Pedro Arias d'. Lettere ... della conquista del paese del mar Oceano scripte ... [Florence?]

CORTÉS, Hernando. La quarta relacion que Fernando Cortes ... embio al ... don Carlos ... Toledo

PIGAFETTA, Antonio. Le voyage et navigation faict par les Espaignolz es isles de Mollucques. Paris

PTOLOMAEUS, Claudius. Geographicae enarrationis libri octo, Bilibaldo Pirckeymo interprete. Strassburg: J. Grüninger for J. Koberger, at Nuremberg

SPAIN. Laws, statutes. Las Cortes de Toledo, deste presente año: de mil y quinientos y .xxv. años. Quaderno. Burgos

Appendix III – A List of American Books Acquired by the British Library in 1837.

American Annual Register for 1832, 1833, New York 1835.
Oliver, Daniel, *First Lines of Physiology*, Boston 1835.
Potter, Elisha R., *Early History of Narraganset*, Providence 1835.
Jones, Silas, *Practical Phrenology*, Boston 1836.
Winslow, Hubbard, *Civil and Social Relations*, Boston 1835.
Oldbug, John, *Puritan*, Vols 1, 2, Boston 1836.
American Journal, Vols 26–28, New Haven 1834, 1835; Nos 59–63, New Haven 1836.
Gall, François John, *On Origin of moral qualities .... of Man*, Vols 1–6, Boston 1835.
Stowe, C.E., *Introduction to Criticism and Interpretation of Bible*, Vol. 1.
Johnson, A.B., *Treatise on Language*, New York 1836.
Everett, Edward, *Orations and Speeches*, Boston 1836.
Sweetser, William, *Treatise on Consumption*, Boston 1836.
Biblical Repository, No. 26, New York and Boston 1837.
North American Review, Nos 93–96, Boston 1836–1837.
Gieseler, J.C.I., *Textbook of Ecclesiastical History*, Translated by Francis Cunningham, Vols 1–3, Philadelphia 1836.
Holbrook, John Edwards, *North American Herpetology*, Vol. 1, Philadelphia 1836.
Lea, Isaac, *Synopsis of the Family of Naides*, Philadelphia 1836.
Biblical Repository, No. 26, New York 1837.
Tanner, H.I., *New Universal Atlas*, Philadelphia 1836.
Dungliston, Robley, *The Medical Student*, Philadelphia 1837.
Story, Joseph, *Commentaries on Equity Jurisprudence*, Vols 1–2, Boston 1836.
Gordon, Thomas F., *Digest of the Laws of New York*, Philadelphia 1837.

Dungliston, Robley, *General Therapeutics*, Philadelphia 1836.
Gordon, Thomas F., *History of Pennsylvania*, Philadelphia 1829.
Gordon, Thomas F., *History and Gazeteer of New Jersey*, Frenton 1834.
Chase, Heber, *Treatise on Radical Cure of Hernia*, Philadelphia 1836.
Edward, David B., *History of Texas*, Cincinnati 1836.
Mahan, D.H., *Treatise on Field Fortification*, New York 1836.
American Biography, Vol. 7, Boston and London 1837.
White, William, *Memoirs of the Protestant Episcopal Church*, New York 1836.
Bliss, Leonard, *History of Reheboth*, Boston 1836.
St George, Mrs A., *Sketch of the Life of Washington*, New York 1834.
Biblical Repository, Nos 20–24, Andover and Boston 1835–1836.
American Quarterly Register and Journal, Vols 1–9 No. 1, Andover 1829–1830, Boston 1831–1836.
North American Review, Nos 1–25, Boston 1815–1819.
American Journal of Medical Sciences, Nos 25–26, Philadelphia 1833, No. 64, New Haven 1837.
Biblical Repository, No. 25, New York and Boston 1837.
Lincoln, W., *History of Worcester*, Worcester 1837.
Gordon, Thomas F., *New York Gazeteer*, Philadelphia 1836.
Chapman, G.T., *Sermons to Presbyterians of all Sects*, Hartford 1836.
Sparks, Jared, *Library of American Biography*, Vols 5, 6, Boston 1836.
Upham, Thomas C., *Manuel of Teace*, New York 1836.
Life on the Lakes, Vols 1, 2, New York 1836.
Cogswell, William, *Assistant to Family Religion*, Boston 1836.
Paulding, James K., *Life of Washington*, Vols 1, 2, New York 1835.
Macey, Abed, *History of Nantucket*, Boston 1835.
American Almanac for 1837, Boston 1837.

Appendix IV – American Publishers Depositing Books in the British Library 1850–1950

Alfred Knopf
Allyn and Bacon
American Book Co.
American Good Government Service
Appleton
Bobbs-Merrill
H.W. Bolton
Britton Publishing Co.
Cassell
Century
Children's Press
Columbia University Press
Continental Publishing
Cornell University Press
Countway-White Publishers
Dodd, Mead
Doran
Doubleday
Duke Univeristy Press
E.P. Dutton
The Encyclopedia Press
Fleming H. Revell
Franklin Watts Inc.
Funk and Wagnall
Ginn
Harper
Harvard University Press
D.C. Heath and Co.
Hearst's International Library Co.
Henry Holt
Houghton Mifflin
Huebsch and the Viking press
John Day and Co.
John Winston
Johns Hopkins Press
Julian Messner Inc.
Liberty and Freedom Press
Lippincott
Little Brown
Longmans Green
Louis Carrier and Co.
McGraw, Hill
Macmillan
Meridian/Thames and Hudson
Michigan State University Press
Municipal Problems Publishing Co.
New American Library
Oxford University Press
Pioneer Publishers
Prentice Hall
Princeton University Press
Progressive National Service
Putnam

Rand, McNally
Random House
Rinehart
Row, Peterson and Co.
Scribner
Stanford University Press
Stanton and Van Vliet
Twentieth Century Fund
University of California Press
University of Chicago Press
University of Michigan Press
University of Minnesota Press
University of North Carolina Press
University of Pennsylvania Press
University of Washington Press
Van Nostrand
Viking Press
Wiley
Yale University Press

Appendix V – Original Files of American Newspapers Published Before 1820, in the British Library

(Locations: files with A pressmarks are in the Newspaper Library at Colindale; all other files are at present kept in the main Library collection.)

CONNECTICUT

Connecticut Mirror (Hartford) 10 July–25 Dec 1809, 26 Jan–3 March 1824. A misc 112
Middlesex Gazette (Middletown) 5 Jan–28 Dec 1809.
 Several numbers mutilated A misc 104
Connecticut Herald (New Haven) 21 Nov 1809, 6 Jan–2 March 1824. A misc 146(63)
Connecticut Gazette and Universal Intelligencer (New London) 1 Nov 1782, 24 Dec 1784–29 Dec 1786. A misc 50
New London Gazette (New London) 2 June 1769. C42 L 1(4)

GEORGIA

Gazette of the State of Georgia (Savannah) 3 March–14 April 1785.
 Imperfect C42 L 1(15)
Royal Georgia Gazette (Savannah)12, 19 Aug 1779, 27 Jul, 3, 31 Aug, 7, 28 Sep, 12 Oct 1780, 7 Dec 1780–22 March 1781.
 C42 L 1(16)

MARYLAND

Maryland Gazette (Annapolis) 29 April, 20 May, 3–17 June, 15, 22 July 1729, 10 May 1749. Burney
Maryland Gazette (Annapolis) 15 Feb 1770, 20 June 1771, 4, 25 March, 9 Sep 1773, 6 July, 17 Aug 1775, 13 June – 3 Oct 1776, 6 March, 10 April, 22 May, 12 June, 7 Aug 1777, 14

Appendix V

May, 11, 25 June, 16 July, 17 Sep, 29 Oct, 12 Nov 1779, 16 Jan – 6 Nov 1783, 2 Dec 1784, 6 Jan 1785 – 10 Aug 1786, 27 Sep 1787 – 29 July 1790.

continued as

Maryland Gazette and Political Intelligencer 7 Jan 1819 – 26 Dec 1822.

Imperfect A misc 139A

Baltimore Evening Post (Baltimore) 25 March – 17 March 1808, 27 Sep 1809 – 31 Dec 1810.

Imperfect A 233

Dunlap's Maryland Gazette or Baltimore General Advertiser (Baltimore) 21 April, 5, 19, 26 May, 25 Aug, 8 Sep 1778, 15 Sep–27 Oct 1778, 12, 19 Sep 1783, 28 June, 29 July 1785, 17 March 1786, 16 Nov, 18 Dec 1787, 8, 19 Sep – 20 Oct, 30 Oct – 6 Nov 1789. A misc 175

Federal Gazette and Baltimore Daily Advertiser (Baltimore) 1 Jan – 31 Dec 1796, 1 Jan – 29 June 1805, 1 Jan – 31 Dec 1806, 1 July 1807 – 30 June 1808, 2 Jan 1809 – 31 Dec 1810, 1 July 1811 – 30 June 1812, 1 Jan – 30 June 1813, 1 Jan 1814 – 30 June 1815, 1 Jul 1816 – 30 June 1817, 1 Jan – 30 June 1818, 1 Jan 1819 – 31 Dec 1823, 1 Jul 1824 – 30 June 1825.

continued as

Baltimore Gazette and Daily Advertiser June 1829, Jan 1835 – Dec 1837 A 235

Maryland Journal and Baltimore Advertiser (Baltimore) 21 Aug 1776, 22 Jan 1777 – 2 Feb, 23 March, 22, 29 June 1779, 25 June, 23 July 1782 – 15 July, 15, 19, 26 Aug – 9 Sep, 24, 31 Oct 1783, 2 Jan – 31 Dec 1784, 8 Feb, 29 March, 8, 12 April, 3–10, 17, 20, 31 May – 1 July 1785, 3 Jan – 8 Aug 1786, 21 Sep 1787 – 27 July 1790.

Supplements 14 April – 19 May 1778, 5 Nov, 24 Dec 1782, 25 Feb, 17 June, 18 Jul 1783, 13 April 1784.

Extraordinary Issues 28 July, 13 Oct – 17 Nov 1778, 25 Sep 1787, 11 Jan, 15 Feb – 4, 18 March, 1 April, 5 Sep – 4 Oct 1788.

Very imperfect A 243

MASSACHUSETTS

Boston Evening Post (Boston) 22 Aug 1743, 29 Dec 1760 – 10 April 1775.
Imperfect A 255
Boston Gazette and Country Journal (Boston) 4–11 Dec 1721, 8–15, 22–29 Jan, 12–19 March, 14–28 May 1722   Burney
Boston Gazette and Country Journal (Boston) 27 May – 17 Jun 1765, 13 Oct 1766 – 20 Feb 1775.
Imperfect A misc 184
(The Newspaper Library has a microfilm edition 1719–1798.)
Boston Gazette, Commercial and Political (Boston) *see* J. Russell's Gazette
Boston News Letter (Boston) 17–24 April 1704
continued as
Massachusetts Gazette and Boston Newsletter 29 Aug, 12, 19, 26 Sep, 10, 17 Oct 1765
continued as
Massachusetts Gazette 7 Nov, 6, 12, 19 Dec 1765, 6 Feb 1766
continued as
Massachusetts Gazette and Boston Newsletter 12 Jun, 17 July, 23 Oct 1766, 21, 28 May, 2, 9 July, 17 Sep, 15 Oct, 19, 26 Nov 1767, 24 March, 15, 21 April 1768
continued as
Boston Weekly News Letter 9, 16, 30 June, 14, 28 July, 18, 25 Aug, 3, 10, 24 Nov, 29 Dec 1768, 2–23 Feb, 2–30 March, 7–20 April, 4 May, 13–27 July 1769
continued as
Massachusetts Gazette and Boston Weekly News Letter 12 Oct 1769 – 1 Feb 1770, 6 April – 14 June 1770, 3 Jan, 7 Nov 1771, 9 Jan – 13 Feb, 29 Oct 1772 – 12 Aug 1773, 11, 18 Nov 1773, 19 May–29 Dec 1774, 13, 20 April, 19 Oct, 9 Nov 1775.
This section is very imperfect
Postscripts 30 June 1768, 20 April 1769.
Supplements 10 Oct 1765, 12 June, 17 July 1766, 4 June, 8 Oct 1767, 9 Feb, 23 March, 4 May, 23 Nov 1769, 1 Feb, 7, 14

June 1770, 5 Nov, 4, 17 Dec 1772, 1 April, 15 July 1773, 1, 15 Sep 1774.
Extraordinary Issues 26 Sep 1765, 17 Nov 1769, 18 Feb 1773.
A misc 186 (1, 4, 5)
(The Newspaper Library has a microfilm edition 1704–1776)
Boston Post Boy and Advertiser (Boston) 17 Feb, 24 March, 28 April, 11 Aug, 13 Oct, 3, 17 Nov, 1, 29 Dec 1766, 16 Feb, 4 May, 13 July, 21, 28 Sep, 12 Oct, 16 Nov, 14, 28 Dec 1767, 1, 22, 29 Feb, 11 April, 20 June, 26 Sep, 28 Nov 1768, 2, 30 Jan – 20 Feb, 22 May, 17 July, 11 Sep 1769.

continued as

Massachusetts Gazette and Boston Post Boy and Advertiser 9 Oct 1769 – 12 Feb 1770, 21 May – 18 June, 17 Sep, 1 Oct 1770, 8 April, 2 Dec 1771, 6 Jan, 3, 10 Feb, 20, 27 April, 12, 19 Oct, 14 Dec 1772, 7/14 June, 6/13 Sep, 27 Dec 1773/3 Jan 1774, 3/10, 17/24 Jan, 28 Feb/7 March, 14/21, 28 March/4 April - 18/25 April, 2/9 May, 27 June/4 July – 25 July/1 Aug, 8/15 Aug 1774 – 6/13 Feb 1775, 20/27 Feb – 6/13 March, 20/27 March – 10/17 April 1775.

Supplements 28 April 1766, 1 Feb, 28 June 1773, 2, 16 May, 29 Aug, 19 Sep 1774, 6 Feb 1775. A misc 185

Massachusetts Centinel and Republican Journal (Boston) 24 March 1784–12 June 1790

continued as

Columbian Centinel 16 June 1790–28 Dec 1839
Imperfect A 259
(The Newspaper Library has a microfilm edition 1784–1790.)

Massachusetts Gazette (Boston) 17, 20 Oct 1786 A 186(3)
Massachusetts Mercury (Boston) 3 July 1798–30 Dec 1800

continued as

Mercury and New England Palladium 2 Jan 1801–8 March 1803

continued as

New England Palladium 11 March–30 Dec 1803, 5 April 1808–31 Dec 1811

continued as

New England Palladium and Commerical Advertiser 1 Oct

Appendix V

1816 – 30 Dec 1817, 1 Jan – 31 Dec 1819, 2 March 1824
Imperfect A 265
Massachusetts Spy (Boston) 7 March 1771 – 1 Oct 1722
continued as
Massachusetts Spy or Thomas's Boston Journal 8 Oct 1772 – 10 June 1773, 2, 16 June, 7 July – 1 Aug, 1, 8 Sep, 6 – 20 Oct, 3 Nov 1774 – 6 April 1775
continued as
Thomas's Massachusetts Spy or Worcester Gazette (Worcester) 1 Jan 1784 – 5 Jan 1786, 3 April 1788 – 25 Feb 1795, 30 March 1796 – 16 May 1821
continued as
Massachusetts Spy 23 May 1821 – 3 Sep 1823
continued as
Massachusetts Spy and Worcester Advertiser 10 Sep 1823 – 16 Feb 1825
continued as
Massachusetts Spy and Worcester County Advertiser 4 Jan 1826 – 26 Dec 1827, 7 Jan 1829 – 29 Dec 1830, 10 March 1858
A 253
New England Courant (Boston) 7 Aug 1721 – 16 Sep 1723 (nos. 1 – 111 wanting 7, 62 and 106). *Ms notes by Benjamin Franklin. See also* Little Compton Scourge or the Anti-Courant (1721) Burney
Repertory (Boston) 3 Feb 1804 – 28 June 1811
continued as
Repertory and General Advertiser 2 July – 31 December 1811 A 267
[Boston Price – Current and Marine Intelligencer] J. Russell's Gazette, Commercial and Political (Boston) 17 April – 6 Oct 1800
continued as
Boston Gazette, Commercial and Political 9 Oct 1800 – 13 April 1801, 25 June 1812 – 1 June 1815
Imperfect A 263
(The Newspaper Library has a microfilm edition 1795 – 1820.)
Weekly Messenger (Boston) 25 Oct 1811 – 13 Oct 1815 A 269

Appendix V

New England Chronicle or the Essex Gazette (Cambridge) 18/
  25 Jan, 1/8 Feb 1776   A misc 110(8)
Essex Gazette (Salem) 4/11 April 1775   A misc 163(49)
Salem Gazette (Salem) 20 March 1783   A283(1)
  (continued at Boston as Massachusetts Gazette)
Salem Gazette (continuation of Salem Mercury) (Salem) 2 Jan
  1801–31 Dec 1802, 1 Jan–31 Dec 1811, 3 Jan–29 Dec 1815,
  7–20, 28 Nov,16, 19, 23 Dec 1823, 2–13, 20, 27 Jan, 3, 6–20,
  27 Feb, 5 March 1824   A 283(2)
Salem Gazette and Newbury and Marblehead Advertiser
  (Salem) 1 July 1774–21 April 1775
  Prospectus 24 June 1774   A misc 56
Salem Register (Salem) 2 Jan 1804–30 Dec 1805   A misc 223
  (The Newspaper Library has a microfilm edition 1800–
  1820.)
Massachusetts Spy (Worcester) Thomas's Massachusetts Spy
  or Worcester Gazette (*See* Massachusetts Spy, Boston.)

MAINE

Eagle (Castine) 14 Nov 1809–14 Dec 1811   A misc 129

NEW HAMPSHIRE

Intelligencer (Portsmouth) 23 Nov 1815   A misc 163(31)
New Hampshire Gazette and Historical Chronicle (Portsmouth) 4 July 1775   C42 L 1 (11)
Portsmouth Mercury and Weekly Advertiser (Portsmouth)
  Jan–Dec 1765   C42 L 2
Portsmouth Oracle (Portsmouth) 18 March 1809
                                                              A misc 146(61)

NEW JERSEY

New Jersey Gazette (Trenton) 22 Nov, 6 Dec 1780 C42 L 1(17)
New Jersey Journal (Chatham) 22 Nov–27 Dec 1780
                                                                   C42 L 1(3)

NEW YORK

Northern Whig (Hudson) 31 Dec 1817 – 24 Dec 1822   A 115
Ulster County Gazette (Kingston) 4 Jan 1800   A misc 157(32)
American (New York) 3 March 1819 – 1 March 1820, 22 Aug 1821   1819–20: A misc 81
    1821: A misc 163(35)
Daily Advertiser (New York) 15 Aug 1786, 6 June–17 July 1801   A misc 133
Herald: A Gazette for the Country (New York) 24 Dec 1796
    A misc 139
Independent Gazette or New York Journal Revived (New York) 10 Jan–14 Feb 1784   A misc 99(2)
Independent Journal or General Advertiser (New York) 24 Jan–21 Feb 1784
Imperfect   A misc 99(3)
Independent Mechanic (New York) 6 April 1811 – 26 Sep 1812
    A misc 80
New York Gazette (New York) 18 Feb 1733–24 April 1738
Imperfect   C 32 L 8(1)
New York Gazetteer and Country Journal (New York) 19–28 Jan, 4–18, 23 Feb 1784
    continued as
New York Gazetteer or Daily Evening Post 14 Aug 1786
    A misc 99(4)
New York Mercury (New York) 3 June 1754, 6 Jan–29 Dec 1755
    continued as
New York Gazette and Weekly Mercury 12 July, 9 Aug, 6, 27 Sep, 11, 25 Oct, 1 Nov, 27 Dec 1773, 24 Jan, 7, 14 Feb, 14 March – 30 May, 13, 27 June, 4, 25 July – 15, 29 Aug, 19 Sep, 10–31 Oct, 5–26 Dec 1774, 9, 23 Jan, 6, 27 Feb, 20 March – 3 April, 5 June 1775, 4, 18 Nov – 2 Dec 1776, 15 Feb 1779, 6 Nov 1780, 18 June – 2 July, 24 Sep, 8 Oct – 5 Nov, 3 Dec 1781, 9, 16 June 1783   A misc 97
(Some additional issues 1753–1786 are available on microfilm in the Newspaper Library)

Appendix V

New York Journal and General Advertiser (New York) 7 July–13 Oct 1777, 11 May 1778–6 Nov 1780, 30 July 1781–6 Jan 1782
    continued as
New York Journal and State Gazette 18 March–23 Sep, 11 Nov 1784–10 Feb 1785
    continued as
New York Journal and General Advertiser 17 Feb–16 June 1785
    continued as
New York Journal or Weekly Register 23 June–11 Jan 1787
    continued as
New York Journal and Weekly Register 18 Jan–6 Dec 1787
    continued as
New York Journal and Daily Patriotic Register 7–28 Dec 1787
    continued as
New York Journal and Weekly Register 31 July 1788–26 April 1790
    continued as
New York Journal and Patriotic Register 4 May–30 Dec 1790
    A 121
(The Newspaper Library has a microfilm edition 1777–1782.)
New York Packet and American Advertiser (New York) 2–9, 16, 23 Feb 1784, 14 Aug 1786   A misc 99(6)
New York Prices Current (New York) 13 May 1797
    continued as
Oram's New York Price Current and Marine Register 9 March 1799
    continued as
New York Price Current 8, 15 June, 6 July, 3, 17, 31 Aug 1799
    A misc 1
People's Friend and Daily Advertiser (New York) 1 Sep 1806
    A misc 163(12)
Rivington's New York Gazetteer or Connecticut New Jersey Hudson's River and Quebec Weekly Advertiser (New York) 29 April 1773 – 21 Sep 1775
Imperfect   A misc 96

Royal American Gazette (New York) 25 Jan 1781, 12, 19 June, 31 July 1783   A misc 99(7)
Royal Gazette (New York) 29 Aug 1778, 30 Aug, 11, 18 Oct, 1–11 Nov 1780, 27 Jan, 17 Feb, 3, 7 March, 23–30 June, 21 July, 22 Sep, 3, 17 Oct–7 Nov, 14–28 Nov, 5 Dec 1781, 23 Nov 1782, 18 June, 20 Sep, 15, 22, 25 Oct 1783   A misc 98
Time Piece and Literary Companion (New York) 13 March – 11 Sep 1797   A misc 72

OHIO

Scioto Gazette (Chillicothe) 28 Dec 1808, 16, 23 Jan 1809
     A misc 146(60)

PENNSYLVANIA

Intelligencer and Weekly Advertiser (Lancaster) 2 Sep 1801– 25 Aug 1802   A misc 89
Lancaster Journal (Lancaster) 29 Aug 1801 – 28 Aug 1802
     A misc 90
Pennsylvania Packet or General Advertiser (Lancaster) *see* Dunlap's Pennsylvania Packet (Philadelphia)
Aurora General Advertiser (Philadelphia) 1 Jan–30 Dec 1796, 1 Aug 1798–31 Dec 1800, 24 April, 1 May, 9–16 July 1801, 8, 9, 11 May 1815   A 325
(The Newspaper Library has a microfilm edition 1790– 1812.)
Daily Advertiser (Philadelphia) 7 Feb–3 July 1797
     continued as
Carey's Daily Advertiser 5 July–11 Sep 1797   A misc 139 C
Dunlap's Pennsylvania Packet or General Advertiser (Philadelphia) 13 Nov 1775, 8 July, 24 Sep 1776, 4 March, 3 June 1777
     continued as
Pennsylvania Packet or General Advertiser 4 Feb 1778–30 Dec 1779, 4, 18 Nov 1780, 13, 16, 30 Jan, 13, 24, 27 Feb, 6 March, 1, 15, 22 May, 9, 28 June, 10, 12, 28 July, 6, 18, 22, 29 Sep, 2 Oct, 1, 10, 13, 22, 24, 29 Nov, 11, 18 Dec 1781, 12,

Appendix V

28 Feb, 2, 12, 16, 28 March, 6, 27 April, 2, 23, 25 May, 1 Aug, 12 Sep, 5, 8, 12, 14, 21, 23 Nov, 3, 14, 17, 28, Dec 1782–4 Jan 1783, 8, 25 Feb, 18 March, 3, 15, 26 April, 10, 31 May, 21 June, 5, 8, 15, 17, 22 July, 2–9, 19, 28 Aug, 11, 20, 25, 27 Sep, 11, 25, 28 Oct, 4, 5 Nov, 12, 30 Dec 1783, 1, 10 Jan, 17 Feb, 10 April, 22 June, 22 July, 12 Aug, 9, 20 Oct 1784, 14 Oct 1785–3 Oct 1786, 14 Oct 1786–31 Dec 1790
continued as
Dunlap's American Daily Advertiser 1 Jan 1791–7 Dec 1793
continued as
Dunlap and Claypoole's American Daily Advertiser 9 Dec 1793–31 Dec 1795
continued as
Claypoole's American Daily Advertiser 1 Jan 1796–31 Dec 1799
continued as
Poulson's American Daily Advertiser 1 May, 2 June–15 July, 14 Oct–15 Dec 1801, 6–15 May 1815   A 309
Federal Gazette and Philadelphia Daily Advertiser (Philadelphia 1 May 1792 – 1 May 1793
continued as
Philadelphia Gazette and Universal Daily Advertiser 1 Jan 1794 – 31 Dec 1799   A 323
Freeman's Journal or North American Intelligencer (Philadelphia) 2, 23 July, 6 Aug 1783, 5 Jan 1785 – 16 May 1792
Imperfect   A 313
Gazette of the United States and Evening Advertiser (Philadelphia) 23 Dec 1793 – 11 June 1794   A 157
(The Newspaper Library has a microfilm 1789–1804)
Independent Gazetteer or Chronicle of Freedom (Philadelphia) 12, 19 July, 9, 16 Aug, 13 Sep, 4, 8, 11–18 Oct, 1, 8 Nov 1783, 5 March 1785, 7 Oct 1786 – 9 Oct 1787
1783, 85 A misc 94
1786–87 A misc 2
National Gazette and Literary Register (Philadelphia) (daily edition) 1 Nov 1820–31 Dec 1841   A 321
National Gazette and Literary Register (Philadelphia) (semi-weekly edition) 5 April–28 Oct 1820   A misc 88

Appendix V 219

New World (Philadelphia) 4 May 1797 A misc 139
Pennsylvania Chronicle and Universal Advertiser (Philadelphia) 16/32 March 1767 Burney
Pennsylvania Chronicle and Universal Advertiser (Philadelphia) 10/17 Sep 1770 C42 L 1(6)
Pennsylvania Evening Herald (Philadelphia) 12 April 1786
C42 L 1(7)
Pennslyvania Evening Post (Philadelphia) 18 Jan, 8, 11 Feb, 4, 11 March 1777 C42 L 1(8)
Pennsylvania Gazette (Philadelphia) 3 Feb 1737, 20 Sep 1750 Burney
Pennsylvania Gazette (Philadelphia) 1 Aug 1754–6 Oct 1757, 27 July 1769, 27 Sep 1775, 10, 17 April, 1 May, 8 Sep 1776, 30 April, 7 May, 25 June 1777, 2 May 1778, 15 Aug, 31 Oct 1781, 1, 22 May 1782, 23 July 1783, 2 Feb, 16 March–18 May 1785, 3 May 1786, 6 Jan 1790–11 Sep 1793
Imperfect A 311
Pennsylvania Journal and Weekly Advertiser (Philadelphia) 25 July 1754, 9 Feb, 5 Oct 1774, 4 Jan 1775 – 28 Aug 1776, 29 Jan, 23 April, 4 June, 3, 23, 30 July 1777, 20 Jan 1779, 29 Nov 1780, 4 June, 12, 17 July, 6, 16 Aug, 6, 10 Sep, 11, 18 Oct 1783, 25 Jan 1786 A misc 179
Pennsylvania Journal and Weekly Advertiser (Philadelphia) 9, 15, 22 Dec 1773, 4 May, 29 June, 13–27 July, 3, 19 Aug, 26 Oct 1774. Postscript 9 Dec 1773 Burney
Pennsylvania Ledger or Virginia Maryland Pennsylvania and New Jersey Weekly Advertiser (Philadelphia) 31 Aug 1776
C42 L 1(9)
Pennsylvania Ledger or Weekly Advertiser (Philadelphia) 26 Nov 1777 A misc 163(50)
Pennsylvania Mercury and Universal Advertiser (Philadelphia) 1 April 1785–28 Dec 1787 A misc 139 B
Pennsylvania Packet (Philadelphia) 20 June, 4, 11, 18 July 1774
Burney
Political and Commercial Register (Philadelphia) 9–11 May 1815 A misc 127
Story and Humphrey's Pennsylvania Mercury and Universal Advertiser (Philadelphia) 14 April, 6 Oct 1775 C42 L 1(10)

True American and Commercial Advertiser (Philadelphia) 14, 16–26 Nov 1803   A misc 128
United States Gazette for the Country (Philadelphia) 5 Jan–28 Dec 1809
Imperfect   A misc 219
(The Newspaper Library has an imperfect microfilm 1801–1838.)

RHODE ISLAND

Newport Mercury (Newport) 6 June 1763, 30 May/6 June 1768, 9 July 1770, 2 Sep, 18 Nov 1771, 6 Jan 1772, 11 Jan, 5 July – 2 Aug, 30 Aug – 25 Oct, 20 Dec 1773, 3, 10 Jan, 7 Feb–14 March, 18 April 1774 – 15 May 1775, 10 June, 28 Aug, 16, 30 Oct, 11 Dec 1775, 5, 19 Feb, 26 March, 30 Sep 1776, 22 March 1783, 31 July, 28 Aug, 4 Sep 1786   A misc 70
Providence Gazette and Country Journal (Providence) 17 Aug, 7 Sep 1776   C42 L 1(12)

SOUTH CAROLINA

Royal Gazette (Charleston) 13 July 1782   C42 L 1(1)
South Carolina Gazette (Charleston) 10–17 Sep 1737, 9 May 1775   Burney
South Carolina Gazette and General Advertiser (Charleston) 3 June 1783, 3/6 Jan 1784   C42 L 1(2)

VERMONT

Burlington Gazette (Burlington) 9 Sep 1814–13 Feb 1817
    A misc 221
Northern Centinel (Burlington) 13 Dec 1810–3 Dec 1812
    continued as
Centinel 10 Dec 1812 – 7 Jan 1814
    continued as
Northern Centinel 14 Jan 1814 – 25 Dec 1829
    continued as

Burlington Centinel 6 Jan – 21 Dec 1832, 3 Jan – 26 Dec 1834
Imperfect A 337
Vermont Centinel (Burlington) 22 Dec 1803 – 25 March 1808
Imperfect A 335

VIRGINIA

Norfolk and Portsmouth Journal (Norfolk) 8 November 1786 C42 L 1(5)
Virginia Gazette and Weekly Advertiser (Richmond) 6 Dec 1787 C42 L 1(14)
Virginia Gazette or American Advertiser (Richmond) 18 Oct 1786 C42 L 1(13)
Virginia Gazette (Williamsburg) 19 Aug 1737 Burney

WASHINGTON DC

City of Washingtion Gazette (Washington DC) 21 June 1820
A misc 146(55)
Daily National Intelligencer (Washington DC) 2 Jan–30 Dec 1815, 7 Jan 1818–31 Dec 1821, 1 Jan 1824–31 Dec 1833, 1 July 1837–1 Jan, 23 March, 1, 19 April 1865 A 203
National Intelligencer and Washington Advertiser (Washington DC) 15 July 1807–24 Nov 1810
continued as
National Intelligencer 27 Nov 1810–31 Dec 1818, 2 Feb, 26 June, 21 Aug 1819, 1 Jan–30 Dec 1820, 3 Jan 1828–27 Dec 1836, 1 Jan 1842–22 June 1869
Imperfect A 204
Washington Federalist (Washington DC) 17 Jan–28 Feb 1809
Imperfect A misc 114

Bibliography of Sources

Adams, Randolph G., *Three Americanists: Henry Harrisse, Bibliographer, George Brinley, Book Collector, Thomas Jefferson, Librarian* (1939).

Adams, Thomas, *The American Controversy: A Bibliographical Study of the British Pamphlets About the Disputes in America 1763–1783* (1981).

——, *American Independence: A Bibliographical Study of American Political Pamphlets Printed Between 1764 and 1776* (1965).

Alden, John, *European Americana: A Chronological Guide to Works Printed in Europe Relating to the Americas, 1493–1776* (1980 proceeding).

American Imprints Inventory: Work Projects Administration Historical Records Survey (1935–1939).

Arber, Edward, *The First Three English Books on America 1511–1555 AD* (1885).

Ayer's Annual Directory of Newspapers and Periodicals (1875–1962).

Barber, Giles, 'Books from the Old World,' *Studies in Voltaire and the 18th Century,* 151–155 (1976), 185.

Barker, Nicolas, 'Americana,' *Book Collector,* 30 (1981), 447.

Barnard, Frederick Augusta, (Introduction to the Catalogue of the Royal Library, 1820).

Barnes, James J., *Authors, Publishers and Politicians: The Quest for an Anglo-American Copyright Agreement 1815–1854* (1974).

Barrow, Lionel C., Jr, 'Our Own Cause: *Freedom's Journal* and the Beginnings of the Black Press,' *Journalism History,* 4 (1977–1978), 118.

De Beer, G.R., 'Early Visitors to the British Museum,' *British Museum Quarterly,* 18 (1953), 27.

———, 'Sir Hans Sloane and the British Museum,' *British Museum Quarterly,* 18 (1953), 2.
Benjamin, Curtis G., 'Book Publishing 1929–1979,' *Publishers' Weekly*, (24 April 1981), 41.
Bennett, G.V., *White Kennett 1660–1728: Bishop of Peterborough. A Study in the Political and Ecclesiastical History of the Early Eighteenth Century* (1957).
Bennett, Henry Stanley, *English Books and Readers 1475–1557* (1952).
Bentley, Richard, *Proposals for Building a Royal Library* (1697).
Besterman, Theodore, *Beginnings of Systematic Bibliography* (1935).
Beswick, Jay W., *The Work of Frederick Leypoldt, Bibliographer and Publisher* (1942).
Bland, David, *History of Book Illustration: The Illuminated Manuscript and the Printed Book* (1969).
Bloomfield, B.C., ed., *Acquisition and Provision of Foreign Books by National and University Libraries in the United Kingdom* (1972).
Bowker, R.R., 'Memories Among English Librarians,' *Library Journal,* 11 (1886), 406.
Bridenbaugh, Carl, *Cities in Revolt: Urban Life in America 1743–1776* (1955).
La Brie III, Henk, 'Black Newspapers: The Roots are 150 Years Deep,' *Journalism History*, 4 (1977–1978), 111.
Brigham, Clarence S., 'Bibliography of American Editions of Robinson Crusoe to 1830,' American Antiquarian Society, *Proceedings*, 67 (1957), 137.
———, *Charles Evans 1850–1935* (Reprinted from American Antiquarian Society *Proceedings*, 1936).
———, *Fifty Years Collecting Americana for the Library of the American Antiquarian Society* (1958).
———, *History and Bibliography of American Newspapers 1690–1820* (1947).
———, *History of Book Auctions in America* (Introduction to American Book Auction Catalogues 1713–1934 by George Leslie MacKay 1937).

——, *Journals and Journeymen: A Contribution to the History of Early American Newspapers* (1950).
Bristol, Roger P., *Index of Printers, Publishers and Booksellers Indicated by Charles Evans in American Bibliography* (1961).
——, (Supplement to Charles Evans' *American Bibliography* 1952).
British Library Acquisitions Department Invoices 30 June 1857, 30 November 1861, 31 October 1862.
British Library Archives, Department of Printed Books Archives 1886.
British Museum, *A List of the Books of Reference in the Reading Room of the British Museum* (1890).
British Museum Central Archives, Original Papers 1886.
 Edward Stanford to the Trustees, 16 April 1886 (8 May 1886), 4 August 1886 (5 August 1886).
 Reports by George Bullen and Richard Garnett, 7 April, 6 May, 8 July, 16 September 1886, ff26–36.
 Trustees Minutes, 8 May, 5 June, 31 July 1886.
 Standing Committee Minutes, July 1885 to May 1887, pp17285–6, 17309, 17359–17361.
Brown, Justin R., *Bibliotheca Americana: A Catalogue of Books Relating to North and South America in the Library of John Carter Brown of Providence, R.I. Parts I–II, 1493–1800* (1st and 2nd editions, 1865–1882).
Brown, Lloyd A., *The Story of Maps* (1949).
Brussel, I.R., *Anglo-American First Editions: Part One East to West; Part Two West to East* (2 vols., 1936).
Brydges, Sir Egerton, *Res Literiae: for May 1821 to February 1822* (1822).
Bryson, William Hamilton, *A Census of Law Books in Colonial Virginia* (1978).
Buchstein, Frederick D., 'The Anarchist Press in American Journalism,' *Journalism History*, 1 (1974), 43–45, 66.
Bühler, Curt F., James G. McManaway and Lawrence C. Wroth, *Standards of Bibliographical Description* (1949).
Butterfield, L.H., 'Historical Editing in the United States,' American Antiquarian Society, *Proceedings*, 72 (1962), 283.

Cappon, Lester J., 'American Historical Editors Before Jared Sparks,' *William and Mary Quarterly*, 30 (1972), 375.

——, 'Geographers and Map Makers, British and American, from about 1750 to 1789,' American Antiquarian Society, *Proceedings*, 81 (1971), 243.

Carpenter, Edward Frederick, *Thomas Tenison, Archbishop of Canterbury, His Life and Times* (1948).

Carpenter, E.H., *Printers and Publishers in Southern California 1850–1876: A Directory* (1964).

Castenada, Carlos, 'Beginnings of Printing in America,' *Hispanic American Historical Review*, 20 (1940), 671.

Chacón, Ramón D., 'The Chicano Immigrant Press in Los Angeles: The Case of "El Heraldo de Mexico", 1916–1920,' *Journalism History*, 4 (1977), 48.

Charvat, William, *Literary Publishing in America 1790–1850* (1959).

——, *The Profession of Authorship in America, 1800–1870: The Papers of William Charvat edited by Matthew Bruccoli* (1968).

Chiapelli, Fredi, *First Images of America* (2 vols., 1976).

Clark, Charles E., 'Newspapers and their Makers: The Evolution of a Social Instrument and an Occupation,' American Antiquarian Society Conference, Printing and Society in Early America, 24–25 October 1980.

Colby, Robert A., 'A Mixture of Nations: Book Collecting, Reading and Society in Old New York,' American Antiquarian Society Conference, Printing and Society in Early America, 24–25 October 1980.

Cole, George Watson, *A Catalogue of Books Relating to the Discovery and Early History of North and South America Forming a Part of the Library of E.D. Church* (1907).

Coote, C.H., *The Voyage From Lisbon to India 1505–1506: Being an Account and Journal by Albericus Vespiccius* (1894).

Cowan, Robert E., *A Bibliography of California* (1952).

——, *Booksellers of Early San Francisco* (1953).

Cowden, Alison, 'British Collections and Lacunae' *Government Publications Review*, 7A (1980), 481.

Crone, G.R., *Maps and Their Makers* (1953).
Cumming, William P., *British Maps of Colonial America* (1974).
Cumming, W.P., S.E. Hillier, D.B. Quinn and G. Williams, *The Exploration of North America 1630–1776* (1974).
Cumming, William P., R.A. Skelton, and D.B. Quinn, *The Discovery of North America* (1971).
Deane, Charles, *An Account of the White Kennett Library of the Society for the Propagation of the Gospel in Foreign Parts* (1883).
Decker, Peter, *Checklist and Short Title Index of Western Americana* (1960).
Dennis, Everette E., and Christopher Allen, 'Puck, the Comic Weekly,' *Journalism History*, 6 (1979), 2–7, 13.
The Dial, 'Literary Notes and News', (Robert Clarke's *Bibliotheca Americana*), 7 (1886), 135.
——, (Review of Henry Stevens, *Recollections of Mr James Lenox*), 7 (1886), 86.
——, 'Justice to Authors,' 7 (1886), 5.
Douglas, D.C., *English Scholars 1660–1730* (1951).
Downs, Robert B., *Books That Changed America* (1970).
——, *Books That Changed the South* (1977).
Drake, Samuel, *Biography and History of the Indians of North America* (1837).
Durie, John, *The Reformed Library Keeper* (1650).
Eames, Wilberforce, *The First Year of Printing in New York* (1928).
Edwards, Edward, *Lives of the Founders of the British Museum; With Notices of its Chief Augmentors and Other Benefactors, 1570–1870* (1870).
——, *Libraries and Founders of Libraries (1865)*.
Eisenstein, Elizabeth, *The Printing Press as an Agent of Change* (2 vols., 1979).
Engley, Donald B., 'George Brinley, Americanist,' Bibliographical Society of America, *Proceedings*, 60 (1966), 465.
Esdaile, Arundell, *The British Museum Library: A Short History and Survey* (1946).
Evans, Charles, *American Bibliography: A Chronological*

Dictionary of All Books, Pamphlets and Periodical Publications Printed in the United States of America 1639–1800 (14 vols., 1903–1959). Supplement, R.P. Bristol, 1952.

Evans, Messrs, *Catalogue of the Very Curious, Valuable and Extensive Library of the Late George Chalmers* (sale catalogue, 1841–1842).

Fay, Bernard, *Notes on the American Press at the End of the 18th Century* (1927).

Febvre, Lucien and Henri-Jean Martin, *The Coming of the Book: The Impact of Printing 1450–1800* (1976).

Fenn, G. Manville, *Memoir of Benjamin Franklin Stevens* (1903).

Finch, Jeremiah S., 'Sir Hans Sloane's Printed Books,' *The Library*, 4th ser., 22 (1942), 67.

Fletcher, W.Y., *English Book Collectors* (vol. 3 of The English Bookman's Library, ed. A.W. Pollard, 1899).

Fortescue, George Knottesford, (Report on paper read to the November meeting.) Bibliographical Society, *Transactions*, 12 (1911–1913), 2.

Foster, James W., and Fielding Lucas, Jr., 'Early 19th Century Publisher of Fine Books and Maps,' American Antiquarian Society, *Proceedings*, 65 (1955), 161.

Francis, F.C., 'The Sloane Collection of Printed Books', *British Museum Quarterly*, 18 (1953), 4.

Garnett, Richard, *Changes at the British Museum Since 1777*, (1877).

——, *Essays in Librarianship and Bibliography* (1899).

——, *Life of Ralph Waldo Emerson (1888)*.

——, *To America, After Reading Some Ungenerous Criticisms* (1898).

Gaskell, Philip, *A New Introduction to Bibliography* (1972).

Gentleman's Magazine, (Review of Rede's *Bibliotheca Americana*), LIX (pt. 2, July 1789), 637.

Gernsheim, Helmut, in collaboration with Alison Gernsheim, *The History of Photography: From the Camera Obscura to the Beginning of the Modern Era* (1969).

Gesner, Karl, *Bibliotheca Universalis* (1545).

Gidley, Mick, *American Photography* (1983).

Gilson, Julius P., (Introduction to the Catalogue of Royal Manuscripts, 1921).
Goff, Frederick R., 'Bishop Kennett and South Carolina,' Bibliographical Society of America, *Proceedings*, 59 (1965), 158.
——, ed. and intro., *The Primordia of Bishop White Kennett, the First English Bibliography on Americana* (1959).
Goodrich, Samuel, *Recollections of a Lifetime* (1856).
Grahame, James, *History of the Rise and Progress of the United States of North America*, (2 vols., 1827).
Greenwood, Robert, *California Imprints 1833–1862* (1961).
Gregory, Winifred, *American Newspapers 1821–1936* (1937).
Grolier Club, *One Hundred Influential American Books Printed Before 1900* (1947).
Growall, A., *Book Trade Bibliography in the United States in the XIX Century* (1898).
Gutharn, Peter J., *British Maps of the American Revolution* (1972).
Gutiérrez, Félix, 'Spanish Language Media in America: Background, Resources, History,' *Journalism History*, 4 (1977), 34.
Harris, P.R., 'The Acquisitions System of the Department of Printed Books in the 1870s,' *British Library Journal*, 7 (1981), 120.
——, *The British Museum Reading Room* (1976).
Harrisse, Henry, *Americus Vespuccius. A Critical and Documentary Review of Two Recent English Books concerning That Navigator* (1895).
——, *Bibliotheca Americana Vetustissima* (1866).
——, *Notes on Columbus* (1866).
Hart, Irving Harlow, 'The One Hundred Best Sellers of the Last Quarter Century,' *Publishers' Weekly*, (29 Jan. 1921), 269.
Hart, James D., *The Popular Book: a History of America's Literary Taste* (1950).
Henry, E. d'A., 'Cincinnati as a Literary and Publishing Center, 1793–1880,' *Publishers' Weekly*, 132 (3–10 July 1937), 22–24, 110–112.

Hester, Al, 'Newspapers and Newspaper Prototypes in Spanish America, 1541–1750,' *Journalism History*, 6 (1979), 73.
Hill, Frank P., *American Plays Printed 1714–1830* (1934).
Horton, Robin, and Ruth Finnegan, eds., *Modes of Thought. Essays on Thinking in Western and Non-Western Societies* (1973).
Howard, Alfred, *Copyright: a Manual for Authors and Publishers* (1887).
Howell, W.S., *Logic and Rhetoric in England 1500–1700* (1956).
Irwin, Raymond, *The English Library: Sources and History* (1966).
Jayne, Sears R., *Library Catalogues of the English Renaissance* (1956).
Jenner, Henry, 'George Knottesford Fortescue – A Memory,' *The Library*, 4 (3rd ser., 1913), 32.
Kaser, David, ed., *Books in America's Past: Essays Honoring Rudolph H. Gjelsness* (1966).
——, ed., *Cost Book of Carey and Lea 1825–1838* (1963).
——, *Joseph Charles, Printer in the Western Country* (1963).
——, *Messers. Carey and Lea of Philadelphia: History of the Book Trade* (1957).
Kelly, James, *American Catalogue of Books Published in the United States 1861–1871* (2 vols., 1866–1871).
Kennett, Richard James, *Catalogue of American Books on Sale at the Low Prices Affixed* (1835).
——, *Catalogue of American Works, Including Those Most Recently Published, Imported and For Sale* (1838).
——, *Catalogue of a Miscellaneous Collection of American Books Recently Imported and Offered For Sale at the Prices Affixed* (1829).
——, *Selection of Miscellaneous New and Second Hand Books in the Various Branches of Literature* (1837).
Kennett, White, *An Account of the Society for the Propagation of the Gospel* (1706).
——, *Bibliotheca Americanae Primordia. An Attempt Towards Laying the Foundation of an American Library, in Several*

Books, Papers and Writings, Humbly Given to the Society For the Propagation of the Gospel in Foreign Parts... by a Member of the Said Society (1713).

———, *The Lets and Impediments in Planting and Propagating the Gospel of Christ* (1712).

Kettell, Samuel, tr., *Personal Narrative of the First Voyage of Columbus to America* (translation of Las Casas' abridgement of Columbus' Journal, 1827).

Krieling, Albert, 'The Rise of the Black Press in Chicago,' *Journalism History*, 4 (1977–1978), 132–136, 156.

LaCourse, Richard, 'Native American Journalism: An Overview, *Journalism History*, 6 (1979), 34.

Leamer, Laurence, *The Rise of the Underground Press* (1972).

Lehman-Haupt, Hellmut, *The Book in America: A History of the Making and Selling of Books in the United States* (2nd ed., 1952).

LeMay, J.A. Leo, 'A Calendar of American Poetry in the Colonial Newspapers and Magazines and in the Major English Magazines Through 1765. Part I: through 1739,' American Antiquarian Society, *Proceedings,* 79 (1969), 291.

Leonard, Thomas C., 'The Newspaper Exposé and the Revolution: A Language for Facts, Ideals and Rogues,' American Antiquarian Society Conference, Printing and Society in Early America, 24–25 October 1980.

Leypolt, Frederick, *American Catalogue of Books* (annual, 1776–1910).

Library of Congress, *Guide to the Microfilm Collection of Early State Records*, Lillian A. Hamrick, ed. (1950).

Luebke, Barbara F., 'Elias Boudinott, Indian Editor: Editorial Columns from the *Cherokee Phoenix,*' *Journalism History*, 6 (1979), 48.

McMurtrie, Douglas, *The First Printers of Chicago* (1927).

———, *History of Printing in the United States* (4 vols., 1936).

Melcher, Frederic G., 'Two Decades of Book Publishing,' *Publishers' Weekly*, (18 Jan. 1941), 211.

Miller, Edward, 'Antonio Panizzi and the British Museum,' *British Library Journal,* 5 (1979), 1.

——, *That Noble Cabinet: A History of the British Museum* (1973).
——, *Prince of Librarians: The Life and Times of Antonio Panizzi of the British Museum* (1967).
Morison, Samuel Eliot, *Admiral of the Ocean Sea* (2 vols., 1942).
——, tr. and ed., *Journals and Other Documents on the Life and Voyages of Christopher Columbus* (1963).
Miscellanea Genealogical et Heraldica, new series, 2 (1870), 287. (White Kennett).
Mott, Frank Luther, *American Journalism. A History of Newspapers in the United States Through 250 Years, 1690 to 1940* (1941).
——, *Golden Multitudes. The Story of Best Sellers in the United States* (1947).
——, *History of American Magazines, 1741 to 1930* (5 vols., 1939–1968).
——, 'The Magazine Revolution and Popular Ideas in the Nineties,' American Antiquarian Society, *Proceedings*, 64 (1954), 195.
Munby, A.N.L., *The Libraries of English Men of Letters* (1964).
Murphy, Sharon, 'Neglected Pioneers: 19th Century Native American Newspapers,' *Journalism History*, 4 (1977), 79.
Naudé, Gabriel, *Instructions Concerning Erecting of a Library*, John Evelyn, tr., (1661).
Newton, A. Edward, *Bibliography and Pseudo-Bibliography* (1936).
Newton, William, *The Life of the Right Reverend Dr White Kennett . . .* (1730).
Norton's Literary Advertiser (Norton's Literary Gazette and Publishers' Circular), Charles B. Norton, ed. (1851–1855).
Norton's Literary Almanac for 1852; Containing Important Literary Information, Accounts of American Libraries etc. continued as *Norton's Literary Register and Book Buyers' Almanack for 1853, 1856*.
Nowell-Smith, Simon, *International Copyright Law and the Publisher in the Reign of Queen Victoria* (1968).

Oswald, John Clyde, *Printing in the Americas* (1968).

Palmer, John E.C., entry for the British Library in *Directory of Rare Book and Special Collections in the United Kingdom and the Republic of Ireland*, M.I. Williams, ed. (1985).

Palmer, Thomas H., *The Historical Register: Being a History of the Late War With Great Britain and a Summary of the Proceedings of Congress* (1814).

Paltsits, Victor H., 'Founding of New Amsterdam in 1626,' American Antiquarian Society, *Proceedings*, 34 (1924), 39.

Panizzi, Antonio, 'On the Collections of Printed Books at the British Museum, Its Increase and Arrangement', in Returns Relevant to the British Museum, Parliamentary Papers, House of Commons, 25 (1846), 5.

Parker, J., *Books to Build an Empire: A Bibliographical History of English Overseas Interests to 1620* (1965).

Parker, Wyman W., *Henry Stevens of Vermont: American Rare Book Dealer in London, 1845–1886* (1963).

Partridge, R.C. Barrington, *The History of the Legal Deposit of Books Throughout the British Empire* (1938).

Patmore, Coventry, 'The Library of the British Museum,' *Edinburgh Review*, 109 (1859), 201.

Payne, John Thomas and Henry Foss, *Bibliotheca Grenvilliana; Or Bibliographical Notices of Rare and Curious Books Forming Part of the Library of the Right Hon. Thomas Grenville* (1842–1872).

Peterson, Gale E., 'American Newspapers: Proposal for a National Project,' *Journalism History*, 1 (1974), 56.

Phillips, P.L., *A List of Maps of America in the Library of Congress* (1901).

Plant, Marjorie, *The English Book Trade: An Economic History of the Making and Sale of Books* (1939).

Pompen, Aurelius, *English Editions of the Ship of Fools. A Contribution to the History of the Early French Renaissance in England* (1925).

Poole, W.F., 'Review of Windsor's Narrative and Critical History of America,' *The Dial*, 6 (1886), 317.

Pride, Armistead S., 'Rights of All: Second Step in Development of Black Journalism,' *Journalism History*, 4 (1977–1978), 129.

Procter, R.G.C., *Jan Van Doesborgh, Printer at Antwerp. An Essay in bibliography* (1894).

Publishers' Circular, (Advertisement for Sampson Low and Co.), 16 Sep. 1889, 1105–1106.

———, (Anglo-American Copyright), 15 March 1887, 356; 1 April 1889, 278.

Publishers' Weekly, (Annual statistics of publishing and report on the book trade), 1872–. (Published in a January issue each year.)

———, (Advertisement for Robert Clarke and Co., Cincinnati) 21 Aug. 1880, 207.

———, (American reprints of British Books), 11 Sep. 1880, 350.

———, (Advertisement for Robert Clarke and Co., Cincinnati), 23 Oct. 1880, 529.

———, (Obituary of Joseph Sabin), 11 June 1881, 620.

———, (Avoiding British Copyright Deposit), 4 Jan. 1890, 9.

———, (American Agents in Britain), 18 Jan. 1890, 49.

———, (Advertisement for Robert Clarke and Co., Cincinnati), 23 Aug. 1890, 233.

———, (American Litrary Invasion of England), 17 Aug. 1901, 285.

———, '*Publishers' Weekly* Thru 50 Years, 1872–1921', 1 Jan. 1921, 9.

———, 'Two Decades of Book Prices,' 20 Sep. 1941, 1069.

Ray, Gordon N., 'The Importance of Original Editions,' in Gordon Ray, Carl J. Weber and John Carter, *Nineteenth Century English Books: Some Problems in Bibliography* (1952).

Rede, Leman Thomas, *Anecdotes and Biography including many Modern Characters in the Circles of Fashionable and Official Life* (1799).

———, *Bibliotheca Americana; or, a Chronological Catalogue of the Most Curious and Interesting Books, Pamphlets, State Papers, etc., Upon the Subject of North and South America,*

From the Earliest Period to the Present, in Print and Manuscript, for which Research has been made in the British Museum, and the Most Celebrated Public and Private Libraries, Reviews, Catalogues etc.* (1789).

Reilly, Elizabeth Carroll, 'The Wages of Piety: The Boston Book Trade of Jeremy Condy,' American Antiquarian Society Conference, Printing and Society in Early America, 24–25 October 1980.

Reynolds, L.G., and N.G. Wilson, *Scribes and Scholars: A Guide to the Transmission of Greek and Latin Literature* (1968).

Rich, Obediah, *Bibliotheca Americana Nova. A Catalogue of Books Relating to America* (2 vols., 1835, 1846).

——, *A Catalogue of Books Relating Principally to America, arranged under the years in which they were printed* (1832).

Roberts, Julian, 'The 1765 Edition of Goody Two Shoes,' *British Museum Quarterly*, 29 (1965), 67.

Rogal, Samuel, 'A Checklist of 18th Century British Literature Published in America,' *Colby Library Quarterly*, 10 (1973), 231.

Roorbach, Orville, *Bibliotheca Americana* (1849).

Royal Commission, *Report of the Commission Appointed to Inquire into the Constitution and Government of the British Museum, with Minutes of Evidence* (1850).

Rye, W.B., (Notes for a study of the growth of the collections) Archives of the British Library Department of Printed Books, 1873.

Sabin, Joseph, *Bibliotheca Americana: A Dictionary of Books Relating to America, from its Discovery to the Present Time* (29 vols., 1868–1936).

Sherman, Stuart C., 'Leman Thomas Rede's *Bibliotheca Americana,*' *William and Mary Quarterly*, 3rd ser., 4 (1947), 332.

Shipton, Clifford K., *Isaiah Thomas: Printer, Patriot and Philanthropist, 1749–1831* (1948).

Shove, R.H., *Cheap Book Production* (1937).

Silver, Rollo G., *The American Printer, 1787–1825* (1967).

——, 'The Boston Book Trade 1800–1825,' (Reprinted from

the Bulletin of the New York Public Library, 1949).
——, 'Efficiency Improved: The Genesis of the Web Press in America,' *American Antiquarian Society, Proceedings*, 80 (1970), 325.
Skelton, R.A., 'The Royal Map Collections,' *British Museum Quarterly*, 26 (1962), 1.
Snow, Peter, *The United States: A Guide to Library Holdings in the United Kingdom* (1982).
Solberg, Thorvald, 'Copyright Report for the Fiscal Year 1919–1920,' *Publisher's Weekly,* 29 Jan. 1921, 291.
Sparks, Jared ed., *Writings of George Washington* (1837).
Steinberg, S.H., *Five Hundred Years of Printing* (1955).
Stevens, Henry, *American Books with Tails to 'Em* (1873).
——, *American Nuggets. Bibliotheca Americana, or a Descriptive Account of my Collection of Rare books Relating to America* (2 vols., 1857).
——, *Catalogue of the American Books in the Library of the British Museum at Christmas 1856* (1866).
——, *Prospectus: Bibliotheca Americana* (1848).
——, *Recollections of James Lenox and the Formation of his Library,* revised and elucidated by Victor Hugo Paltsits (1951).
——, *Schedule of Two Thousand American Historical Nuggets* (1870).
——, *Stevens' American Bibliographer,* nos. 1, 2 (1854).
——, 'Twenty Years Reminiscences of Panizzi and the British Museum, 1845–1865,' Library Association of the United Kingdom, *Transactions and Proceedings*, 1884, 117.
Stevens, Henry Newton, *The First Delineation of the New World and the First Use of the Name America on a Printed Map* (1928).
——, *Ptolemy's Geography: A Brief Account of all the Printed Editions Down to 1730* (1908).
Stevens, John D., 'The Black Press Looks at 1920s Journalism', *Journalism History*, 7 (1980), 109.
Stillwell, Margaret B., *Incunabula and Americana 1450–1800* (1931).
Stoddard, Roger E., 'Notes on American Play Publishing

1765–1865,' American Antiquarian Society, *Proceedings*, 81 (1971), 161.

Sutton, Walter, *The Western Book Trade: Cincinnati as a 19th Century Publishing and Book Trade Center 1796–1880* (1961).

Tanselle, G. Thomas, 'Some Statistics on American Printing, 1764–1783,' in Bernard Bailyn and John B. Hench, eds., *The Press and the American Revolution* (1980).

Taylor, E.G.R., Edition of Roger Barlow 'A Brief Summe of Geographie,' Hakluyt Society, 2nd ser., no. 119 (1932).

——, *Tudor Geography 1485–1583* (1930).

Tebbel, John W., *A Compact History of American Newspapers* (1969).

——, *History of Book Publishing in the United States* (4 vols., 1972–1981).

Ternaux, Henri, *Bibliothèque Américaine ou Catalogue des Ouvrages Relatifs à l'Amérique qui ont paru Depuis sa Découverte Jusqu'à l'an 1700* (1837).

Thatcher, John Boyd, *Christopher Columbus* (3 vols., 1903–1904).

Thomas, Isaiah, *History of Printing in America* (2 vols., 1810).

——, *Three Autobiographical Fragments by Isaiah Thomas*, M.A. McCorison, ed., (1962).

Thomas, P.D.G., 'Parliament and the British Museum in 1774,' *British Museum Quarterly* 23 (1960), 1.

Thompson, Lawrence S., *Printing in Colonial Spanish America* (1962).

Thomson, M.A., *Some Developments in English Historiography during the 18th Century* (1957).

The Times, (Editorial on the British Museum, 31 May 1887).

Tooley, R.V., *Maps and Map Makers* (1949).

Trent, William P., *A History of American Literature: Supplementary to the Cambridge History of English Literature* (1918).

Trübner, Johann Nicolaus, *Trübner's Bibliographical Guide to American Literature* (1855, 1859).

Tryon, W.S., and William Charvat, *The Cost Books of Ticknor and Fields* (1949).

Tyler, Moses Coit, *A History of American Literature During the Colonial Time, 1607–1765* (2 vols., 1878).
——, *The Literary History of the American Revolution, 1763–1783* (2 vols., 1897).
United Society for the Propagation of the Gospel, Archives (Letters relating to White Kennett and Sir Hans Sloane, 1712, 1715, and to the White Kennett Library, 1855, 1916).
Vail, R.W.G., *The Voice of the Old Frontier* (1949).
Waldman, Milton, *Americana: The Literature of American History* (1926).
Wall, Alexander J., Jr, 'William Bradford, Colonial Printer: A Tercentenary Review,' American Antiquarian Society, *Proceedings*, 73 (1963), 361.
Wallis, Helen, 'The Map Collections of the British Museum Library,' in Helen Wallis and Sarah Tyacke, eds., *My Head is a Map* (1973).
Weimerskirk, Philip John, Antonio Panizzi's Acquisitions Policies for the Library of the British Museum, (Unpublished Columbia University DLS thesis, 1977).
Weiss, Roberto, *Humanism in England During the Fifteenth Century* (1941).
Welch, D'Alté A., *A Bibliography of American Children's Books Printed Prior to 1821* (1972).
Wightman, W.P.D., *Science and the Renaissance* (2 vols., 1962).
Willison, Ian R., *On the History of Libraries and Scholarship: A Paper Presented Before... the American Library Association, 1979* (1980).
——, 'The Development of the United States Collection, Department of Printed Books, British Museum,' *Journal of American Studies*, 1 (1967), 79.
——, 'The political and cultural context of Panizzi's reform of the British Museum Department of Printed Books as a national research library,' in *Wolfenbütteler Schriften zur Geschichte des Buchwesens*, 8 (1982), 53.
Wilson, C. Edward, 'The Boston Inoculation Controversy: A Revisionist Interpretation,' *Journalism History*, 7 (1980), 16.

Winship, George P., *The Cambridge Press, 1638–1692* (1945).
Winterich, John T., *Early American Books and Printing* (1935).
Winsor, Justin, *Narrative and Critical History of America* (8 vols., 1884–1889).
Wiseman, John A., Henry Stevens and the British Museum (United Kingdom Library Association Fellowship thesis, unpublished, 1973).
Wright, L.H., *American Fiction 1774–1850: A Contribution Toward a Bibliography* (1939).
——, 'A Few Observations on American Fiction, 1851–1875', American Antiquarian Society, *Proceedings*, 65 (1955), 75.
Wright, Louis B., *The First Gentlemen of Virginia* (1940).
——, *The Cultural Life of the American Colonies 1607–1763* (1957).
Wright, Thomas Goddard, *Literary Culture in Early New England, 1620–1730* (1920).
Wroth, Lawrence C., *An American Bookshelf, 1775* (1934).
——, *The Colonial Printer* (1938).
——, *The First Century of the John Carter Brown Library: A History with a Guide to its Collections* (1946).
——, *History of Printing in Maryland 1686–1776* (1976).
Wynne, James, *Private Libraries of New York* (1860).

INDEX

Abbot, John, 169
Abbott, Robert S., 139–140
Adams, D.K., *American Newspaper Holdings in British and Irish Libraries*, 133
Adams, Henry, 147
Adams, John, 179
Adams, John Quincy, 70
Adams, Samuel, 179
Adams, Thomas, *American Controversy*, 23
Addison, Joseph, *Cato* (American edition), 24
Albany, imprints, 34, 54
Alcott, Louisa May, 79
Alden, John, *European Americana*, 5, 120–121
Allen, Hervey, *Anthony Adverse*, 69
Alman, Miriam, *Guide to Manuscripts Relating to America in Great Britain and Ireland*, 155
Almanacs, 22, 24, 33, 92
American Antiquarian Society, 43, 75, 132, 155
American Bookseller, 42
American Magazine, 149
American Museum, 149
American Periodicals 1741–1900, 102, 130, 149
American Revolution, 2, 21–23, 114, 122, 126, 148–149, 154, 164, 167–170, 178–180
American Trust for the British Library, 6, 88, 138, 143
American Women's Club Magazine, 146
Americana, definition, 3, 31, 58–59

Ames, J.G., *Comprehensive Index to the Publications of the U.S. Government*, 125
Ames, Joseph, *Typographical Antiquities*, 58
Amherst, Lord Jeffrey, 116
Anderson, Adam, 178
Andover, NH, imprints, 54
Andrews, Charles M., 152, 155; *Guide to the Manuscript Materials for the History of the United States to 1783 in the British Museum*, 157
Andriot, John L., *Guide to U.S. Government Publications*, 125
Anghiera, Pietro Martire d', *See* Peter Martyr
Anthony, Susan B., 144
Antwerp, 17
Areopagitica, 24
Arnt, Karl J.R., *German Language Press of America*, 23
Arr, E.H. (Ellen Chapman), *New England Bygones*, 110
Ascham, Anthony, *A Lytel Treatise of Astronomy*, 17
Atherton, Gertrude, 182
Atlantic Monthly, 148
Ayer's Annual Directory of Newspapers, 133
Ayscough Catalogue, 30, 151–152
Ayscough, Samuel, 152

Baber, Rev. Henry, 47
Bacon, Francis, 12
Bacon, Nathaniel, 176
Bailyn, Bernard, *The Press and the American Revolution*, 22, 135

Index

Balfour, Lord Arthur, 182
Baltimore, imprints, 34, 54
Bancroft, George, 4, 153
Bancroft, H.H., 74
Banks, Sir Joseph, 47, 176
Barcelona, 11
Barlow, Roger, *A Brief Summa of Geographie*, 17
Barnard, Frederick, 32–33
Barnes, Timothy, loyalist newspapers, 135
Barrie, J.M., 69
Bartlett, John Russell, 45, 56
Basel, 17
Bay Psalm Book (Whole Book of Psalms), 19, 45
Behaim, Martin, 16
Belgium, 120
Bennett, James Gordon, 135
Berkeley, Gov. William, 18
Best sellers, 69, 80, 85
Bible, 25, 45, 92, 122
Bierce, Ambrose, 79; *Devil's Dictionary*, 64
Birch, Thomas, 177
Blaise, 99
Blanqui, Louis, 66
Bloomer, Amelia, 143
Bodley, Sir Thomas, 29
Bohemian Club, 64
Bolton, Theodore, *American Book Illustrations*, 109
Boni, Albert P., 75
Book auctions, 43
Book collecting, 4, 21, 27–28, 31, 45, 57–58
Book illustration, 17, 109
Book output, American colonies, 21–22, 25; United States, 37, 41, 67–69.
Book prices, 42, 63
Book trade, 67–68, 112
Book Review Digest, 75
Booksellers, 43; *See also* Henry Stevens and Benjamin Franklin Stevens; John Russell Bartlett, 45; Richard Kennett, 34, 130; William Pickering, 34–35, 49; Bernard Quaritch, 76; Orville Roorbach, 43; Joseph Sabin, 50; Nicholas Trübner, 76; Wiley and Putnam, 34–35, 49
Books in Print, 44
Boston, 19, 147; book trade, 23; imprints, 34, 37, 54, 83
Boston Athenaeum, 147
Boudinot, Elias, 142
Bouquet, Henry, 157, 178–179
Bowditch, Nathaniel, *American Practical Navigator*, 115
Bowdoin College, 139
Bowker, Richard R., 44, 46, 76
Boyle, John, 187
Bradford, Gov. William, 188
Brady, Matthew, 107, 110–111
Brant, Sebastian, *Narrenschiff* (Ship of Fools), 5, 12
Bray, Rev. Thomas, 23
Brigham, Clarence, *Bibliography of American Newspapers*, 131–133
'Brigham' newspapers in the British Library, list, 209–221
Bright, John, 181
Brinley, George, 45
Bristol, Roger P., Supplement to *American Bibliography*, 5, 21–22, 75
British books in American, 19–20, 23, 37, 39, 41–42, 51, 69
British Library, budget and funds, 47, 55, 62–63, 81–82; catalogues, 5, 30, 46, 59–60, 91–100, 106, 108, 116, 124–126, 128–130, 132, 151–152, 156; Department of Oriental Manuscripts and Printed Books, 120; Garnett appointed Keeper of Printed Books, 75; general spending on printed books, 47, 55, 62–63, 81, 91; lists of American books received 1846, 52–53; Manuscripts Department, 114, 116, 118, 151–152, 154–156; Map

Index

Library, 112, 116; Newspaper Library, 93, 108, 130–132; numbers of American books, 51–57, 60–63, 81–88; spending on American books, 51–57, 62–63, 81–82; state 1830s–1840s, 35–36, 46–47; Stevens agent for, 1; subject catalogue, 96–100, 110
British Library Catalogue (Saur), 96
British Library Subject Catalogue (Saur), 99
British Museum, 3–4, 29, 47; archives, 3; *Catalogue of Prints and Drawings*, 104; foundation, 6–7, 29, 151; reading room, 4, 56, 76; Trustees, 78
British Publishers Archives (Chadwyck-Healey), 103
British Union Catalogue of Periodicals, 93
Brooker, William, 133
Brother Jonathan, 42
Brown, John Carter, 45–46
Brown University, 155
Brunet, Jacques Charles, *Table Méthodique*, 96
Brussel, I.R., *Anglo-American First Editions*, 79
Brymner, Douglas, 179
Buckland, James, *Account of the Discovery of a Hermit*, 25
Buell, C.C., *Battles and Leaders of the Civil War*, 109
Bullen, George, 78
Burney, Dr Charles, newspaper collections, 32, 35, 101, 209–221
Butler, Gov. Nathaniel, 173
Butterick pattern books, 107
Byfield, Nathanial, 168

Cable, George Washington, 66, 107
Caesar, Sir Julius, 165, 178
California, 113, 121, 162; as a centre of publishing, 64–65
Calvert, George, 174
Cam, Diego, 16
Cambridge, Mass., first printing press, 18; imprints, 54
Campbell, John, 133
Caribs, 14
Carnegie Institution, 155
Carvajal, Bernardino, 16
Carver, Jonathan, 176
Cary, Mathew, 40, 148–149
Catalogue of Maps etc. in the Library of George III (King's Library), 116
Catalogue of Printed Maps . . . in the British Museum to 1964, 116
Catalogue of Printed Music in the British Library (Saur), 118
Cato's Letters, 134
Cecil, William, 165
Census Schedules, 129
Century Magazine, 110, 148
Chalmers, George, 177; *Political Annals of the United Colonies*, 153; *Revolt of the Colonies*, 35, 153; sale of library, 35–36
Charleston, imprints, 54
Checklist of U.S. Public Documents, 125
Chicago, fire of 1871, 64; imprints, 183
Children's books, 25, 40
China, Treaty of Nanking, 48
Christophers, R.A., *How to Use the Catalogue*, 92, 94
Church, Dr Benjamin, 179
Cicero, *Cato Major* (American edition), 24
Cincinnati, as a centre of western publishing, 25–26, 38, 65–66; imprints, 34, 54, 65–66
Civil War, 41, 139–140, 144, 181
Clarke, Robert, 74; list of titles published 1880, 65
Cobden, Richard, 181
Coke, Sir Edward, 27, 58
Cole, William, 176
Columbus, Christopher, 26, 57; attempts to calculate longitude,

Index

1503, 14–15; bookseller and mapmaker, 13; claim to the benefits of his discoveries, 15; discovery of Americas, 11, 14; English version of his name, 17; geographical knowledge, 14
Columbus, Fernando, 14
'Columbus letter', 11, 15–16
Columbus, Ohio, imprints, 34
Conan Doyle, Arthur, 69
Concord, 41
Condy, Jeremy, 23
Congress (United States), 30
Congressional Committee Hearings 1839–1869, 125
Congressional Committee Prints 1829–1870, 125
Congressional Globe, 126
Connecticut, 166; first printing, 20
Contarini, Giovanni Matteo, 57, 115
'Contarini' map, 115
Cook, Captain James, 114, 169
Cooper, James Fennimore, 40, 79, 146
Cooper, Rev. Myles, 164
Copyright, 39, 70; British works in America, 24, 40, 70; International Copyright Agreement, 1891, (Berne Convention), 39, 73
Copyright Acts, 34, 67, 70, 73, 78
Copyright deposit, 4, 29, 34, 46, 63, 67–68, 74, 77–85, 91, 108, 116, 118, 131, 207–208
Cornish, Samuel, 139
Corpus Juris Secundum, 126
Cosa, Juan de la, 113
Cotton, Sir John, 6
Cotton, Sir Robert, 6, 27, 158–159
Cotton, Sir Robert Bruce, 158
'County Histories', 128–129
Cowden, Alison, *American Studies Collections in the University of London*, 7
Crampton, J., 170
Crick, Bernard, *Guide to Manuscripts Relating to America in Great Britain and Ireland*, 155
Cumulative Book Index, 75

Dana, Richard Henry, 40
Dati, Giuliano, *Questo e la Historia*, 11, 58
Davenport, Francis G., *Guide to Manuscript Materials for the History of the United States to 1783 in the British Museum*, 155
Davis, John, 165
Daye, Mathew, 18
Daye, Stephen, 18
Deane, Charles, 190
DeBrahm, William Gerard, 114, 164
De Bry, Theodor, 16–17, 57, 173
Dee, John, 158
Deering, C., *Union List of American Serials in Britain*, 93, 149
Delaware, first printing, 20
Dennett, Mary Ware, 182
D'Ewes, Simonds, 161
Dewey, Melvin, 46, 59
Dickens, Charles, 37
Dilke, Sir Charles, 181
Discovery of America, and printing, 12; Columbus' 1st voyage, 11; Columbus' 3rd voyage, 14; first named on map, 11–12; fraudulent claims, 16
Donne, John, 'Valediction of the Book', 15
Douglas, Frederick, 139
Drake, Sir Francis, 158, 163, 165–166
Drake, Samuel, 45, 187–189; 'Chronicles of the Indians of North America' (ms), 178
Drieser, Theodore, *Sister Carrie*, 73
Durant, Will, *Story of Philosophy*, 69
Dutton, John, 'Atlas of the United States' (ms), 178
Duyckinck, Evert A., and George C., 148

Index

Early American Imprints (Readex), 75, 101
Early American Newspapers, 131
Ecuador, 18
Eden, Rechard, 16; tr., *Historie of the West Indies*, 17; tr., *Treatise of the Newe India*, 17
Eden, William, (Lord Auckland), 157, 179
Edinburgh Review, 74, 145
Educational publishing, *See* Textbooks
Edwards, Arthur, 29, 32
Eighteenth Century Short Title Catalogue, 122
El Paso, Spanish press, 142
Emerson, Ralph Waldo, 40–41, 79; Garnett's biography, 76; in England, 70
Encisco, Martin Fernandez de, *Suma de Geographie*, 13
Encyclopedia Americana, 40, 51
English Cartoons and Satirical Prints (Chadwyck-Healey), 104
Evans, Charles, *American Bibliography*, 5, 21, 26, 41, 75, 101–102, 132
Evans, Hilary and Mary, *Picture Researcher's Handbook*, 106
Everett, Edward, 4, 147–148

Fagan, Louis, 76
Farrar, John, *Map of Virginia*, 113
Fiction, 23, 41–42, 60, 66–69, 73, 80, 85, 87, 102
Filkin, Richard, 178
Florida, 166
Force, Peter, 45, 127
Fortescue, George Knottesford, 96–97; *Subject Index . . . to the Library of the British Museum*, 97
Foster, John, 19, 187
Fox, Charles James, 181–182
France, 24, 120, 143
Franklin, Benjamin, 134, 164;
collected writings, 34
Franklin, James, 134, 191–193
Frederick, Harold, 79
'Freeman's Oath', 19
Freidel, Frank, *Harvard Guide to American History*, 110, 125
French and Indian War, 114
Frobisher, Martin, 158, 161, 165, 174
Froude, J.A., 154

Garnett, Richard, 46, 75–79, 189
Garrick play collection, 32
Garrison, Wendell Phillips, 148
Garrison, William Lloyd, 101–102, 139, 148
Gautier of Metz, *Mirrour of the World*, 15
Gentleman's Magazine, 30
George III, library of, 32
George, Henry, *Progress and Poverty*, 66
Georgia, 140–141, 169, 175; first printing, 20
Germany, 120, 122, 143
Gernsheim, Helmut, *History of Photography*, 106
Gesner, Karl, *Bibliotheca Universalis*, 26
Gladstone, William Ewart, 157, 181
Gonzales, Ester B., *Annotated Bibliography on Cubans in the United States*, 121
Gorges, Fernando, 153
Gibson, Charles Dana, 108
Gidley, Mick, *American Photography*, 106
Goodrich, Samuel, 'Peter Parley', 42, 70; *Recollections of a Lifetime*, 42
Gordon, George Hamilton, (Lord Aberdeen), 181
Grahame, James, *History of the . . . United States*, 35–36
Greeley, Horace, 135–136

Gregory, Winifred, *American Newspapers*, 133
Grenville, George, 181
Grenville, Thomas, 31–32, 115; acquisition of library by British Museum, 57–58
Grenville, William Wyndham, 182
Growall, Adolf, 44

Hakluyt, Richard, 16, 28, 57; *Voyages*, 58
Haldimand, Sir Frederick, 106, 157, 178–179
Hall, David, 23
Handbook of Latin American Studies (Library of Congress), 122
Hardwick, Earls of, 157, 180
Hargrave, Francis, 167, 176
Hariot, Thomas, *Virginia*, 58
Harley, Edward, 2nd Earl of Oxford, 6, 160
Harley, Robert, 1st Earl of Oxford, 6, 27, 160
Harper's Weekly, 107, 110
Harper's Monthly, 146
Harris, Benjamin, 19, 133
Harris, P.R., 'Acquisitions system of the Department of Printed Books 1870s', 56–57; *The British Museum Reading Room*, 6
Harrisse, Henry, 16, 31, 122; *Bibliotheca Americana Vetustissima*, 44; interest in maps, 112, 115
Harte, Bret, 70, 79
Hartford, imprints, 54
Harvard College, 18, 147
Hawkins, Sir John, 159, 165
Hawthorne, Nathaniel, 40, 79; 'Marble Faun' (ms), 178; *Scarlet Letter*, 4; *Twice Told Tales*, 54
Hearn, Lafcadio, 59
Hench, John B., *The Press and the American Revolution*, 22, 135
Herrera, Diane, *Puerto Ricans and Other Minority Groups in the Continental United States*, 121
Hickey, General William, 126
Higden, Ranulf, *Polichronicon*, 15
Hill, Frank Pierce, *American Plays Printed Before 1830*, 104
Hillsborough, Lord, 153
Holland, 120
Holmes, Oliver Wendell, 40, 79; *Contagiousness of Puerperal Fever*, 58
Homer, Rev. Arthur, 30
Homer, Winslow, 109
Hoosier novels, 64
Hope, Anthony, 69
Howells, William Dean, 66
Hubbard, William, *General History of New England*, 189; 'History of New England' (ms), 170; *Narrative of the Indian Wars*, 5, 54, 114, 187–190
Hunter, Joseph, 'Early History of the Founders of New Plymouth' (ms), 178
Hunter, Gov. Robert, 163
Huskisson, William, 180
Hutchinson, Thomas, 157, 168–169, 180; *History of Massachusetts*, 54, 153

I.F. Stone's Weekly, 149
Index Catalogue of the Library of the Surgeon-General's Office, 96
Index to Manuscripts in the British Library (Chadwyck-Healey), 156
Indian captivity narratives, 25
Indiana, 64
Indians, 17
Irvin, Washington, 40, 79
Italy, 120

Jamaica, 14, 28
James, Henry, 80, 147, 182; in England, 70
Jameson, Franklin J., *The American*

Revolution Considered as a Social Movement, 155
Jefferson, Thomas, *Notes on the State of Virginia*, 81
Jenkins, William S., 127
Jenkinson, Charles, 157, 180
Jenkinson, Robert Banks, (Lord Liverpool), 180
Jewett, Charles Coffin, 51
Jewitt, Sarah Orne, 107
Johnson, R.U., *Battles and Leaders of the Civil War*, 109
Johnson, Dr Samuel, 1, 32–34
Jones, John Paul, 178
Jones, John Winter, 56–57, 91

Kansas, 137
Keith, George, *Truth Advanced*, 24
Kelly, James, *American Catalogue*, 44, 51
Kennett, Benjamin Franklin, 34
Kennett, Richard, 34–35, 130; list of newspapers sold to British Museum, 209–221
Kennett, White, 26–29, 165–167; *Bibliothecae Americanae Primordia*, 26, 28–31; *Compleat History of England*, 27; *Parochial Antiquities*, 27
Kipling, Rudyard, 69
Knapp, Samuel, 189
Knox, Henry, 23

Layard, Austen Henry, 180
Law books, 30, 60
Laws, proceedings etc., 18, 20, 23–24, 84, 94, 124–129
Leclerc, Charles, *Bibliotheca Americana*, 122
Lennox, James, 45–46, 57
Leypolt, Frederick, *American Catalogue*, 44
Libraries, *See also* British Library
Libraries, American Antiquarian Society, 43, 132; Bodleian, 7, 76, 78; British Patent Office, 144; Brown University, 51; Cambridge University, 7, 76, 78; Cottonian, 27, 29, 32, 158–159; dispersal of monastic libraries in Britain, 26; Faculty of Advocates, Edinburgh (National Library of Scotland), 78; founding of libraries in West Indies and America by SPG, 23, 28; Grenville, 31–32, 57, 115, 187; Harleian, 27, 160–164; John Carter Brown, 45, 74; King's, 26–27, 115; London School of Economics, 129; Trinity College, Dublin, 78; libraries in American colonies, 23; Library Company of Philadelphia, 51; Library of Congress, 67, 74, 78, 154; New York Public, 45, 58, 74, 154; Oxford and Cambridge Colleges, 26; Peterborough Cathedral, 29; Rhodes House, 7; Royal (Old Royal Library), 29, 187; Society for the Propagation of the Gospel, 28, 29; University of London, 7; University of Virginia, 189–190
Library Association of the United Kingdom, 76
Library Journal, 76
Lieber, Francis, 40
Life, 108
Lily, 143
Lima, 18
Lisbon, 11
Literary World, 148
Littlefield, Daniel F., *American Indian and Alaskan Native Newspapers*, 141
London, book trade, 23, 34; imprints of American books, 71, 77, 85, 87; specialist libraries, 6
London Quarterly Review, 145
Longfellow, Henry Wadsworth, 40, 70, 80, 146
Longman, Thomas, 23

Los Angeles, Spanish press, 142
Louisiana, 120
Louvain, 17
Loyalists, 22–23, 35, 45, 122, 135, 148, 153–154, 164, 168–170, 176
Low, Sampson, list of books distributed in Britain, 1899, 71
Lowell, James Russell, 80, 146–148
Lowell, Mass., 128
Lowell Offering, 143
Lyte, A.D., 111

McCarthy, Justin, *History of Our Own Times*, 66
McCarty, Clifford, *Film Composers in America*, 118
McClure's Magazine, 106–107, 148
McHugh, Hugh, *John Henry*, 73
Magellan, Ferdinand, 17
Maine, 168, 181
Mandeville, Sir John, *Travels*, 16
Maps, 13, 68, 112–117
Marlborough, Dukes of, 183
Martin, Gov. Josiah, 181
Martines, John, 161
Martyr, Peter, (Pietro Martire d'Anghiera), 11, 16–17, *Decades*, 16
Marx, Karl, 48
Maryland, 173–174; first printing, 20
Massachusetts, first printing, 20
Massachusetts Historical Society, 147
Massachusetts Magazine, 149
Mather, Cotton, 57, 153
Mather, Increase, 191, 193
Mayer, Michael C., *Bibliography of United States-Latin American Relations*, 122
Medical books, 37, 39, 58–59, 72
Mela, Pomponius, 15
Melville, Herman, 80, 148; in England, 70; *Moby Dick*, 4
Mencken, H.L., 1
Mexico, 121

Mexico City, 18
Miller, Edward, *Prince of Librarians*, 4; *That Noble Cabinet*, 6
Miller, Francis Trevelyan, *Photographic History of the Civil War*, 110–111
Miller, Joachim, 80
Miller, John, 'New York Considered and Improved' (ms), 178
Mitchell, Sir Andrew, 176
Monthly Catalog of U.S. Government Publications, 125
Moodie, Edith, 155
Mooney, James E., *Short-Title Evans*, 75
More, Thomas, *Utopia*, 12, 17
Morris, Gouverneur, 179
Mott, Frank Luther, *Golden Multitudes*, 69; *History of American Magazines*, 147
Mowbray, J.M., *Journey to Nature*, 73
Müller, Johann, *See* Regiomontanus
Munich, 48
Munster, Sebastian, *Treatise of the Newe India*, 17
Murray, Alexander, 162
Music, 68, 118–120

Narrenschiff, *See* Brant, Sebastian
Nast, Thomas, 108
Nation, 149
National Union Catalog, 75, 93–94, 133
Nevins, Allan, *Century of Political Cartoons*, 108
Newcastle, Duke of, 157
New England, 18, 20, 128, 134, 161–162, 168, 170–175, 178–179; religious publishing, 25; transcendentalists, 37, 147
New England Historic Genealogical Society, 189
Newfoundland, 161–162, 168
New Grove Dictionary of American Music, 118

Index 247

New Hampshire, 154, 168; first printing, 20
New Jersey, 154, 162; first printing, 20
New London, imprints, 54
New Mexico, 142
New Orleans, imprints, 34; pictures by Pennell, 110
Newspapers, 19, 24–25, 34, 37, 65, 68, 93, 108, 120, 126, 130–150; Burney collection, 130, 134; Colonial American Newspapers in the British Library, list, 209–221; *Newspapers in Microfilm*, (Library of Congress), 133; *America*, 146; *America Abroad*, 146; *American and Colonial Gazette*, 146; *American Commercial and Chemical Journal*, 137; *American Eagle*, 146; *American Gazette*, 146; *American Herald*, 146; *American Home News*, 146; *American Humorist*, 146; *American News*, 146; *American Referee*, 146; *American Register*, 146; *American Settler*, 146; *American Society in Europe*, 146; *American Trade Review*, 146; *American Traveller*, 146; *American Visitor*, 146; *American Visitor's News*, 146; *American Weekly Mercury*, 134; *Anglo-American and Continental Courier*, 146; *Anglo-American Illustrated News*, 146; *Anglo-American Times*, 146; *Anglo-American Traveller*, 146; *Anglo-Californian*, 146; *Anglo-Colorado Mining . . . Guide*, 146; *Anglo-Saxon*, 146; *Baltimore Afro-American*, 139; *Boston Gazette*, 34, 133; *Boston Guardian*, 139; *Boston Newsletter*, 133; *Cherokee Phoenix*, 140–141; *Chicago Defender*, 139–140; *Clamor Publico*, 142; *Coloured American*, 139; *Commercial Advertiser*, 145; *Crepusculo de la Libertad*, 142; *Daiy Graphic*, 111; *Dallas American*, 139; *Freedom's Journal*, 138; *Gaceta de Mexico*, 142; *Heraldo de Mexico*, 142; *Houston Informer*, 139; *Indianapolis Recorder*, 139; *Liberator*, 101, 138–139, 148; *London American*, 146; *Maryland Gazette*, 134; *Mountain Messenger*, 137; *Musical World*, 137; *New England Courant*, 134; *New Iowa Bystander*, 139; *New York Age*, 139; *New York Evening Post*, 73; *New York Gazette*, 134; *New York Herald*, 135–137; *New York Tribune*, 135–137; *New York Weekly Journal*, 24; *North Star*, 139; *Peaceful Revolutionist*, 144; *Pennsylvania Gazette*, 134; *Philadelphia Tribune*, 139; *Public Occurrences*, 19, 133; *Revolution*, 144; *Rhode Island Gazette*, 134; *Rights For All*, 139; *San Francisco Elevator*, 139; *South Carolina Weekly*, 134; *Southern Vineyard*, 137; *Spiritual Telegraph*, 137; *Type of the Times*, 137; *Virginia Gazette*, 134; *Warren Telegraph*, 136; *Washington Bee*, 139
New York, 24, 66, 68, 113, 137, 163, 174, 178; abolition of slavery, 139; first printing, 20; imprints, 34, 37, 54, 83–84
New York Conspiracy, 81
New Yorker, 108
Nicaragua, 137
Nicholson, E.B., 76
Nile's Weekly Register, 149
North, Lord, 153, 165
North American Review, 4, 147
North Carolina, 169, 181; first printing, 20

248　　　　　　　　Index

North West passage, 161, 172, 174
Norton, Charles B., *Norton's Literary Advertiser*, 43
Norton, Charles Eliot, 147
Nuremberg Chronicle, 16
Nye, Bill, 107

Of the Newe Landes, 17
Oglethorpe, James Edward, 172
Oliver, Peter, 169–170
Olson, May E., *German Language Press of America*, 122
Oregon, 181
Oviedo Y Valdes, Gonzalo Fernandez de, *Historie of the West Indies*, 17

Paine, Thomas, 143
Palmer, Gregory, *Bibliography of Loyalist Source Material*, 135, 177
Palmerston, Lord, 182
Pamphlets, 22–24, 39, 54, 61, 67–68, 81–84, 126
Panizzi, Antonio, 75–76, 79; acquisition of the Grenville Library, 57–58; and Henry Stevens, 46, 49–50; appointment as Keeper of Printed Books, 3, 47; appointment as Principal Librarian, 3, 47; arrival in Britain, 3, 48; catalogue of printed books, 91, 95; ideal of a national library, 1–2, 47–51; report of 1846, 36, 48–49
Pap, Leo, *Portuguese in the United States*, 121
Parins, James W., *American Indian and Alaskan Native Newspapers*, 141
Parker, Mathew, 27
Paris, 48
Parliament, 6, 24, 47, 84
Paullin, Charles O., *Guide to the Materials in London Archives for the History of the United States Since 1783*, 155, 164

Paxson, Frederic L., *Guide to the Materials in London Archives for the History of the United States Since 1783*, 155, 164
Payne, Will, *Story of Eva*, 73
Peel, Sir Robert, 157, 181
Penn, William, 169, 172
Pennell, Joseph, 109
Pennsylvania, 174; first printing, 20; religious publishing, 25
Pennsylvania Historical Society, 154
Pennsylvania Magazine, 143
Periodicals, 54, 65, 67, 84, 93–94, 101–103, 106–109
'Peter Parley', *see* Samuel Goodrich
Philadelphia, book trade, 23; establishment of a paper mill, 19; imprints, 34, 37, 54, 83; pictures by Pennell, 110
Pickering, William, 34
Pigafetta, Antonia, tr. Richard Eden, 17
Pilot books, 114
Pine-Coffin, R.S., *How to Use the Catalogue*, 92, 94
Pinelo, Antonio de Léon, *Epitome de la Biblioteca*, 26
Pino, Frank, *Mexican Americans*, 121
Planta, J., 159
Plumier, Charles, 173, 178
Poe, Edgar Allen, 40, 80, 146–147; in England, 70
Pollard, A.W. and Redgrave, G.R., comps., *A Short Title Catalogue . . . 1475–1640*, 104
Polo, Marco, 16, 57
Poole, W.F., *Index to Periodical Literature*, 107, 149
Portugal, 120–121
Povey, Thomas, 169
Pownall, John, 153
Pownall, Thomas, 164
Precis, 99
Printers, William Bradford, 24; Mathew and Stephen Daye, 18;

Index

Jan van Doesborch, 16; John Foster, 18; James Franklin, 134, 190–192; Samuel Green, 18; Daniel Greenleaf, 189; Juan Pablo, 18; Richard Pynson, 17; Isaiah Thomas, 21; James Rivington, 22; Christopher Saur (Sower), 57, 122; Wynken de Worde, 17; Augustin Zamorano, 121

Printing, and the discovery of America, 12–17; English printing of American books, 23–24; first printed books about America, 11–12; first printing in British colonies, 20; first printing in the New World, 18, 120–121, 142; in British colonies, 2, 18–26; in the United States, growth in the 19thC, 25; of laws and statutes etc., 18, 20, 23–24; spread during the Revolution, 21–22

Proceedings of the American Antiquarian Society, 132

Providence, Rhode Island, 45

Ptolemy (Claudius Ptolemaeus), *Almagest*, 13; *Geographies*, 13

Public Record Office, 4, 19, 126, 133, 153–155, 160

Publishers, Aldine, 43; American Book Company, 64; Appleton, 38, 42, 84; Mathew Cary, 40; A.S. Barnes, 38; Richard Bentley, 182; Boni and Liveright (Modern Library), 68; Chicago UP, 69; Robert Clarke, 65–66; Columbia UP, 69, 84; Cornell UP, 41; Thomas Crowall, 41; John Day, 69; Dodd and Mead, 38, 66; Doran, 68; Doubleday, 68, 84; Dutton, 41; Farrar and Rinehart, 69; Funk and Wagnell, 41; Ginn, 41; Harcourt Brace, 68; Harpers, 38, 84; Henry Holt, 41, 84; Houghton Miflin, 41, 84; Alfred Knopf, 68, 84; Lippincott, 38, 66, 84; Little and Brown, 38, 84; Longmans, 84; Sampson Low, 70–73, 78–79; Alexander McClurg, 39; McGraw Hill, 68, 84; Macmillan (England), 70, 182; Macmillan of America, 41, 84, 182; William Morrow, 69; W.W. Norton, 69; Pennsylvania UP, 69; Princeton UP, 69, 84; George Putnam, 39, 84; Rand McNally, 41; Random House, 69; Routledge, 70; Scribner, 38, 84; Simon and Schuster, 68; Edward Stanford, 77–78; Tichnor and Fields, 38; Truman and Smith (American Book Company), 38; Van Nostrand, 38; Viking, 68; Wiley and Putnam, 38; H.W. Wilson, 75; Yale UP, 69

Publishers' Circular, 73

Publishers depositing in the British Library, list, 207–208

Publishers' Trade List Annual, 44, 103

Publishers' Trade List Annual (Meckler), 103

Publishers Weekly, 41, 43–44, 66–67, 70, 73

Publishing industry, 37–43, 64–69

Puck, 108, 148

Punch, 149

Purchas, Samuel, 16, 28, 57

Puritans, 19–20, 42

Purvis, Captain George, 161

Putnam, Herbert, 74

Quary, Robert, 162

Raimo, John W., *Guide to Manuscripts Relating to America in Great Britain and Ireland*, 155

Raleigh, Sir Walter, 158, 165

Ramusio, Giovanni Battista, 16

Rastell, John, *A New Interlude and a Mery of the Nature of the Four Elements*, 17

Index

Readers' Guide to Periodical Literature, 149
Reading, Lord, 182
Rede, Leman Thomas, *Bibliotheca Americana*, 30, 33, 36
'Red Line' map, 114
Regiomontanus (Johann Müller), *Ephemerides*, 14–15; tr. *Almagest*, 13
Register of Debates in Congress, 126
Reis, Claire R., *Composers in America*, 118
Religious books, 20, 39, 60, 66
Remington, Frederic, 109
Rhode Island, 163; first printing, 20
Ribault, Jean, 174
Rice, Sir Cecil Spring, 182
Richardson, Joseph, 23
Richardson, Samuel, *Pamela* (American edition), 24
Riley, James Whitcomb, 80
Rivington, James, 22
Robinson, George (Marquis of Ripon), 181
Robinson, John, 180
Rolfe, John, 'A True Relation of Virginia' (ms), 164
Rome, 13, 16
Roorbach, Orville, *Bibliotheca Americana*, 41, 43–44, 51
Rosselli, Francesco, 115
Rotz, John, 'Book of Hydrography' (ms), 164
Royal United Services Institution, map collection, 115
Rules for Compiling the Catalogue, 91–92
Russia, 122–123
Russwarm, John, 139
'Ruysch' map, 13

Sabin, Joseph, 44–45, 51, 75; *Bibliotheca Americana*, 5, 44
San Antonio, Spanish press, 142
Sandys, George, tr. Ovid's *Metamorphoses*, 19

San Francisco, pictures by Pennell, 110; Spanish press, 142
Sanger, Margaret, 182
Scientific American, 109
Scientific books, 30, 33, 60, 67
Scott, Sir Walter, 37
Scribner's Magazine, 148
Scribner's Statistical Atlas, 77, 116
Seidensticker, Oswald, *First Century of German Printing in America*, 122
Shakespeare, William, American edition of complete works 1794, 24; Boston edition 1844, 54
Shaw, Ralph R., *American Bibliography*, 1800–1820, 75, 102
Shaw, Renata, *Picture Searching*, 106
Shelburne, Lord, 164
Sheridan, Richard B., *School for Scandel* (American Edition), 24
Ship of Fools, See Brant, Sebastian
Shipton, Clifford H., *American Bibliography*, 75; *Short-Title Evans*, 75
Shoemaker, Richard H., *American Bibliography 1800–1820*, 75, 102
Shove, R.H., *Cheap Book Production*, 42
Sinclair, Sir John, 176
Sloane, Sir Hans, 6, 28, 172–173, 175, 190–194; *Catalogus plantarum quae in insula Jamaica*, 28
Slocum, Joshua, *Sailing Alone Around the World*, 148
Smirke, Sir Robert, 47
Smith, Captain John, 153, 173
Smith, Rev. Sydney, 74–75
Smith, William, 153
Snow, Peter, *The United States: a Guide to Library Holdings in the United Kingdom*, 7
Social Science and Humanities Index, 149

Society for the Propagation of the Gospel, 23, 25, 27–28
Society of Antiquaries, 158
Soto, Ferdinand de, *Florida*, 58
South Carolina, 174; first printing, 20
Spain, 120–121
Spanish in America, 11–12, 15–17, 26, 120–121, 142
Sparks, Jared, 4, 46, 49, 147; *Diplomatic Correspondence of the American Revolution*, 40; *Library of American Biography*, 40; *Writings of Washington*, 40
Spectator, 134
Spencer, Herbert, 66
Spofford, A.R., 74–75
Springer, Balthazar, 16
Stamp Act, 171–172, 180
Stanton, Elizabeth, 144
State Constitutional Conventions 1776–1976, 128
State Paper Office, *See* Public Record Office
State Records Microfilm Project, 127
Stephenson, Robert Louis, 64
Stevens, Benjamin Franklin, 46, 55–56, 61, 154–156; 'Stevens Transcripts', 154, 179–180
Stevens, Henry, agent for the British Museum Library, 1, 46, 49–57, 63, 85–86, 88, 187; *American Maps in the . . . British Museum*, 116–117; and R.R. Bowker, 76; and Panizzi, 49–50; arrival in Britain, 4, 49; *Catalogue of American Books, 1856*, 55–56, 59; death, 77, 80–81; exchange of official publicatons, 127; interest in literary manuscripts, 178; interest in maps, 112; list of desiderata, 1845, 50; newspaper collection, 1858, 135–138; Oxford and Cambridge libraries, 7; visit to the United States, 1857, 55–56
Stevens, Henry, senior, 4, 45–46
Stevens, Henry Newton, 80
Stockton, Frank R., 80
Stopes, Marie, 182
Stowe, Harriet Beecher, 80; *Uncle Tom's Cabin*, 4–5, 70, 188
Strachey, William, 'History of Travaile Into Virginia', 173
Strahan, William, 23
Switzerland, 120
Syphilis, 12

Tanselle, G. Thomas, 'Statistics on American Printing', 22
Tebbel, John, *History of American Publishing*, 42
Tenison, Thomas, 27, 29
Texas, 121
Textbooks, 25, 34, 39, 42, 64, 67
Thackeray, William Makepeace, 37
Thomas, Isaiah, 21, 148–149; *History of Printing in America*, 43, 132
Thompson, Maurice, *Alice of Old Vincennes*, 73
Three Centuries of English Plays, 104
Thurloe, John, 176
Tindall, Robert, 163
Today's Ladies Book, 143
Toronto, imprints, 54
Tracts, *See* Pamphlets
Trask, David F., *Bibliography of United States-Latin American Relations*, 123
Treaty of Guadalupe Hidalgo, 121, 142
Tudor, William, 147
Twain, Mark, 64, 70, 79, 170

United States Consular Despatches 1790–1906, 125
United States Federal Government Publications, 124–126
United States Government Publications (Non-Depository), 125
Utah, 137

Van Doesborch, Jan, 16–17
Vattemare, Nicolas Allexandre, 127
Velegas, Captain Bartholomew, 162
Vespucci, Amerigo, *Mundus Novus*, 11, 16–17, 57
Virginia, 113, 161–164, 168, 170–174, 178–179; first printing, 20
Virginian, 109
Votes and Proceedings of the American Continental Congress, 126

Waldseemüller, Martin, *Cosmographiae*, 11–12
Wallace, Lew, *Ben Hur*, 66
Wanley, Humphrey, 27
Warren, Joseph, 179
Warren, Josiah, 144
Washington DC, imprints, 38, 54, 83
Washington, George, 176; collected writings, 34; Weem's *Life*, 40, 54
Watt, Robert, *Bibliotheca Britannica*, 96
Watts, Thomas, 46, 50–51, 56–57, 59, 91
Webster, Noah, 1, 149
Weems, Mason Locke, *Life of Washington*, 40, 54
Weitenkampf, Frank, *Century of Political Cartoons*, 108

West Indies, 24, 28
Wharton, Edith, 182
Whistler, James McNeill, 80
Whiteford, Caleb, 179
Whittier, James Greenleaf, 80
Whole Book of Psalms, See *Bay Psalm Book*
Wilgus, Curtis W., *Historiography of Latin America*, 121
Wilkes, John, 24, 179
William, Edward, *Virgo Triumphans*, 113
Wilmot, Sir John Eardley, 176
Winslow, Edward, *Good Newes from New England*, 58
Winthrop, John, 173
Wiseman, John A., 'Henry Stevens and the British Museum', 50–51
Woman's Advocate, 143
Woman's Journal, 144
Worcester, Mass, 43
Wrench, Sir Evelyn, 182
Wright, Lyle H., *American Fiction*, 102
Wright-Molyneux map, 113

Zenger, Peter, *Brief Narrative of the case and trial of . . .*, 24, 134